Organizational Change and Strategy

The Coghlan and Rashford book on organizational levels and strategy is an important addition to the literature on how to help organizations make the necessary changes to survive in a more turbulent world. This is one of the very few books that deals realistically with the need to make changes at the individual, group and organizational levels and to take seriously the interconnections between these levels.

> Edgar H. Schein, *Sloan Fellows Professor of Management Emeritus, MIT Sloan School of Management, USA*

This book takes a holistic approach to change, looking at the organization through a systemic lens. Thus there are no anodyne solutions for managing change but instead the authors provide a framework for understanding the inter-relating dynamics that can either help or hinder organization change. These insights are presented in an accessible and user friendly language and take the reader through a carefully crafted process in which they learn how action research helps them understand the organization and simultaneously create organization change. It is essential reading for anyone tasked with changing and developing their organization, whether as a consultant or senior manager.

> Professor Kim Turnbull James, *Director, Centre for Executive Learning for Change, Cranfield School of Management, UK*

Exploring the discontinuous nature of forces for change – both in the external global environment and in the internal environment – which make organizational growth, development and even survival a skilled activity, this book guides the reader through the intricacies of this complex subject.

In this text, strategy and organizational change are bridged using a framework of organizational levels. The authors focus on how the strategy and change process involves individuals (CEO, senior managers and others), teams (senior management team, board, other teams), the inter-departmental group (inter team) and the organization (in its external relations) in systemic interactions.

Expertly combining theory with practice, this will be a vital text for all those concerned with strategy and change.

David Coghlan is a member of the faculty of the School of Business Studies, University of Dublin, Trinity College, Ireland.

Nicholas S. Rashford is University Professor at Saint Joseph's University, Philadelphia, Pennsylvania, USA.

Organizational Change and Strategy

An interlevel dynamics approach

David Coghlan and
Nicholas S. Rashford

Routledge
Taylor & Francis Group

LONDON AND NEW YORK

First published 2006
by Routledge
2 Park Square, Milton Park, Abingdon, Oxon OX14 4RN

Simultaneously published in the USA and Canada
by Routledge
270 Madison Ave, New York, NY 10016

Reprinted 2007

Routledge is an imprint of the Taylor & Francis Group, an informa business

© 2006 David Coghlan and Nicholas S. Rashford

British Library Cataloguing in Publication Data
A catalogue record for this book is available from the British Library

Library of Congress Cataloging in Publication Data
Coghlan, David
Organizational change and strategy: an interlevel dynamics approach/David
Coghlan and Nicholas S. Rashford.–1st ed.
    p. cm.
  Includes bibliographical references and index.
  1. Organizational change. 2. Communication in organizations. I. Rashford,
Nicholas S. II. Title.

HD58.8.C6 2006
658.4'06–dc22   2005026414

ISBN10: 0–415–37816–8 (hbk)
ISBN10: 0–415–37817–6 (pbk)

ISBN13: 978–0–415–37816–1 (hbk)
ISBN13: 978–0–415–37817–8 (pbk)

Contents

Illustrations

Figures

Tables

The authors

David Coghlan is a member of the faculty of the School of Business Studies, Trinity College, University of Dublin, Ireland, where he specializes in organization development and action research and works internationally with both communities. He has an MSc from the Manchester School of Management (UK), an SM from MIT's Sloan School of Management and a PhD from the National University of Ireland. He is currently on the editorial review boards of the *OD Practitioner, Journal of Applied Behavioral Science, Action Research* and *Systemic Practice and Action Research*. His most recent books are *Changing Healthcare Organisations* (Blackhall, Dublin, 2003), *Managers Learning in Action* (Routledge, London, 2004), and *Doing Action Research in Your Own Organization* (Sage, 1st edn 2001, 2nd edn 2005).

Nicholas S. Rashford is University Professor of Management at Saint Joseph's University, Philadelphia and was President and CEO from 1986 to 2003. He was formerly Dean of the School of Management at Rockhurst University, Kansas City. He has an SM from MIT's Sloan School of Management and a ScD from Johns Hopkins. He is Visiting Professor of Management at Universidad Alberto Hurtado in Santiago, Chile. He is a former Chairman of the Delaware River Port Authority and a Commissioner of the Philadelphia Regional Port Authority. He has consulting experiences with companies such as AT&T, Butler Mfr, Blue Cross Blue Shield, Equitable Trust, Philadelphia Insurers.

Acknowledgements

We are grateful to colleagues, friends, clients and participants on our courses with whom we have discussed our ideas and who supported and challenged them. David thanks Paul Coughlan and Joe McDonagh for their friendship and colleagueship and for contributing to the development of some of the case material. Nicholas thanks Helen, Isabel, Trish and Linda, who read and typed and corrected much of the material; Christine Russo, who opened doors, added constructive suggestions and who has been a student, supporter and friend. He thanks the President's cabinet and all of the people at Saint Joseph's and the Board and staff at the Delaware River Port Authority. We both thank Gerard McHugh, Head of School of Business, University of Dublin, for the funding for Nicholas to spend time at the School and the Irish food board, Bord Bia, who, at a later stage, gave him a place to write and learn. We both thank Jesuit communities in Dublin, Philadelphia and Santiago for their support.

We are very grateful to the groups with which we have worked and who contributed to testing the frameworks as they reflected on their own experience and worked enacting change in organizations. Nicholas thanks all of the Saint Joseph's and Alberto Hurtado's graduate students who made the live cases possible and who taught more than they learned. He thanks Erivan and Helga Haub for their support and Christian Haub for the opportunity to work with A&P and for spending many days teaching in the Executive MBA at Saint Joseph's.

We thank Warren Bennis and Bill Torbert for permission to draw on their work and Christian Haub for his generosity and willingness to present the A&P case.

We owe a deep debt to our intellectual mentors, Ed Schein and the late Dick Beckhard, who formed a sense of process and a spirit of inquiry in us that has transformed both our lives.

We acknowledge the invaluable help and support of the Routledge editorial and production teams, especially Francesca Heslop, Emma Joyes and Steve Thompson.

Overture

The overture of an opera or a musical typically provides listeners with an introduction to the major musical themes or tunes of the work. We are drawing on the notion of an overture to provide an introduction to this book. So at the outset, you, the reader, are beginning the cycles of taking in what we want to say, of making sense of it both in terms of organization development and change (ODC) theory and practice and of shaping the actions you take, whether as a manager, a non-executive member of an organization, an ODC consultant or a student. There are three major content themes, which are reflected in the three main parts of the book. Part I, comprising two chapters, introduces the construct of organizational levels. Part II, with three chapters, explores the subject of change in organizations. Part III, with seven chapters, takes up the subject of strategic planning and its required strategic change. Part IV concludes the book with a comprehensive case example and the finale.

There are several process themes that deal primarily with methodology and perspective. We are taking an action research approach to this book whereby we invite you, the reader, to reflect on your own situation in the light of the concepts and case situations presented and see how they inform your own assessment of what is going on and what action you might plan to take. The methodological framework under which you may be doing this may have different titles: action research (Coghlan and Brannick, 2005), action learning (Marquardt, 2004), clinical inquiry (Schein, 1987), work-based learning (Raelin, 2000), action inquiry (Torbert, 2004), appreciative inquiry (Watkins and Mohr, 2001), collaborative research (Adler *et al.*, 2004), to name a few. While we are using the term 'action research', we are using it inclusively to cover the many applications of action-oriented research that exist. We provide a diagnostic and action template for this action research activity. We suggest four perspectives (Beckhard, 1972):

1   Senior managers.
2   Organizational members (i.e. those not in senior management positions).

3 ODC consultants.
4 Outcomes.

Levels and interlevels

The first theme comprises two tunes. If you walk around an organization you see individuals at work, whether they are sitting at desks working at computer screens, selling goods to customers, or leaving the building to work with customers or clients elsewhere. You might seek an interview with a senior manager who might say that the workforce is highly skilled and is very effective at its work. We know that these individuals have a formal relationship with the organization through a contract of employment that sets out details of salary, holidays and leave, pension contributions and other human resource elements. If you talk to them and listen to what they say you find that they have experiences and feelings about what it is like to work in this organization. For some their work and career in the organization has them feeling good; for others their job and role in the organization is not experienced as good, but as rather uninteresting and something to be tolerated, or perhaps is very interesting but is highly stressful. For some their personal experience of recent events in the organization, such as how a previous change was managed, has left them feeling angry or distrustful. For some of these people their experience of their life in the organization is related to their age or their position in the organization's hierarchy. Some have been in the organization a long time and see retirement on the horizon; others see the organization as an opportunity for pursuing a promising career. For others their experience of the organization can be viewed primarily in relation to interests outside of the formal working role in the organization. Perhaps they have hobbies or pastimes which take pride of place in their lives. This range of issues, which is easily accessible when you listen to members of organizations, of whatever position on the hierarchical ladder, illustrates how complex the relationship between a member of an organization and the organization is (Schein, 1978). Yet, in this walk about the organization you see that focusing on the individual does not provide the total picture of the organization.

Individuals in organizations work with other individuals in groups and teams, and the quality and output of their work together are significant. So how teams work in terms of how they perform and the processes they adopt to maintain effective collaborative relationships are significant elements of how to understand and work in an organization. Indeed, they may be seen as being more complex than what we considered regarding the individual, because all of what we considered there is already present in individual team members, with now the added complexity of collaborative working mechanisms.

Yet focusing on individuals and teams does not answer all the questions about organizations. In this walkabout you see teams at work in different locations, performing different forms of tasks, while at the same time needing to relate to one another, to exchange information and to move the partly completed task from one stage to another. If you listen to team members in any particular functional area, you may find that their understanding of other functional areas may be quite limited and their propensity to speculate and attribute motivation to them echoes how ethnic cultures frequently refer to other ethnic cultures. Many of these functional areas speak their own technical language and have different frames of reference, which to the outsider appear alien (Schein, 1996, 2004). So the view of organizations comprising individuals who are also members of teams which exist in an inter-team environment illustrates an increasing degree of complexity.

Yet this view of organizations comprising individuals who are also members of teams which exist in an inter-team environment within the organization is not the total picture. Organizations exist in an external environment and so are constantly interacting with external forces in a world where change is the only constant – economic, political and social – and with multiple stakeholders' groups, such as customers/clients, competitors, suppliers and government. The primary task of the organization is to be successful in this external world, with survival as the minimum requirement and success being defined within specific categories of financial ratios, market share and customer satisfaction.

Our opening tune, therefore, is to remind you that organizations comprise these four levels of analysis and that as a manager, as an organizational member or as an ODC consultant you are constantly working with each of these levels, making them work more effectively (Rashford and Coghlan, 1994). This involves being able to see which one might be having difficulty at any given time, knowing how to intervene to deal with the relevant issue and being skilled at a range of interventions and styles. But experience tells us that these levels are not only discrete and separate but they are also interdependent and interrelated. This is our second tune.

What happens at one level has an impact on each of the others. So a recession or slow-down in the global economy leads to a reformulation of strategy, a realignment of operations across the interdepartmental group, a change in the work of teams, and change for individuals, some of whom may be laid off and so their relationship with the organization ceases, while others may benefit through re-skilling and professional development. If a team is working well, that contributes positively to the motivation and participation of the individual members; the reverse is also true. The work of one team affects the work of others. So each level is systemically linked to each of the others and events at one level are both cause and effect of events at other levels.

Organization development and change

Our second theme is the familiar organization development and change (ODC) theme (Rothwell and Sullivan, 2005). There are many approaches to viewing the field of organizational change. Some focus on the development and maximization of economic value, which Beer and Nohria (2000) call Theory E. Other approaches, which Beer and Nohria (2000) call Theory O, focus on developing organizational capabilities. Traditionally, the latter approach was referred to as organization development (OD). However, OD has developed to deal with changing organizational conditions and now works with both business/economic and organizational issues (Worley *et al.*, 1996; Greiner and Cummings, 2004). Accordingly, it is more contemporary to refer to ODC as an approach that integrates Theory E and Theory O. In this book, we intend such integration.

How do large systems change? What are the kinds of thinking and actions that managers, organizational members and ODC consultants can do to help an organization survive and thrive in a world of discontinuous change? We need to understand something of how change happens, in individuals, teams, the interdepartmental group and an organization, and how large-system change can be led and facilitated to recognize why change is required, what the desired outcome of change is, what needs to be done to achieve that outcome and how the transition period in getting there can be managed (Beckhard and Harris, 1987; Nadler, 1998). These are recognized as central to making large-scale organizational change work. An important tune within this theme is how strategy is conceived and enacted. So this theme explores how large-system change comprises complex iterations of individual, team, interdepartmental group and organizational action.

Strategy and the formation and implementation of strategic action

There has been a change in the management literature on strategy formulation. One reason for this change is the changing conditions in which organizations find themselves in the modern complex global environment. The second reason is the self-understanding of organizations that has developed over the past 25 years. The new approaches to planning view organizations as complex adaptive systems and draw on biology, quantum physics and chaos theory, particularly theories of self-organization, non-equilibrium and the 'butterfly effect' of minute fluctuations creating large-scale change, rather than the mechanistic and militaristic approaches which dominated strategic thinking in the latter decades of the twentieth century (Pascale *et al.*, 2000).

In this theme, primarily in Part III, we explore the processes by which managers, organizational members and ODC consultants craft strategy (Floyd *et al.*, 2005) and in particular, how they create a picture of who the organization is, express that picture, analyse the external and internal environments, choose and implement actions and evaluate outcomes. We view these processes not as linear steps, but as cyclical and systemic strategic actions, which involve iterations of individual and team actions and action between teams, the whole organization and with customers.

Template for diagnosis and action

Our fourth theme is a template for diagnosing and taking action. Forty years ago Blake and Mouton (1964) taught us that it is not enough to concentrate on the tasks we have to do, but that we also need to have an eye on the relationships which are needed to complete the task, whether these be interpersonal in a team, inter-team or inter-organizational. So our first tune in this theme is to note that actions need to be taken to complete tasks successfully and to build and maintain relationships on which completing the tasks depend (Table 0.1).

After more than 50 years of ODC we are well attuned to the distinction between content and process (Schein, 1999). Content refers to *what* is done, while process refers to *how* it is done. Content and process apply to both task and relational issues. So we can usefully identify *task content*, which refers to what the organization, interdepartmental group, team or individual is intending to do: its mission, the task to be done, the problems arising around clarity of mission, assignment of functions to meet tasks and analysis of information. We can note how *task process* points us to how the organization, interdepartmental group, team or individual engages in defining mission, setting goals, completing tasks, reviewing progress, etc. These issues require attention if the tasks are to be completed satisfactorily.

Relational content refers to the particular roles members of an organization

Table 0.1 Template for diagnosis and action

	TASK	RELATIONAL
Content		
Process		
Culture		

play with regard to other members. *Relational process* overlaps somewhat with interpersonal content and focuses more on what is happening in the team, interdepartmental group or organization and how they function in relation to the members: how people listen or don't listen to each other, how they agree or disagree over specific issues, and how they support each other or support some people more than others.

Yet what we see and hear is not the whole picture on content and process issues. Much of what goes on in organizations is grounded in collective assumptions that constitute the organization's culture. They become embedded in the organization and in the different teams and interdepartmental groups that make up the organization. As Schein (2004) has shown, these assumptions become taken for granted and accordingly disappear from consciousness. They are passed on to new members and in effect become a structured way of thinking and behaving. Culture is, as Schein (2003) terms it, the DNA of an organization. It pertains to the organization's survival in the external environment and, therefore, focuses on the issues of mission, goal setting, task accomplishment and problem solving. So within task issues there is *task culture*, which points to the basic assumptions that have formed around critical task issues. Similarly, *relational culture* points to how authority and peer relationships are defined and how subcultures within functional areas and occupational communities relate to one another. As Schein points out, if you want to understand an organization's culture, go to a meeting and notice who talks to whom (or doesn't), who listens to whom (or doesn't), how decisions are made and so on. Argyris (2000) illustrates how defensive routines, which serve to save face and to protect people from embarrassment, abound in organizations and become undiscussable and embedded in how the organization functions. Uncovering the embedded taken-for-granted patterns of behaviour that enable or inhibit the organization's change efforts while an organization is creating and implementing strategy is essential for managers and ODC consultants.

Action research

Our fifth theme is an action research approach. As the name suggests, action research is an approach to research which aims at both taking action and creating knowledge or theory from that action. Shani and Pasmore provide a definition of action research that echoes our description of the theory and practice of organization development and change.

> Action research may be defined as an emergent inquiry process in which applied behavioural science knowledge is integrated with existing organizational knowledge and applied to solve real organizational problems. It is simultaneously concerned with bringing about change in organizations, in developing self-help competencies in organizational members

and in adding to scientific knowledge. Finally it is an evolving process that is undertaken in a spirit of collaboration and co-inquiry.

(Shani and Pasmore 1985: 439)

Action research is a well-established approach to understanding organizations and helping them change. The steps of action research are:

1 Articulating an initial setting of the context and purpose.
2 Working with other members of the system as to what the data means (a sort of 'shared diagnosis').
3 Deciding together what needs to be worked on in order to change the system in the desired direction.
4 Making planned interventions collaboratively in the system on the basis of the planned action to achieve those desired changes.
5 Evaluating both intended and unintended outcomes and reviewing to see what needs to be done next, and so repeating the cycle.
6 Standing back to reflect on steps 1 to 5, and reviewing what learning is taking place and what knowledge is being generated. (This step is particularly important, and indeed essential if the work is being submitted as a dissertation for an academic award.)

Action research and ODC are intimately intertwined, both theoretically and through the work of those scholar-practitioners who have shaped the development of both approaches. Action research works through a series of cycles of consciously and deliberately (i) planning, (ii) taking action and (iii) evaluating that action, leading to further planning, action and evaluation. A second dimension of action research is that it is participative, in that the members of the system participate actively in the process. The action research approach is powerful. It engages people as participants in seeking ideas, planning, taking actions, reviewing outcomes and learning what works and doesn't work, and why. These are in stark contrast with programmed approaches that mandate following pre-designed steps and which tend not to be open to alteration. These approaches are based on the assumption that the system should adopt the whole package as designed. Action research and ODC, on the other hand, are based on the assumptions that each system is unique and that a change process has to be designed with that uniqueness in mind and adapted in the light of experience and learning.

By taking an action research approach in this book we mean that we invite you, the reader, whether you are a senior manager, a non-executive organizational member, an external ODC consultant or a student, not only to understand the concepts developed in this book, but also to engage in learning-in-action by inquiring into what is going on around you, both inside and outside the organization, drawing on concepts which help you make sense of your experience and then engaging in action, evaluating outcomes, reflecting on learning and developing knowledge (Coghlan *et al.*, 2004). We recommend that you do not do this on your own and keep your reflections private, but that you engage others in conversations of shared reflections.

The action research activities at the end of many of the chapters will enable you to reflect on an organization with which you are familiar. Indeed, we invite you, where possible, to engage in these action research activities on the same organization throughout the book, so as to build up your diagnostic skills. Appendix 1 provides some additional support for insider reflection and action (Coghlan and Brannick, 2005). If you are external to the organization, either as an ODC consultant, a student or as an action researcher in the mode of collaborative research (Adler *et al.*, 2004), then your reflections are in collaboration with the local managers'. The vignettes within chapters and the cases at the end of chapters provide illustrations and aim to provoke further reflection and discussion.

Action research distinguishes between four territories of experience (Fisher *et al.*, 2000):

1   *Intentionality*: This is the territory of purpose, goals, aims and vision.
2   *Planning*: This is the territory of plans, strategy, tactics, ploys and schemes.
3   *Action*: This is the territory of action, behaviour, implementation, skills and performance.
4   *Outcomes*: This is the territory of results, outcomes, consequences and effects.

The parallel equivalent for organizations is visioning, strategizing, performing and assessing. The central process of action research is to develop our awareness, understanding and skills in each of these territories. Inquiry helps us to understand our intentions, develop our capacity to plan and develop strategies that reflect our aspirations, reflect on the skills of our implementation and to see the impact of our actions. Inquiry can also take us through how each of the territories are linked. A first or single inquiry loop can begin from outcomes and inquire into how we acted to produce those outcomes. A second or double inquiry loop can take us from outcomes to action to what we planned. A third or triple inquiry loop can take us from outcomes, through action, through strategy to ask questions about our intention, aspirations and values. Throughout the book we adopt this three-level inquiry approach and invite you to connect outcomes with action, with strategies and with intentions.

So our overture comprises these five themes – level and interlevel dynamics, ODC, strategy, the template of content, process and culture with regard to task and relational issues and a spirit of inquiry in action. Let us now proceed to the first theme.

Action research activity 0.1

Take an organization with which you are familiar and see how you can apply the themes of the Overture to it.

1 Apply the construct of organizational levels.

  a Who constitutes the individual level? Pick a particular individual you know and describe his/her formal role in the organization and what you know of his/her self-expressed experience of being a member of the organization.
  b Of what teams is that individual a member?
  c To what others teams does that team relate in terms of the design of work flow?
  d How does the work of the individual, the team and the other teams contribute to the overall goal of the organization in its external environment?

2 How does change impact on this organization, particularly on what it is and how it makes choices about how it functions in its environment?
3 What difference does it make to your view of change if you are inside or outside the organization, and if inside what role you have?

Part I

Levels and interlevels

Chapter I

Organizational levels

Theory and practice

Conceptual foundations

In the Overture we made the point that when we think in terms of levels in organizations, we should not only distinguish between hierarchy/echelon and complexity, but focus on complexity as a more fruitful way to analyse organizational phenomena and organizational change processes. Levels of complexity – individual, group, inter-group, total organizational – are frequently used as frameworks for understanding organizational processes (Leavitt, 1978; Tuohy, 1999; Klein and Kozlowski, 2000; Harrison, 2005). Several essential points need to be clarified about the concept and usage of the term 'organizational levels'. The notion of levels must be distinguished from that of echelon or hierarchy (Rousseau, 1985). Echelon refers to position on a chain of command in an organization, such as worker, supervisor, middle manager, etc.

Levels of organizational behaviour, however, describe levels of complexity, as, for instance, described by Miller (1978) with regard to biological systems. He identifies seven levels: cell, organ, organism, group, organization, society and supernatural. They are hierarchical in that each system is composed of interrelated subsystems in a hierarchical order, i.e. organs are composed of cells, organisms composed of organs, etc. The hierarchical nature of the system also means that if any of its subsystems ceases to carry out its function, the system would cease to exist. Accordingly, a cancerous cell affects the functioning of the organ, affects the life of the individual person and has an impact on that person's family and friends. Therefore, a dynamic notion of levels of complexity is needed to more fully understand, appreciate and manage behaviour in a complex organizational system. The subsystems that make up an organization as a living system are: the individual, the face-to-face working team, the interdepartmental group of teams and the organization. Clearly the notion of levels extends beyond the individual organization. An industry sector, such as financial services, healthcare, telecommunications, education, etc., where the participants are governed by common regulatory laws, faces common challenges and at times may present a common front in order to negotiate with regulatory bodies, may be considered to be a fifth level. In this book we are focusing primarily on four levels, drawing on this fifth level when appropriate.

The construct of organizational levels, therefore, is (a) a point of view so one can look at an organization from which ever level one chooses, (b) a platform for analysis and (c) an entry point for change. Because it focuses on complexity, rather than hierarchy, it enriches the perspective of organizations as living systems (de Geus, 1997; Burke, 2002) as it accounts for the multiple patterns of complexity and unpredictability of participation in organizations.

Four levels of organization behaviour

We are presenting levels in terms of how people participate in organizations (Rashford and Coghlan, 1994; Coghlan, 1996). Moreover, we will discuss how linking the levels to one another provides an additional useful tool and core skills for managers and ODC consultants. This framework describes four levels of participation – individual, face-to-face team, interdepartmental group and organization. These four levels can be viewed as degrees or types of involvement, subsystems or as degrees of complexity. It depends on one's perspective.

Within each level there are tasks. These tasks are doubled-sided. There is the task from the viewpoint within each level, such as the individual's task to be an individual or the team's task to function well, and there is the task from the outside viewpoint at each level, such as management's requirement that an individual belong or that a team be effective. These dual tasks co-exist at each level and create a tension between them. These tensions have been well described by Fox (1985). Within a unitary frame of reference, the tension is between individual and organizational goals, the resolution of which comes through effective human resource management. Within a pluralist frame the tensions are between competing political self-interest groups, the resolution of which is through bargaining and negotiation. Within the radical frame, the tension fundamentally cannot be resolved within the organizational context and so it is enacted on the wider stage of society and politics. Organizational levels can be viewed through the many lenses through which people's participation in organizations can be viewed (Bolman and Deal, 1997).

Each organizational level can be viewed from four different perspectives – manager, organizational member, ODC consultant and outcomes. The input perspective tends to be from the smaller system to the larger, while the output is perceived from the larger system to the smaller. From the point of view of the individual, the least complex approach to participation is the membership which the individual has with the organization in order to meet personal life goals (Level I). The more complex approach exists in establishing effective working relationships in a face-to-face team, while also maintaining personal integrity (Level II). An even more complex involvement exists in terms of the interdepartmental group or divisional type of interface where teams must be coordinated in their efforts in order to achieve complex tasks and maintain a balance of power among competing political interest groups (Level III). A further complexity from the point of view of the individual is the relationship of the total organization to its external environment, in which other organizations are individual competitors, competing for scarce resources to produce similar products or services. The key task for any organization is its ability to adapt to environmental forces driving for change (Level IV). When one approaches the question from the point of view of the individual member who is not in a senior executive position member, the key issue is involvement in the organization (Table 1.1).

CEOs and other senior managers grapple with issues of content and process as they attempt to integrate their use of power, knowledge and trust (Zand, 1997). So when one views organizational levels from the point of view of senior management, the key issues are how different forms of participation in the organization are achieved (Table 1.2). From senior management's perspective (the output perspective in systems terms), the core issue is one of involvement. The most basic form of involvement is to get a person committed to the goals, values and culture of the organization. The second level of involvement is to establish good, working face-to-face relationships in functional teams. The third level of involvement is the group or divisional level in which complex information and data systems are used to extend the knowledge and to coordinate the functions of the total working

Table 1.1 Individual members' tasks at each of the four organizational levels

Level	Task
I Individual	Membership and participation
II Face-to-face team	Creating effective working relationships
III Interdepartmental group	Coordinating joint effort
IV Organization	Adapting

Table 1.2 Management tasks at each of the four organizational levels

Level	Task
I Individual	Involvement
II Face-to-face team	Productive team functioning
III Interdepartmental group	Coordination of effective output
IV Organization	Competitive advantage

group, made up of multiple face-to-face teams. Finally, the most complex of all is the unified effort of all participants in an organization towards the goal of making the organization profitable, growth-oriented and functional in its external environment. This set of complex behaviours, then, is separated into a cognitive map – a mental construct of different types of participation and involvement – by the use of the concept of levels.

ODC consultants view the four levels in terms of how they fit systemically with one another in relation to the successful management of change (Table 1.3). The 'matching' process between individuals and the organization are key to attitudes to the change process and how the attitudes influence action. Team effectiveness is critical to the change process, whether in formal statutory teams or in task forces or project teams set up to assist the change. Inter-team coordination and minimal conflict is also critical to the change process. Ultimately the change process is aimed to achieve better adaptation to a changing environment, with possible collaboration with other organizations.

The outcomes of the successful achievements of the tasks at each level describe the four tasks at each of the four organizational levels (Table 1.4). The four key tasks of *matching needs*, *creating a functioning, working team which is productive*, *coordination* and *adaptation* form a complex pattern.

It is in the working out of these tensions and the completion of the relevant tasks that participation at each level is most successful. For example, at Level I, in a career interview, the manager must suppress the need to praise or rebuke productivity performance if the focus of the interview is on how the

Table 1.3 ODC consultants' perspectives at each of the four organizational levels

Level	Task
I Individual	Matching needs
II Face-to-face team	Productive team functioning
III Interdepartmental group	Coordination
IV Organization	Adaptation to changing environment

Table 1.4 Outcomes at each of the four organizational levels

Level	Task
I Individual	Matching needs
II Face-to-face team	Creating a functioning team
III Interdepartmental group	Coordination
IV Organization	Adaptation

individual can improve his or her own personal development and growth. For example, at Level II a team can work through its internal dynamics and create a cohesive, functioning unit, while at the same time meet the organization's demands to be effective in terms measured by others outside the team. Within each level are behaviours that contribute to the successful completion of the level's tasks.

Interventions

The levels framework provides important insights into the types of intervention which are desirable in any given organization development and change programme. Each level demands its own most appropriate or 'key' intervention in terms of helping to fulfil the primary task of that level and also suggests the most relevant interventions to help link the tasks of the levels to one another. In our view, some interventions are more useful than others in resolving the core issues which define each level. An ODC consultant utilizes interventions according to the joint diagnosis by consultant and client as to what is needed in a given situation (Schein, 1999). Our notion of key intervention does not attempt to predetermine or limit a consultant's ability to intervene effectively in the concrete situation of any given consultation.

Level I – Individual

Individuals within organizations have life-tasks, needs and wishes which extend far beyond their participation in any given work setting. Each individual struggles to find unique and personalized satisfactions in this regard. Management's perspective at the same point, however, is that individuals somehow belong to the organization in an appropriate psychological contract. When the tasks at this level are reasonably and adequately met, individuals can allow the organization and its goals to be a source of personal goal motivation. Individuals will still retain their own individuality while 'belonging' to the organization. In contrast, the awareness and utilization of motivational techniques are the basic functions of management towards each individual in the organization in the hope that they will enhance growth and effectiveness. Therefore, management's ideal goal is to create a matching process in which people are able and encouraged to become involved, and find that the work situation develops them as human beings while the organization benefits from such an involvement (Schein, 1978, 1995). Not all individuals relate to management's goal in this regard, and some prefer to define the relationship with the organization in political and adversarial terms around issues of power and control (Fox, 1985; Bolman and Deal, 1997).

There is an inevitable serious tension in this matching process. Individuals attempting to be themselves bring unique aspects of themselves to the organization and, at the same time, adapt to organizational norms. One common difficulty here is that the plurality of views and theories-in-use of how people are motivated produces contradictory approaches and undermines the growth process (McGregor, 1960). The manager who thinks that motivation is external and applied by force is in sharp contrast to the manager or subordinate who thinks that motivation comes from within the person. The point becomes even more critical if in unexamined behaviour a manager proposes in speech one point of view and in action the other. The critical need is for managers to reflect on how different people might be motivated in diverse and changing situations. The more ownership and awareness that individuals have of their lives, the more capable they are of contributing their unique aspects which are so necessary for organizations to change and develop.

The key intervention on this level is the *career interview* in which the dynamics of the life-cycle, the work-cycle and the family-cycle are located and placed in juxtaposition so that the individual can locate his/her career in the context of his/her life (Schein, 1978). Through the person-centred nature of the interview, the individual can be facilitated to take ownership of his/her life and career and adopt positive coping responses to the tasks facing him/her. It can empower individuals to initiate and promote change in the organization. At the same time, managers can utilize the process to reflect on and restructure managerial assumptions and behaviour. A technique such as the career anchor exercise, based on the individual's work experience, needs and values, is of great significance (Schein, 1993). In the career anchor, that aspect of work which produces a sense of identity and self-concept in work is located by the individual and can be used in the setting of the contract between the individual and the organization for his/her contribution to the corporate endeavour and the organization's response.

An electrical engineer in a high-tech company was promoted to a managerial position. After some time in the job, he reported to his superior that he was unhappy in this role and that he preferred to be back in the technical area of product design where he felt at home in the field of technological research. Because his superior knew and understood him, this request was granted. This recognition by the superior that he was happier as an engineer than as a manager (which in career anchor terms means that his career anchor was technical functional, rather than managerial) enabled the organization and the individual to reconfigure the relationship between them so as to achieve a better match of the individual's desires, skills and motivations with the organization's needs.

Level I applies throughout an organization. It works differently at different points on the chain of command. A secretary's or worker's commitment to the organization is typically different from that of the CEO. If a Level I dysfunction from the individual's side occurs at senior management, its consequences are different than if a similar problem were occurring for the warehouse clerk. If the dysfunction emanates from management policy, the effects can vary throughout the organization. By Level I dysfunction is meant that because of assumptions, attitudes or behaviours of either the individual or the organization's management, the Level I task of matching needs is frustrated with consequential negative results for working relationships, inter-team collaboration and ultimately the functioning of the organization.

In conclusion, the issues at the individual level are usefully viewed through the four perspectives (Table 1.5). Senior managers view them in terms of attaining and maintaining performance. Organizational members view them in terms of their own career and development. ODC consultants view them in terms of the effect of managerial behaviour on members and their reciprocal response. The outcome is appropriate matching needs.

Level II – Face-to-face team

From the individual's perspective, entry into the work activity involves interfacing with other individuals in clearly defined units. Face-to-face teams are typically formal groups and defined in terms of:

1 Face-to-face interaction.
2 Common objectives.
3 Psychological awareness of other members.
4 Self-definition as a team with member/non-member boundaries clearly defined.

Level II is a more complex level than Level I because of the increased number of participants and interactions. Teams form part of a wider system in

Table 1.5 Perspectives at individual level

Perspective	
Leader	How do we create the conditions for high motivation and commitment to attain and maintain high performance?
Member	How does working in this organization meet my needs and enhance my development?
ODC consultant	What effects does management behaviour have on members' motivation and commitment to the goals of the organization? Does employee behaviour reinforce management behaviour?
Outcome	How are organizational and individual members' goals matched?

organizations and some of the dysfunctional issues which arise within the team may originate beyond the team in its technological and political interface with other teams. Problems which arise between teams are considered at Level III.

From the managerial perspective, any individual's task within the face-to-face team is to contribute to the collective ventures of the team. Management requires the team to be efficient, flexible and cooperative in its output towards the overall organizational tasks. Effective team functioning requires the team to be successful in accomplishing its tasks and skilled in learning from its experience in building and maintaining working relationships. While we are focusing primarily on the team as a face-to-face working unit, these process issues apply to what is termed 'virtual teams' (Duarte and Snyder, 1999) or teams which utilize information technology as primary communication mechanisms (Johansen *et al.*, 1991).

The team's process, then, focuses on becoming a functioning work unit to build on success and learn from mistakes. It is critical for face-to-face teams to develop the appropriate skills of self-reflection and correcting their own dysfunctions. Such skills typically constitute the definition of successful teams. Level II dysfunctions occur when assumptions, attitudes and behaviour of team members towards one another and the team's effort frustrate the team's performance. Generally the discovery of negative information is not valued in many organizations as people then tend to confront one another. This results from the learned patterns of inference, attribution and the placing of blame. Behaviours such as blaming, withholding information, inappropriate team leader style, misplaced competition, sexism, racism and lack of trust can negatively affect the team members' capacity to work well together and also inhibit team development. Furthermore, within any given team the interaction skills of task achievement and maintenance function may not be equally developed. In most organizations, performance is not measured on the team level. Subsequently, rewards may be divisive in teams, break up teams through the transfer of successful individual members, and impose restrictive norms and practices. The team dynamics described above are relevant to all teams, whether at the senior management or middle management echelon or at the worker-maintenance areas in an organization; or in formalized permanent teams within an organization's structure or temporary project teams or task forces. A particular challenge for teams is to maintain flexibility in situations where membership configurations change on a frequent basis, with new members joining and others leaving, as in temporary task forces or project committees.

The key intervention on the face-to-face team level consists in formally building up and maintaining team skills. Team-building is the title given to a wide range of activities which are aimed at improving a work team's effectiveness. Team skills comprise four activities in order of importance (Beckhard, 1972; Nadler *et al.*, 1998):

1 Setting goals and priorities.
2 Analysing and allocating work.
3 Examining the team's process.
4 Developing the interpersonal relationships among team members.

Team building is the key intervention because it deals with members' participation, with the team's goals and work allocation and how the team can be productive. Other interventions focus on less comprehensive issues and provide team process skills in communication, problem-solving, decision-making, member roles and functions, cultural rules of interaction, norm evaluation, conflict management, leadership style and the exercise of influence, and initiating and managing change (Schein, 1999). Team development provides a framework for understanding the growth stages of the collective personality that is the team (Wheelan, 1999) and through cultural analysis uncovering the hidden assumptions that constitute its relationship to its external and internal environment (Schein, 2004).

The four tasks of setting goals and priorities, analysing and allocating work, examining the team's process and developing the interpersonal relationships among team members can be viewed from the perspective of the manager, the team member, the ODC consultant and outcomes (Table 1.6).

A working party established by a bishop to create a pastoral plan for the diocese invited Coghlan to work with its members because the group was experiencing interpersonal difficulties. Meetings were proving to be stressful; members frequently felt hurt by others' comments and several were reported to be on the verge of resigning. After being briefed by a delegation of the working party, Coghlan designed a process for a two-day review meeting. At the outset he invited each member to write down what he or she thought were the working party's mission and purpose. He did this to ground any later exploration of interpersonal relations in the working party's mandate, the way it structured its tasks and the way the process worked. When members shared their perceptions of the working party's mission and purpose, both Coghlan and the group noticed that there were practically as many versions of the mission as there were members, and that many of the perceptions were incompatible. It emerged that the purpose of the working party had changed since it was originally established, and that some members were working from a new definition, some from the original one and other from a variation on both. The two-day meeting was then devoted to clarifying and articulating a common purpose for the working party and its work. Very little time was subsequently devoted to the subject of interpersonal relations. Coghlan, presenting the team-building framework outlined above, pointed out that if the goals and mission of the group had remained unclear, then any work on interpersonal relationships within the group would at best be temporary and the problems would resurface. Subsequent reports indicated that interpersonal relations did improve as the working party launched into its work with a clearer and agreed statement of purpose.

Table 1.6 Perspectives on tasks at team level

Perspective	Setting goals	Allocating and implementing work	Team process	Interpersonal relations
Leader	How much do I set the goals and invite opinions?	Who is responsible for what? Who does what? Who manages what? How do I allocate . . .?	What processes do we need to make the team work – meetings, communication mechanisms . . .? Does the team have the ability to change membership and be flexible to subdivide the work and add people for specific tasks? How do I deal with team dysfunction? What extra resources do I need?	How can interpersonal relations assist the work and not inhibit it? Can it relate to other teams?
Member	What is expected of me? Can I respond to other tasks if required?	Are my goals and tasks clear? Have I the competence and resources to complete my tasks? How will I be evaluated?	How do we communicate? Can I be critical? What happens if we have conflicts? Will I be listened to and heard?	Can I work with people I don't like or who have different approaches to me?
ODC consultant	Are the goals clear? Are they agreed upon?	Is there a match between goals and roles? Is talent optimized? Is it flexible to reconfigure membership for other tasks?	How does the team work – communicate, give feedback, solve problems, make decisions, manage conflict . . .? What hidden norms are operative?	Do the different personalities, styles, etc. work together? Do they appreciate difference?
Outcome	Clear and agreed goals	Effective implementing of goals	Effective team working and achievement of goals in multiple situations and tasks	Effective interpersonal relations appropriate to goal achievement

Level III – Interdepartmental group

From the team's point of view, to be effective and enter the organization's life is to work within a larger system. This third level is made up of any number of face-to-face working teams which must function together to accomplish a divisional purpose, such as manufacturing, sales or marketing, or it is a collection of individual work teams that provide a strategic business unit function for an organization. The interdepartmental group level needs to:

1   have the ability to sense critical information not directly experienced;
2   pass beyond the barriers of individual teams in order to implement pro-grammes through coordination;
3   project at a range beyond their direct contact, i.e. deal with people not in their immediate group team or functional department;
4   manage work, information and resource flows.

In large organizations, where size and distance dissolve immediate personal relationships, it is imperative that this level functions well. From manage-ment's view, the team's tasks within the group is to perform as a team, while having a sense of belonging to the interdepartmental group from which it receives the scarce resources enabling it to function. When this third level is working effectively, the interdepartmental group or division is capable of obtaining information and converting it into decision processes, enabling the implementation of complex programmes or operations. The task of this level is to map the flow of information and partially completed work from one unit to another. Management requires that these units form a coordinated aggregate. The process of performing a complex function and making an appropriate distribution of scarce resources, such as personnel and money, is the key venture of the group level. It is a highly political situation in which the in-built structural conflicts of multiple interest parties need to be resolved. As an interdepartmental group, this diversified mass of differing functions and interests must negotiate an outcome that adequately reflects the balance of power among competing coalitions and a just distribution of resources. An essential element in Level III dynamics centres on issues of power and how power is exercised in the allocation of resources and the accessibility of infor-mation.

From management's view, the technical issues at this level require an ability to locate dysfunctions. Dysfunctions occur in the flow of transferring information and partially completed work or services from one team to another. The entire function must be viewed, understood and successfully handled in order to produce the product or service. Because of a huge number of individuals engaged in particular functions in a large organization, this process is often very difficult to see. The interdepartmental group's process then must focus on becoming a functioning work unit to build on successes and learn from mistakes. Difficulties also arise at this level from the lack of reflective and corrective skills. Discovery of negative information is difficult because it is often hidden in the interfaces that exist between one team and another. The organizational rewards system often does not reflect the actual needs of particular functioning units within the larger group.

Severe dysfunctions on an interdepartmental group level are most often solved through the use of an ODC consultant who can help the group configure its information and its materials handling processes, and restructure itself, if necessary to a new configuration. Knowledge of content is essential. For example, a consultant must be conversant with the content of the technology in an information flow or decision-making process.

A construction company which manufactured modular factory/warehouse units and competed with companies which manufactured stand-alone units uniquely suited to each operation provides an example of this intervention. The problem posed was that, through the process of manufacturing the modules and making adaptations to fit customers' requirements faster than competitors, deliveries were not being made on time. Accordingly, a consultant gathered the heads of each major departmental area and facilitated a detailed mapping of each step in the process from input to output. Time delays and the reasons for them were identified. The inadequacies of meeting others' needs, the points of differences and conflict between the department areas were carefully worked out. After some thoughtful reflection it became apparent that while there were unique requirements for each customer, there were some common elements among customers. If sales sat down with engineering and talked about what the customer's needs were, often pre-designed engineering solutions were available and could fit the customer's needs without requiring extremely time-consuming engineering projects. Out of this mapping process intervention the time it took to build modified units dropped significantly.

Level III interdepartmental group dysfunction does not, of necessity, take place only within the workflow process, but often can take place within the resource flow. For example, a major research unit of a large university was functioning within one of its schools. The dean of the school had established a process where there was an associate dean in charge of finance. The associate dean's function was to make sure that the expenditure of funds matched the university's needs and requirements. The individual had good financial skills for managing the resources of the university. The research group, on the other hand, comprised faculty members who wanted flexibility in terms of dealing with financial matters and wanted a quick response in terms of having access to the resources that the institution was garnering from outside sources. There was a great deal of frustration and anger directed at the associate dean because of his failure to understand the dynamics of the group when he insisted on financial accuracy to match internal consistency on how the funds were being used. The group, in turn, had requirements to match funding processes at other institutes with which they collaborated for the grants. In this situation, rather than an internal mapping process, intervention focused on the research group articulating its need for support from the financial function of the dean's office and on the other hand hearing some requirements from the dean's office to have common reporting practices across the school's units.

A common expression of failures at Level III is the perennial issue of information technology enabled change. Research and experience over decades have shown that (a) most investments in information technology fail to deliver on time and within budget and (b) that this failure is due to the lack of integration between the technology and the human and organizational dimensions of organizations (McDonagh, 2001). A primary dynamic of this failure is the existence of subcultures within organizations, especially executive and technical occupational communities, each of which has its own assumptions, language and perspective on information technology (Schein, 1996). The inherent difficulties of enabling these occupational communities to communicate with one another on information technology have proved to be complex and enduring (Coghlan and McDonagh, 2001). The framework of organizational levels enables the dynamics of information technology in organizations to be identified in how IT affects the work of individuals, teams, the access and sharing of information across the interdepartmental group and contributing to organizational effectiveness and competitiveness (Coghlan, 1998a).

The key intervention on this interdepartmental group level consists of internal mapping. This framework focuses a process whereby individual heads of work units or team leaders are asked to plot the workflow through their section, and to do this in such a way that from the beginning of a work process to its finish, all the intermediate links between different functioning teams are plotted, and all the members of the group then have a chance to jointly own the dysfunctional areas and work in small task forces to address the dysfunctions. This process requires each manager to put down each input and output from their own area on a large sheet. These sheets are connected together in an interdepartmental group meeting and the quality and effectiveness of each point of connection between teams are evaluated. The correction process of dysfunction is to set up a marker or flag at each point of dysfunction and put together a task force of affected individuals to correct the dysfunction. Most often the dysfunction is *between* working teams and not in them.

Another important intervention at this level is the use of large group processes (Bunker and Alban, 1997; Coghlan, 1998b), such as 'search/future search conferences' (Emery and Purser, 1996; Weisbord and Janoff, 1995), 'whole-scale change' (Dannemiller and Tyson Associates, 2000), 'open space' (Owen, 1997). Organizational members from all functional and geographical areas come together for a number of days to:

- review the past
- explore the present
- create an ideal future scenario
- identify common ground, and
- make action plans.

The significance of these approaches is that they enable the whole system to engage in strategic thinking and planning in an integrated manner in a defined period of time in a manner that is dialogical, participative, draws on metaphoric approaches as well as rational ones and builds ownership of strategy and change agendas.

The tasks at the interdepartmental group level can be viewed from the four perspectives (Table 1.7).

Senior management group

There is a certain amount of discussion as to whether senior management teams are actually teams or not. Hambrick (1994) suggests that the constellation of executives at the top of an organization may not constitute a team, but

Table 1.7 Perspectives at interdepartmental group level

Perspective	
Leader	How do I lead effective coordination across the organization and minimize any inter-functional conflict and political turf-protection that jeopardizes the enterprise? What technologies do we invest in to achieve effective coordination?
Member	How do I work across functions? What technologies do I have to coordinate information across functions?
ODC consultant	What coordinating technologies are in place? Are they effective? How well do functional areas understand other areas? How do the occupational communities engage in working together? Would a large group intervention be appropriate?
Outcome	Coordination across functions, technologies, operations, business units, geographical units, subcultures, occupational communities . . .

rather a group. In the same vein, Katzenbach (1998) outlines a number of myths pertaining to senior management groups which negate the notion that these groups are teams. While staying with the term 'executive team', Nadler *et al.* (1998) highlight synthetic and cosmetic teamwork, under-designed teams, consensus management, good plough–wrong field, inertia and succession overhang as the main problems with senior management groups. In the light of these issues it is more useful to think of the senior management group as a collection of individuals, each representing a constituency and with his/her own goals and preferences – the CEO with the board (Hambrick *et al.*, 1998) and the senior managers with their departments.

Finglestein and Hambrick (1996) identify three critical issues with respect to an understanding of senior management groups. First, the composition of the senior management group needs to be clear – who is a member and why. Second, the power dynamics among a group of executives at the top of an organization are central. Third, the nature of the interaction within the senior management group is key.

Composition: While it is clear that this group is at the strategic apex of the organization, its membership may vary according to the nature of the strategic decisions under consideration. In relation to particular areas of decision, different individuals may be included or excluded according to their area of expertise and hierarchical position within the organization. The selection of members, the boundaries of who is included and/or excluded, and indeed the formation of group norms is largely created by the chief executive.

Power dynamics: The distribution of power among the members of the senior management group is not equal. The play of power among a CEO, line managers, staff analysts, support staff and others is acted out, not only through an active voice in decision-making, but also through advice-giving, sponsorship and alliances in the internal coalition which forms the structure of an organization. When strategic decisions are unstructured and ambiguous, the role power plays is greater. There is greater potential for competition for scarce resources, self-interest and institutional enhancement. Accordingly, conflict can not only be about substantive issues relating to the content and process of the policy, but can also be emotive. Amason (1996) concludes that quality of decision in senior management group depends on the encouragement of substantive conflict with a restraining of emotive conflict.

There is a complex relationship between the CEO and the members of the senior management group. CEOs are the leaders of the groups. They design the composition, structure and process of the group. When the group meets, they chair and shape the dynamics. As a senior management group typically does not spend much time together and its members work apart from each other most of the time, CEOs also shape the dynamics when the group is not in meeting. At the same time, the group members are dependent on their

CEOs, whose decisions are final. Their tenure is uncertain and their continued membership of the senior management group depends on their CEOs. Senior managers have limited exit options; they can only move down or out, so they need to build a good working relationship with their CEOs.

Interaction: When executives interact in a senior management team or group on unstructured tasks such as policy formation, implementation and review, the dynamics are complex. As Ancona (1990) points out, there are social complexities whereby with a high ego involvement there is a high potential for disagreement and a need for individuals to be able to stand back from their own perspectives and biases. There are political complexities as a great deal may rest on the individuals in terms of their careers.

In our view, Level II is defined by the common task and interaction in a small group or team, whether formal or formal, permanent or temporary. When the senior management group engages in the process of strategy formation, implementation and review, it can be understood in terms of a Level III membership attempting Level II process working on Level III and IV content. That is to say, the issues of strategic and policy analysis and decision, organization and coordination of resources and action are discussed and acted upon by a working group which forms a political coalition from the functional areas of members which they represent as it engages in strategic conversation. Therefore, group and team process issues of how goals are set, how the group process works, how information is communicated, decisions are made and so on are pertinent and critical to how the content issues of strategic analysis, decision, implementation and review are considered and put into practice (Nadler *et al.*, 1998).

Level IV – Organization

The fourth level is the organizational goals, policy or strategy level. It is the final fusion of the three previous levels together to form a working, cohesive organization which functions as a complex adaptive system in a discontinuous world. As Pascale *et al.* (2000) argue, organizations operate at the edge of chaos and must exhibit a capacity for self-organization in the face of multiple complexities. In their view equilibrium means death and therefore the creation of variety is paramount for organizations to learn and adapt to the many unexpected changes.
    The organization's task is:

1   To be cohesive.
2   To live in a competitive environment.
3   To exchange a product or service to obtain scarce resources.
4   To reflect on its own strengths and weaknesses.

5   To engage in a proactive relationship to determine the opportunities and
    threats from the external environment.

Strengths and opportunities are matched in a selection process that determines programmes, services, products aimed at accomplishing the goals of
the organization and servicing the external environment with its products
and services. An awareness of the cultural assumptions that underlie an
organization's policies, strategies, structures and behaviours contributes to
the successful completion of the tasks at this level (Schein, 2004).

The key intervention is open systems planning, performed in terms of the
organization's core mission, with its internal and external constituencies
that make demands on the organization. Open systems planning comprises elements of identifying key environmental stakeholders and analysing
the demands they are currently making on the organization, the projected
demands they will make, the current responses to those demands, creation
of a desired future and action planning (Beckhard and Harris, 1987; Nadler,
1998).

The tasks at the organization level can be viewed from the four perspectives
(Table 1.8).

In Part III we develop the open systems perspectives in terms of five
strategic foci – framing the corporate picture, naming corporate words,
doing corporate analysis, choosing and implementing corporate actions,
and evaluating corporate outcomes. The central theme of the book is to
link these processes to the process of change, whereby the strategic foci
are the means by which managers and consultants enact change in their
organizations.

Table 1.8 Perspectives at organization level

Perspective	
Leader	Where are we going?
	What does the horizon look like?
	What's over the horizon?
	What advantages do we have over the competition?
	Do we understand whom we serve?
	Do we have the capabilities to achieve our goals?
Member	How do I contribute?
	Do the plans include me?
ODC consultant	Do they know the competition?
	Do they understand the customer?
	Is there good strategic thinking?
	Is there good involvement of all?
Outcome	Does the organization learn and adapt in a changing environment?

A pharmaceutical company began as a single product company, manufacturing a calcium supplement. As the product was successful and the operation grew, a conscious programme of acquisitions was begun. A company that manufactured a chairlift for stairs and one that manufactured eyeglasses were purchased. These organizational components would generally be classified in the medical or health field. After a period of significant growth, there was a flat period at the company in which this wide range of activities was difficult to manage. The president brought the senior management group into his office to discern the company's core mission. They decided to be an ethical pharmaceutical company and began a systematic placement of themselves in that business. The first approach was the development of new ethical prescriptions from R&D. The period from the initiation of the basic research to the production of a marketable product lasted 14 years. A second strategy was evolved to acquire from abroad other products that could be manufactured and sold in the United States under license. This process produced a marketable product in three years. This strategy combination of R&D and product license was used systematically to shape the organization from within and simultaneously develop the strategic advantage. It placed itself in a particular competitive marketplace while developing a strong market position with strong new products.

In developing the core mission, the company found out it could not sustain being a medical company. A medical company was too broad with too many supply channels and marketplaces on which to focus as a single organization. Second, it realized that the product the company was selling was sold over-the-counter through pharmacies and that this, in turn, was a very different market from the ethical drugs prescribed by physicians and sold in pharmacies under prescription. Both these insights contributed to the refinement of the company's core mission. The company decided that the most lucrative market was the specialized ethical drugs sold through pharmacies under physicians' prescriptions. The result of this decision was that the other products which were no longer consistent with the company's mission were sold off, and the funds from the sales were used to obtain products which would be within the pharmaceutical specialty. The long phase of research and testing in order to obtain certification that a drug was safe for use was such that it was not possible to make up ground quickly on competitors. The ten years of basic research and ten years of testing meant that most new products would only come on the market 20 years after inception. Careful discussion and thought-provoking focus enabled the company to decide to purchase the rights to drugs already in the testing process in foreign countries, and so reduce the 'catch-up' time to four or five years.

> The strategy of using foreign drugs is a precise example of setting an interim state between the present and future states. In this situation the ability to start from scratch and form new ethical drugs was still a distant dream. An intermediate point, but moving in that direction, was to take drugs already in existence with some original testing finished for their accuracy, and bring them into the marketplace on a quicker basis by doing the testing required by the United States FDA, a process which shortened the time and gave the pharmaceutical company an intermediate life.

Inter-organizational networks

A dynamic within the organization level is the increasing development of participation in inter-organizational networks, such as strategic alliances, in inter-organizational collaboration supply chain management through the extended manufacturing enterprise (EME). Supply chain management seeks to align deliberately and strategically the value-adding activities in different stages of the supply chain, with the expectation of improving the performance and, eventually, the service delivered to customers (Lane, 2001). Due to changing market and competitive demands, individual companies have found it necessary to focus on their core business in order to remain competitive, while, at the same time, developing relationships with other firms with complementary competences (Nohria and Eccles, 1992). Consequently, competition is moving increasingly from inter-firm rivalry to collaboration between supply chains and networks (Ring and Van de Ven, 1992; Christopher, 1998). In the field of manufacturing, such collaboration between firms may develop into an EME, a chain or network comprising all the relevant functions of the partners. Developments in information and communication technology have facilitated both process improvement within organizations and between organizations. In this inter-organizational network the modes of collaboration, i.e. through technology such as EDI, and its quality, i.e. the levels of inter-organizational trust, partnership, are key to successful completion of the task at this level (Huxham and Vangen, 2005).

The 'key' individual, team, group/division and organization

We have made the critical distinction between organizational levels and echelon and pointed out that they are not the same. There is a strong connection. Positioning on an organization's hierarchy has an impact on functioning or dysfunctioning. When an individual has a problem the higher ranking he/she is, the greater the impact is on the organization. The charismatic founder/entrepreneur is legendary in having an impact on an organization's life, style and functioning. The higher ranking one is or the more power one team has, the greater the influence is to bring about change. The problem of an interdepartmental group or divisional leader is more than a Level II issue for his or her team. The representatives of an organization in building and sustaining inter-organizational networking are central to the creation and maintenance of trust and good inter-organizational relations.

To develop that idea further we refer to the notion of the 'key' individual (individuals who by virtue of power, position, charisma or expertise can influence more than other individuals). The notion of the key individual allows for how leadership is spread around an organization and how it is embedded in teams and groups, rather than in the heroic individual (Raelin, 2003).

Similarly, within an organization there is the notion of the 'key' team and the 'key' group. In engineering organizations, the lead engineering group may be the key group. In manufacturing organizations, over different stages of the life-cycle, the key group may shift from design engineering to production to sales. In universities there is typically competition between academics, administration and finance as to which is the key group. In competitive markets where organizations compete for clients and customers, there are 'key' organizations (i.e. those organizations which are pre-eminent, the market leader from which other organizations tend to position themselves). In organization development, process interventions must be owned in the organization from the top. If an intervention is to be successful, the issues around key individuals must be understood and dealt with first.

Conclusions

In this chapter we have discussed organizational membership through the notion of the four levels of behaviour and distinguished it from rank. We have also outlined the organizational processes which take place at each level. We have characterized these processes in terms of a key word to define the essence of each level: Level I *matching needs*, Level II *functioning team*, Level III *coordination* and Level IV *adaptation* (see Table 1.5). Finally we have noted that within the issues of each level there is a twin focus: actions which enable completion of the relevant tasks at each level and actions which facilitate the significant interrelationships between each level.

This construct of four organizational levels is essential for understanding the dynamic interrelationship between individuals, teams, aggregations of teams and an organization's strategic endeavours in a complex world of discontinuous change. It integrates the disciplines of individual and group psychology with those of strategic management, technology and industrial relations. In our view, it is located at the cutting edge of organization development and the management of change.

Action research activity 1.1

	Organization	Interdepartmental group	Team	Individual
Organization				
Interdepartmental group				
Team				
Individual				

Take an organizational change issue with which you are familiar.

1   Name a change issue from the perspective of the organization for its performance and success.
2   Now work diagonally along the shaded boxes. What demands does it make on interdepartmental group coordination? How does it impact on the work of teams? What are the consequences for individuals?
3   Where would you put your energies to advance the progress of the change and heal dysfunctions?
4   Develop strategies to implement change at each level.

Case: Omega Foundation

In an ODC intervention in the Omega Foundation, a European healthcare organization which provides residential care for people with physical and sensory disabilities, organizational levels were central.

In 1997 Omega was going through a period of serious change. Internally, this resulted in a change in governance structure, in policies and procedure, employment and funding operations. A major internal force for change was identified in the service users' changing needs and expectations with regard to the service provided by Omega. In response to these forces for change, an organization development project was initiated, with its agreed objective to build the capacity for change through creating a shared learning experience for participants which would be grounded in Omega values and mission enabling it to develop capabilities and processes for continued organizational learning and change.

The aim of the project was to (a) create conditions in which the stakeholders could engage in conversation and listen to each other on what is important in the life of Omega and (b) how it could create actions from the conversations in order to move purposefully into the future.

Each individual, whether resident, staff member, trustee, volunteer, member of a management committee, had a relationship to the organization. This relationship was experienced very differently by members of the different groups and varied from individual to individual. Some individuals related to others as part of staff teams. Others related to the organization as individuals with responsibility and many were recipients of the care provided by others. The project aimed at strengthening the relationships in ways that were appropriate to the different constituencies by the process of creating the open space in which conversation and listening could take place. The project also aimed at addressing the functional and residential groups and teams in which individuals worked and lived. Therefore, there was attention to the strategic and operational issues of how each centre functioned, how committees worked and how people worked together to deliver the service to the residents. It also attended to how the different groups coordinated their efforts, whether resident, staff and management committee within a centre or the many centres within the national organization, or between the head office and the local centres. Finally, the ultimate aim of the project was to help the strategic and operational adaptation of the whole organization in a changing world. The ODC project attempted to create an open space for conversation across and between all levels. The project created a structure to facilitate conversation about the present and desired future states of the organization, to enable stakeholders to take ownership of the change issues and to begin to empower themselves to map courses of action.

Questions for reflection and discussion

1   Map what you think are the different expressions of the individual and teams levels in Omega.
2   What are the complexities of Level III in Omega?
3   How does Level IV in Omega comprise the effective workings of Levels I, II and III?
4   How would you structure working with each level in an ODC project as outlined above?

Chapter 2

Interlevel dynamics

The notion of organizational levels is common in organization development and change (ODC) texts. Many of these texts have their chapters constructed around interventions at different levels, for example, individual interventions, group interventions, inter-group interventions and total system interventions (French and Bell, 1999; Cummings and Worley, 2004). It appears that this approach uses organizational levels as a set of convenient headings under which various ODC activities can be categorized. Organizational levels in this context become a rather static notion. In the latter part of the last century, the focus was on individual, team and organization, but not on the systemic interconnectedness and interrelationship between them. By contrast, we are endeavouring to describe the dynamic nature of the four organizational levels. A significant element in this dynamic nature is the relationship between levels. Therefore, when we talk about any particular level, we are simultaneously dealing with an interlevel reality.

The conceptual basis for the interconnectedness of organizational levels is found in systems dynamics (Senge, 1990; McCaughan and Palmer, 1994; Jackson, 2003). As system practitioners point out, the key insight in a systems approach is to see interrelationships occurring in feedback loops rather than seeing linear cause-and-effect chains. For instance, an individual's relationships within a team are both affected and caused by the team's relationships with individual members. Within organizational systems, the interconnectedness of departments, functions, positions in the hierarchy, demonstrate the centrality of complex feedback loops, each having an effect on the other. In the framework of the four organizational levels, each level is related to the other three. The individual is affected by his/her relationship with the team, by how the team works in the interdepartmental group and by how the organization functions in its external environment. The face-to-face team is affected by how the individual functions in his/her relationship with the organization and vice versa, how the interdepartmental group functions and how the organization succeeds in its mission. The interdepartmental group is affected by how the organization relates to its environment, how its constituent teams function, and how the individuals and the organization match their respective needs. In our view these dynamic relationships are constitutive of the organization as a living system.

Interlevel dynamics, or levels of aggregation as they are sometimes called, enrich the perspective of organizations as living systems, as they focus on patterns of interaction among people, and so are open to the complexity and unpredictability that all human relationships potentially have. We cannot be mechanical about relationships, we can only adopt an organistic approach which tries to work collaboratively with people rather than control them. The patterns of participation in organizations – the individual with the organization and vice versa, the individual with fellow team members and vice versa, teams with other teams in the interdepartmental group, and the organization with its external environment and vice versa – are determined by the system itself. They can work together in the interest of the whole or work against one another and fragment the whole. They have their own internal cognitional activity which shapes what we call culture and they select what they consider to be important, sometimes to the frustration of senior management. Above all, they are capable of learning and changing. How they do so is the subject of this book. A premise underpinning the integration of interlevel dynamics and action research in this book is that interlevel dynamics are integral to creating 'communities of practice' (Wenger, 1998) and 'communities of inquiry' (Friedman, 2001) and are central to the use of parallel learning structures (Bushe and Shani, 1991).

The interconnectedness between positions in the hierarchy and levels of complexity exists in the role of the key individual. The key individual is a general term to connote those whose role involves crossing boundaries from one subsystem to another and linking one subsystem to another, as instanced by Likert's (1961) famous linking pin framework. The team-leader, supervisor, manager, administrator crosses the boundary from his/her area of responsibility to those of other functions or higher management. That is a crossing of boundaries on the hierarchical echelon. At the same time, these individuals are interacting in interlevel dynamics. They bring individual issues to a team, and team issues to the interdepartmental group. When an individual represents his/her own team to a broader function, he/she crosses from a team to an interdepartmental group level, and the dynamics of that interaction may lead to a reassessment of the individual level. Examples of such interlevel interaction are described by Lewin (1948) as the 'gatekeeping' role, by Allen (1977) as the 'technological gatekeeper' and by Ancona and Caldwell (1988) as external functions such as 'sentry', 'scout' and 'ambassador', whereby information is brought into the team from the external environment. New information, especially disconfirming information, may cause the individual to be rejected by the team, thereby producing conflict in the team. We will return to the notion of the key individual in chapter 5, when we examine how the process of change moves across the four levels.

Level I effects – functional and dysfunctional – on other levels

The matching needs task at Level I implies an interconnectedness between the individual and the organization. The individual brings his/her life tasks to the organization and enters into a psychological contract with the organization. The feedback loop from the organization's management communicates that the person is of value and is worthy of compensation. Thereby the formal contract of employment is set up and enacted through conditions of employment, socialization, training and development, career planning, promotion opportunities and other human resource management processes.

Dysfunctions at Level I can come from either side of the relationship. Issues particular to an individual can come from person's maladaptive coping with the dynamics of the life, work and family cycles of adult development (Schein, 1978). From management's side, managerial assumptions about human motivation, actual management behaviour, and the conditions of employment and compensation create the conditions for, or inhibit, an effective Level I (McGregor, 1960).

Level I can affect any of the other three levels (Figure 2.1). Depending on the individual's place in the organization's hierarchy, this effect can be more or less significant. If a dysfunction on the individual level concerns the chief executive, then the Level II senior management group, the coordination of the entire organization at Level III and the organization's competitive

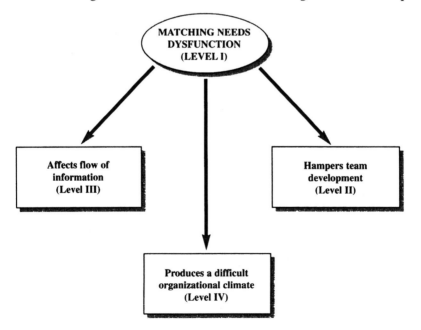

Figure 2.1 Level I dysfunctions affecting other levels.

performance at Level IV are affected. When an individual level dysfunction occurs at the operational level, the effects may be more localized.

How Level I affects Level II

As the individual enters into a face-to-face working team (Level II), issues of team membership predominate for the individual. The individual struggles to satisfy particular emotional needs – identity, power, control and influence, individual needs versus team goals and acceptance-intimacy (Schein, 1999). How these issues are resolved on a continuing basis sets the psychological contract between the team and the individual member. From management's view, the task is to be effective in achieving the team's tasks, and the focus is more on uniting around common goals and effective process. When individuals do not integrate into a team the outcome can be team dysfunctioning (Level II) or a dysfunctioning in the matching needs relationship at Level I among the team members. Yet if a dysfunction persists for a long period of time or does not yield to team process interventions, then most often Level I dysfunction is operative.

How Level I affects Level III

As individuals interact with a wider and more complex system, depending on their position in the organization, there is a growing sense of alienation and of non-belonging. The average individual's identification with his/her own team, section or function typically means that the individual's interaction with the interdepartmental group primarily operates through the membership of a team. As already mentioned, this scenario is different for key individuals, such as supervisors and middle and higher level management. In this context, Level III dynamics centre around issues of information availability, resource allocation and inter-team power alignment as management attempts to orchestrate the aggregation of multiple teams at Level III.

In a university the president operated on an authoritarian top-down detailed analysis mode of operating. He worked that way himself and that philosophy spread through the university. His successor worked from a participative model, whereby problem-solving and decision-making through consensus were implemented. He had an uphill battle in transforming the norm from the individual controlling his/her own area in isolation to one where interdependence created a need for interactive information-sharing and decision-making by consensus. This was apparent through all levels of the university as well as up and down through the hierarchy. The ten years' practice of guarding one's turf and working in isolation was difficult to overcome.

How Level I affects Level IV

The chief executive of an organization plays a key role in forming the organization's strategic position in its external environment.

> Howard Head was an inventor and entrepreneur. In establishing the Head Ski company he influenced how the company was perceived. He wanted his skis to be black so that colour would not detract from the design and marketing would be centred on the engineering of the skis. If he had had his way the only customers would be professional skiers. This insight into Head the engineer is essential to understanding the Head Ski Company (Rashford and Coghlan, 1994).

Level II effects – functional and dysfunctional – on other levels

Team dynamics occur throughout the organization. They are found in the workings of the senior management group, teams within each department, the organization of the cleaning shifts, formal and informal committees, task forces and so on. The face-to-face team level is connected to the individual, interdepartmental group and organizational levels (Figure 2.2).

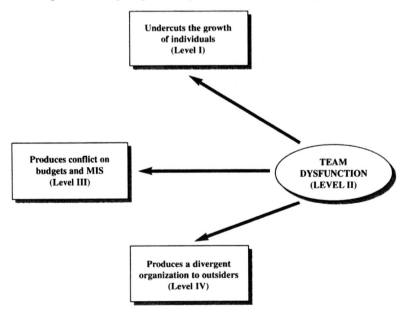

Figure 2.2 Level II dysfunctions affecting other levels.

How Level II affects Level I

A team's norms may result in behaviour that discriminates against particular individuals and creates a dysfunction from the team back to the individual. The famous Asch experiments have shown how a group can enforce conformity on individuals even to the point of the individuals doubting sensory evidence. Such pressure from the group can enforce conformity on individuals to participate in the group's defensive routines by colluding with a sense of success (groupthink) by not surfacing questions of concern or by not raising issues which are considered to be undiscussable (Argyris, 2000).

A sales installation team of a large telephone company comprised one woman in an otherwise all-male team. The men were avid sports enthusiasts and constantly made use of sporting analogies and imagery. In fact, the sports chat was the price of admission to the team's conversations. Their female colleague, who had no interest in sports and was barraged by sporting models, felt that she was being made to feel excluded. The lack of sensitivity on the part of the males forced the withdrawal of the woman from active participation in the team. For her part, she explained the difficulties that she was having to her MBA organizational behaviour professor. He suggested that she confront the men's behaviour in front of the team and talk out the issues involved. The ability to raise and articulate the issues enabled the woman to return to her team, confront the men with their behaviour in a gentle way and show how it produced a feeling of exclusion in her. While this confrontation resulted in some sensitivity and opened the door for a greater participation in the team on the woman's part, it did not eclipse all the prejudice and behavioural practices which had built up in an all-male organization over a long period of time. The climate had grown over many years. The role of operators was limited to women and the role of installer was limited to men. In this intervention, it was not a prescriptive solution that was brought to bear, but an awareness on the part of all concerned that an equal team participation was required.

How Level II affects Level III

In a large organization, the interdepartmental group's effectiveness depends on the quality and timeliness of information and resources from the teams which make up the interdepartmental group, so that any interdepartmental group-level dysfunctioning may be due to a particular team's dysfunctioning in achieving its tasks. For instance, when a finance department delays purchase or payment for purchases, new purchases are not received on time for particular projects. A finance team's context is always at the interdepartmental group and organizational levels: receiving information; providing it for other parts of the organization; making judgements regarding financial criteria for the operation (Level III) and relating it to external auditors, the board of management and the CEO (Level IV).

How Level II affects Level IV

The interlevel interaction between the team and organizational levels can be found in those teams whose role is to work on policy and strategy, e.g. senior management groups, sales teams and other boundary functional teams.

A construction company, in its building division, was going through a difficult period. Competition was focused on the custom building, in which the company manufactured modular buildings. The engineering team met to determine how to approach dealing with its problems. A meeting with the sales and manufacturing departments was called. In a separate venture which included the same people, the management training section had put together a management training session and asked Rashford to act as facilitator. The first session comprised an exercise of tinker toys to encourage the development of team skills. The senior management group elected to stay together as a group. As the exercise proceeded the company's president got up, left the group and began to pace the room on his own. He then returned to the group with an answer on what the group should use the toys to build and how it could sell the idea (the task of the exercise). The group complied. In the review and discussion that followed, it was reflected that the president's behaviour in the exercise was his common way of behaving and that the company's senior management group operated in this manner also. In fact, the real issue in the company's inability to develop custom building was that the divisions represented by senior management wanted to do their work as individuals and did not have the skills to work together. Working together was essential in order to produce custom building for the customer.

Level III effects – functional and dysfunctional – on other levels

The interdepartmental group level is the most political of levels and is where interlevel interaction is most critical (Figure 2.3). Interdepartmental group-level dynamics are commonly enacted in team-level settings where representatives of different functions or departments meet to coordinate and

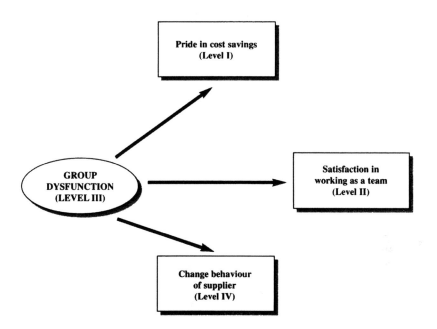

Figure 2.3 Level III dysfunctions affecting other levels.

review plans and activities. Success at this level requires political manoeuvring and bargaining in order to achieve an adequate political balance between information availability, resource allocation and the maintenance of power and influence of particular interests. An instance of the interdepartmental group level interacting with the individual level is where department heads experience their suggestions and proposals blocked, and their frustration with the inability to get ideas through leads them to withdraw from the arena and perhaps leave the organization.

How Level III affects Level I

The effect of Level III on Level I is most often seen in the budgeting process or the management of information. The organization that finds resources scarce and begins to change the allocation process will soon affect one team more than another. Individuals begin to worry about their relationship with the organization. The ability of the organization to be a place of personal growth appears to diminish.

How Level III affects Level II

The working of the interdepartmental group can affect the working of a team. Obvious examples like late or incomplete information at the interdepartmental group can impede effective task completion by a team which is dependent on the reception of that information accurately and on time.

An organization's senior management group set up a team to design and coordinate a company-wide training programme on environmental awareness. After six month's work the team invited Coghlan to do some team-building work. It was reported that morale was low; one member had resigned and others were on the point of following her. The consultant met the team and inquired into the team's process – its goals, its way of working and so on. What became very apparent to the consultant was that this team had been very active and had fulfilled its brief effectively. At the same time its work did not appear to be having an impact on the organization. Few members were taking up the opportunity for the training that the team was organizing. What emerged was that while the senior management group had given the team its brief and told it how important its role was, it has not communicated this to the rest of the organization. Consequently the training programme was perceived across the organization as outside of the mainstream priorities of the organization and therefore something that one could take or leave as one chose. Subsequently, the team met the senior management group and discussed the lack of clarity. This case illustrates how the team's problems lay not in the Level II processes within the team but in the interface with the senior management group, whose own behaviour in not communicating the importance of the training to the organization as a whole had led to the crisis within the team.

How Level III affects Level IV

Interdepartmental rivalry or conflict can sabotage an organization's ability to compete in its external market. An industrial dispute can cripple an organization when it loses its share of the market during closure or its good name for reliability suffers so that when the dispute is ended it finds it difficult to recover its former position. The terms of settlement may put severe strain on the organization's resources.

Sometimes the effect of Level III on other levels is positive.

A greeting card manufacturing company using large quantities of paper purchased on rolls measured in tonnes set up an interdepartmental group management information system to detect paper losses throughout the production process. Each roll was purchased within parameters of length and thickness while conforming to weight specifications. The company wanted to increase its production by controlling and reducing the amount of waste. As the paper moved along the production process, whenever presses were out of register or there were other failures, the length of the amount of paper that had to be scrapped was measured and detailed against the weight of the original roll. This led to a reduction of waste. The printing foremen and their teams were put under pressure not to produce waste (Level III affecting Level II). At the same time, there was considerable tension between the production people and card design people as production blamed card design for not making designs that were easier to produce (Level III affecting Level II in another function).

The control of scrap and the measurement of the length of paper to provide a better manufacturing control mechanism turned out to have the desired effect, but not in the way it was expected. The paper manufacturer, through its sales people that had worked in the card company, heard that the greeting card company was measuring the length of each roll in order to ascertain how much loss there was. Fearful of losing the greeting card company's business, the paper manufacturer evaluated its process and found it had allowed the paper to be produced thicker. The roll was shorter, producing fewer cards for the card company while it was the same weight. The card company wanted length for more cards. The paper company changed its manufacturing process in order to produce a thinner paper with the same strength but with a longer length on the roll. As a consequence, the card company improved its productivity by thousands upon thousands of impressions, and hence produced more cards. This effect from the change on Level III affected Level IV in the card company by putting it strategically in a better position regarding its competitors. A change also happened in the paper manufacturing company.

The above case is an example of the interdepartmental group level of one organization affecting Level III change in another organization. The case is interesting because it demonstrates feedback from one organization to another and shows how the control or attempted control of a production process, when shared with a supplier, ended up with the supplier having a greater change impact on the organization than the internal change efforts that had caused so much interdepartmental group conflict in the original situation. The interdepartmental production group in the paper company learned a valuable lesson and had to change.

Level IV effects – functional and dysfunctional – on other levels

The organizational level depends on the individual, team and interdepartmental group levels working adequately (Figure 2.4). The organization's attempt to exist, to survive and to fulfil its mission in a competitive environment requires a strategic balance between the subsystems within it. It is contingent on coordination at the interdepartmental group level (Level III), so that the many departments, functions and interest groups maintain a working relationship which contributes to the organization's ability to fulfil its mission (Level IV). Such coordination depends on each team being effective in its own area of responsibility (Level II), which, in turn, depends on an adequate formal and psychological contract between the individual and the organization (Level I).

Often, Level IV dysfunction emanates from the competitive environment and then affects the other levels. When a radical shift in the market necessitates a change in the material being used, engineering and manufacturing functions are drastically affected. For example, the material that tennis racquets are made of went from wood to aluminium to graphite in a matter of 20 years (Rashford and Coghlan, 1994).

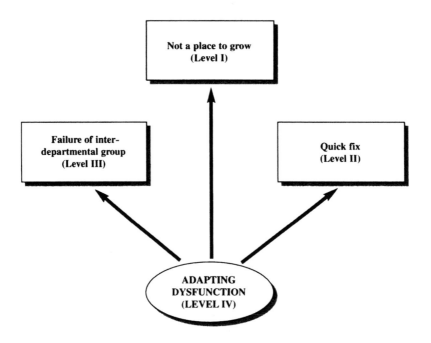

Figure 2.4 Level IV dysfunctions affecting other levels.

How Level IV affects Level I

A special relationship exists between the organizational policy level and the individual level. The individual's identification with the organization's mission and culture is dependent upon how the organization functions in its external environment and how that then gets transferred back through the three levels. The ability to function at Level IV requires a sense of mission, stability and viability. When this is threatened, individuals review their most basic commitment to the organization. The relationship between these two levels is typically referred to as 'organizational climate'.

In a national health service, when funds from the exchequer were reduced in an effort to control public spending, there was less money to go around the different sectors of the health service (Level III). This resulted in particular units receiving less money and having to work on reduced resources, both financial and personnel (Level II). Consequently, many units were placed under a great deal of strain. This in turn resulted in a growing anger and alienation among nursing staff, a decrease in the matching needs relationship and many seeking to leave the system and work elsewhere (Level I).

How Level IV affects Level II

Environmental forces can play a significant part in the functioning of a senior management group and are often mediated through the interdepartmental group. A discussion on how the changing environment is affecting the organization can evoke protective action in the senior management group's behaviour as each function represented tries to protect its own group from forthcoming changes.

How Level IV affects Level III

Mergers and acquisitions provide particular challenges between Levels IV and III. What was hitherto a Level IV organization becomes a Level III unit within the merged or acquired organization. The challenges arise from disparate groups being thrust together, the forced merging of cultures and traditions and the change demands made on what is considered to be the minor partner.

Conclusions

In this chapter we have shown how the four organizational levels are implicitly interconnected. Each level is linked to each of the others (Figure 2.5 overleaf). An understanding of how the loops feed back from one level to another is essential for the manager or consultant in assessing the workings of each level and in preparing and implementing interventions.

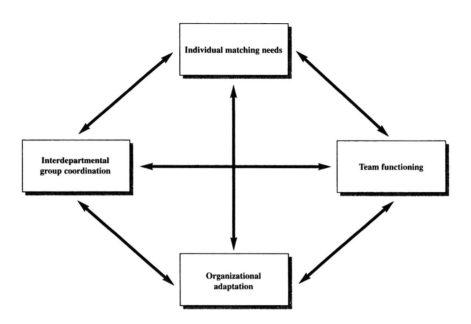

Figure 2.5 Interlevel dynamics.

Action research activity 2.1

	Individual	Team	Interdepartmental group	Organization
Individual				
Team				
Interdepartmental group				
Organization				

In an organization with which you are familiar:

1 Name a change issue with regard to an individual.
2 Now work diagonally along the shaded boxes. How does one level have an impact on the others?
3 Where would you put your energies to advance the progress of the change and heal dysfunctions?

Action research activity 2.2

1 Name a change issue which applies to the whole organization.
2 Now work diagonally along the shaded boxes. How does one level have an impact on the others?
3 Develop strategies to implement change at each level.

Case: The IT investment (adapted from Coghlan, 2000)

An IT consultant was invited to an organization to advise its senior management on the selection of an updated IT system. He initially met the managing director, and then in turn interviewed the managers of the manufacturing, marketing and finance functions respectively, each of whom were members of the senior management group. He also met the IT director, who was not a member of the senior management group.

From these interviews he formed the following picture. The senior management group was an intensely political arena; some of the members disliked other members. They were unanimous in their distrust of the managing director. They did not readily share information with one another, and, in fact, individual managers had little sense of what was going on in functional areas other than their own. None of them had much idea of what they required of a new IT system. Each commented that they left IT matters to the IT director. The IT director felt very frustrated. He experienced that while IT issues were being left to him, he could not get enough information or policy directions from the senior managers on which to make recommendations. It subsequently emerged that the capability of the current IT system, which was now to be replaced, was largely underutilized. His expectation was that this would happen again with the new system and a significant capital investment would not reap its potential benefits.

It is clear from this case that the IT agenda for this organization is secondary to the organizational issues. In other words, any efforts to resolve the technological issues of choosing a new IT system may well be doomed to failure unless some key organizational issues are resolved first.

Questions for reflection and discussion

1   What are the Level I, Level II, Level III and Level IV issues in this organization?
2   How do they affect the issues of IT investment?
3   How do the level issues identified in Q. 1 affect one another?
4   At what level do you think the IT consultant should intervene?

Case: Interlevel dynamics in extended manufacturing enterprise (EME) (adapted from Coghlan and Coughlan, 2005)

A company worked in the capital equipment industry competing in both the military and the civil market. The company employed over 1500 people, and had grown by 20 per cent over the previous two years. The industry is characterized by low-volume, high-value products with a life cycle of up to 30 years in the military sector and of up to 15 years in the civil sector. Strict quality requirements are reflected in a need to certify and to trace each component part, each piece of raw material and each operation performed. Consequently, only certified suppliers can be employed, making the management of the supply base complex. Entry into the civil market in the 1980s required a change in the company strategy with a move from vertical integration to choosing a different network of suppliers for each programme. As a consequence, purchasing had grown over 100 per cent in the past five years, indicating the increasing importance of supplier relationships for the company. The supplier was a specialist in high technology metalwork parts, design and engineering, starting from 3D models provided by customers. The set of activities performed depended on the requirements of the customer. Products were usually prototypes or small series of mechanical parts with high technological content. The system integrator (SI) accounted for 45 per cent of its total turnover. The relationship with the SI was considered strong, stable and strategic with dedicated investments in design and process technology and equipment.

The company, as a system integrator in the supply chain engaged with a supplier in an action learning process, whereby a group comprising senior purchasing managers from the system integrator and senior managers from the supplier met in an action learning set to explore collaborative improvement in the supply chain between them. Through participation in regular meetings of the action learning set, both parties had the opportunity to present outcomes of their initiatives for constructive questioning and reflection.

Two collaborative improvement cycles were undertaken through the action learning process. The first related to reduction of delays; the second related to management of personnel qualifications.

First cycle: reduction of delays

Disrespect for delivery times regarding materials, drawings and documents was seen as a major cause of delays. The initiative was concerned with mapping the overall order process and monitoring times and dates in order to identify possible causes for delay. The supplier was responsible for ensuring that all documents and parts were received on time. The SI felt that the supplier needed to be more proactive and recommended more frequent and more direct lines of communication. It was agreed to monitor all orders for three months in order to identify all the delivery dates of the parts and the dispatch date of documents, materials and drawings. The activity steps were as follows:

- Analyse the causes of the delays noticed and then meet to discuss these causes.
- Develop an improvement proposal relating to order management including implementing the new order management system, analysing the improvement activity and its results.

As the result of this activity, delays on the specific part considered for the pilot initiative were reduced by 75 per cent.

Second cycle: Management of personnel qualifications

For certain product programmes, staff involved needed specific qualifications and certification. The goal was to create a database detailing the staff and processes in both the SI and the supplier, including the qualifications necessary for performing welding, surface treatment and chemical treatment tasks. Data were to include a list of the people involved, medical checks necessary, nature and duration of qualifications, validity and expiration of qualifications and a list of applicable product programmes for this database. This database would allow the SI and the supplier to access current data and to plan with greater visibility of employee status. The activity steps were as follows:

- Define the data needed and identify the data fields.
- Create the database.
- Upload the data.

This task took approximately one month to complete. They began to use the database and to monitor and evaluate its use. On the basis of this evaluation, the database was extended to include information about process, process steps and the types of qualifications and certifications needed for different product programmes. It was hoped that this database could be rolled-out to larger suppliers if successful.

Questions for reflection and discussion

1   What are the levels present in the EME action learning group?
2   Place yourself in the role of one of the SI's purchasing managers. What interlevel issues do you face in this action learning process?
3   How are interlevel dynamics useful in understanding and managing EME processes?

Part II

Interlevel change

Chapter 3

The process of change and learning

As change and learning are central to organizational survival and development, it is important for managers and consultants to draw on knowledge of how change and learning take place. How change and learning take place applies not only to individuals, but also to teams, between teams and to organizations.

Change

Before we explore issues relating to organizational change there are important categories of change we need to consider. These are orders of change, planned and unplanned change, context of change, frequency of change, content of change and process of change. We now describe each of these in turn.

Orders of change and learning

There are different orders of change and learning. From the work of Bateson (1972) and others who have developed his work, a distinction between change or learning which deals with routine issues and that which involves a change of thinking or adoption of a different mental model is typically defined as a distinction between single- and double-loop learning (Argyris and Schon, 1996) and first- and second-order change (Bartunek and Moch, 1987), adaptive and generative change (Senge, 1990) and continuous and discontinuous change (Nadler, 1998; Nadler *et al.*, 1995).

First-order change occurs when a specific change is identified and implemented within an existing way of thinking. For example, Bartunek *et al.* (2000) describe management-led action research in a bank regarding communication problems with clients. Through the processes of participative data gathering, data analysis, feedback and action planning, intervention and evaluation, the named problem was addressed and improvements made.

It is realized that sometimes concrete problems are symptoms of complex attitudinal and cultural problems that must be addressed, and that problem resolution involves organizational transformation. *Second-order change* occurs when a first-order change is inadequate and the change requires lateral thinking and questioning and altering the core assumptions that underlie the situation. In another example, Bartunek *et al.* (2000) describe a manager-led change project which initially aimed at improving a manufacturing system by increasing volume while maintaining flexibility as well as enabling automated material control and improved planning. As the data were being analysed, it became evident that these changes would involve creating a radically new way for the company to do business. Accordingly, through the change process, materials personnel, assemblers, testers and supervisors/managers participated in diagnosis, analysis and feedback resulting in the implementation of a new integrated manufacturing system. Due to the success of this project, a similar methodology was applied to other change projects in the company. Second-order change is equivalent to a change in culture (Schein, 2004). What can happen is that a second-order change is implemented as a one-off event and becomes normative and embedded in the system as unchangeable. The creative leap or lateral thinking gets embedded in operational practice and takes on a first-order identity. Hence there is a need for organizations to develop the skills of being able to renew themselves continually.

Third-order change occurs when the members of an organization learn the habit of questioning their own assumptions and points of view and developing and implementing new ones. In contemporary terms this is where organizations act as complex adaptive systems existing on the edge of chaos (Stacey, 2001; Burke, 2002). Pascale *et al.* (2000) point to the characteristics of such organizations:

1   Complex adaptive systems are at risk when in equilibrium. Equilibrium is a precursor to death.
2   Complex adaptive systems exhibit the capacity for self-organization and emergent complexity.
3   Complex adaptive systems tend to move toward the edge of chaos when provoked by a complex task.
4   One cannot direct a living system, only disturb it.

Planned and unplanned change

By 'planned change' is meant change that is a deliberate decision. It does not mean, as some critics maintain, that everything can be planned. Because there is some dissatisfaction with the present state, either because of the emergence of existing or anticipated problems or because of a vision of a preferred future, a deliberate process of change is embarked upon. Unplanned change refers to unintentional or accidental change, where events force reaction and change is in effect necessitated by the forces for change.

Context of change

The context of change refers to (a) the external forces in the socio-economic and political environment which drive change, such as capital market demands, developing customer needs, etc., and (b) the internal environment, such as budget overruns, low morale among staff, excessive dysfunctional political inter-group rivalry, etc. The external and internal contexts draw together Theory E and Theory O, which we introduced in the Overture.

Frequency of change

There is considerable discussion as to how frequently change occurs. Tushman and Romanelli (1985) developed the punctuated equilibrium model which states that organizations proceed through short periods of second-order change between which are periods of equilibrium. In a not dissimilar vein, writers like Nadler (1998) and Weick and Quinn (1999) suggest that change is episodic as external environmental forces infrequently exert pressures for second-order change. On the other hand, continuous change tends to occur at the micro-level effecting incremental modifications in how employees do their work (Orlikowski, 1996). Episodic change affects the work of senior management and creates changes in strategic activity, such as redefinition of mission, strategic positioning of markets and cultural change. Lewin's notion of quasi-stationary equilibrium, where any stability is temporary and is upset by forces driving for change, is an appropriate way of viewing the challenge of change for many organizations. Throughout this book we will draw on the case of Saint Joseph's University as a traditional mature organization that exists in quasi-stationary equilibrium and is confronted by episodic change. Complex adaptive systems exist in continuing discontinuous change. Throughout this book we study the experience of VerticalNet, an Internet company, which went through rapid unpredictable change in a short space of time.

Content and process of change

Content of change refers to what changes. For organizational systems, formal content areas of strategy, policy, technology, organizational structure, work patterns, job design, HR systems, financial systems may be the targets and mechanisms for change. At the informal level attitudes, norms and culture may be the focus for change. Process refers to how a system changes and is the subject of this book.

We now turn to exploring the subject of how people change. What kinds of issues do they consider? What psychological processes go on when people move from one set of ways of thinking and behaving to another?

Understanding change

There are several sources of motivation to planned change. There can be an experience of pain or dissatisfaction with a present situation, so the driving force for change can be a desire for relief. The dissatisfaction can come from a perceived discrepancy between what is and what ought to be. There can be external pressures to change. The move to change can come from the internal thrust toward wholeness or development. This latter point echoes Maslow's finding that motivation is not always deficiency-driven as by lower order needs, but can be driven by higher order drives for self-actualization. This is important for organization development and change as appreciative inquiry builds on such assumptions. Appreciative inquiry is an approach which rejects the focus on problems and seeks to engage the life-giving forces of a living system by building on experiences of the positive, by engaging participants in creating shared images of a preferred future and by finding innovative ways of creating the future (Watkins and Mohr, 2001).

When change is mandated by others

Of course, not all change is self-initiated. Within organizational settings change is frequently if not typically mandated by others, particularly senior management. What are the dynamics of the change process for those who are being mandated to change by their managers?

For individuals, teams and the interdepartmental group, there are three critical process elements: perception of the change, assessment of its impact on the individual and response (Figure 3.1).

The first is *perception*:

*   This comprises the *meaning* the change has for those mandated to change, the degree to which they have control over the change and the degree of trust in those promoting the change. How the organizational members perceive what the change might mean is directly dependent on the amount of information provided. When managers say, 'there will be a lot of change around here' and do not elaborate what they have in mind, listeners to that statement are left to make their own inferences and create whatever meanings they wish. Some may infer that their job is under threat and thereby create a negative perception. On the other hand, if managers say, 'there is a continuous bottleneck at the order processing stage which we need to address to speed up our customer delivery service', then the listeners know what is meant and can position themselves in relation to the change which might follow from this problem definition.
*   The second element of perception of the change has to do with the *degree of control* the organizational members have over the change. For instance, if the mandated change affects the way subordinates do their

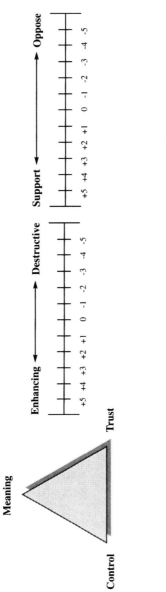

Meaning

Control

Trust

Enhancing ⟷ Destructive

+5 +4 +3 +2 +1 0 -1 -2 -3 -4 -5

Support ⟷ Oppose

+5 +4 +3 +2 +1 0 -1 -2 -3 -4 -5

PERCEPTION ⟶ IMPACT ⟶ RESPONSE

Figure 3.1 When change is mandated by others.

job and they have not been consulted and they think that their ability to do their job and deliver a quality service is being inhibited by the change, then their perception is likely to be negative. Degrees of control lie along a continuum; at once extreme is no control and at the other full control. Selecting the appropriate position on the continuum varies from situation to situation.

• The third element of perception is the *degree of trust* that organizational members have in those mandating the change. When managers in effect say 'trust us' and everything they have been doing over the past few years has had the opposite effect, why should anyone trust them in this case? Change puts extra pressure on existing relationships. If there is low trust before change, then the change process will not, of itself, increase trust. Trust may be viewed as a continuum, with high trust at one extreme and low trust at the other and varying degrees in between. In putting these three elements together we can see that if managers do not provide adequate information about the proposed change, do not involve the subordinates and have a low trust relationship with them, then the perception of the change is likely to be negative.

Perception of the change leads to *an assessment of the impact of the change.* Any assessment is not simply black or white, good or bad. Rather, there is a continuum along which assessment is made. The change may be assessed as positively enhancing at one end of the continuum or threatening or destructive at the other. In between are varying degrees of positive and negative assessment. It is uncertain, though probably positive or probably negative. If the perception is negative, then the assessment of the impact is likely to be so also. Lack of information, lack of control and low trust is likely to lead to a negative assessment. Schein (2004) refers to this as 'survival anxiety', meaning that if there is no response to the disconfirming information, then some important elements of the system will fail. Schein makes the point that 'survival anxiety' alone does not suffice for change to take place. A system can be blocked by what Schein calls 'learning anxiety', which is that form of anxiety which promotes defensiveness, resistance and paralysis. A person may experience learning anxiety from the pain of unlearning, from feeling temporarily incompetent, a fear of losing one's identity or losing team membership or a fear of being punished. Increasing such learning anxiety has the effect of increasing paralysis and resistance. The implication for managers is to reflect on how they behave (Schein, 1992). It is easy for managers to create disconfirmation; they have the strategic perspective and the hierarchical clout to assert that things are not going well or that change has to happen. They are also well positioned to create anxiety. What they typically tend to be less skilled at is creating psychological safety and so minimize defensiveness, resistance and survival anxiety.

Perception and assessment lead to *response.* Responses range along a continuum. At one extreme is active and positive embracing of the change; at the other extreme is open opposition. In between are varying degrees of support, acceptance, toleration, resistance, dodging and denial.

The overall point is that for organizational members to change at the behest of their superiors, the response to change is dependent on (a) how the change is perceived (which itself is dependent on the degree of information provided, the amount of local control over the change and the degree of trust in the change initiators) and how the impact of the change is assessed. These three elements are influenced heavily by the availability of information about the change and the process of communication between those promoting the change and those affected by it. Absence of information and a lack of a sense of participation create learning anxiety, uncertainty, hesitation and resistance, and increase any lack of trust that might exist.

Four psychological reactions to change

Traditional change theory has been built around Lewin's (1948) model which states that the change process has three stages or sets of issues: being motivated to change, changing, and making the change survive and work. Any change process can be conceptualized as comprising three stages:

1   A stage of seeing the need for change and assenting to its relevance (what Lewin called 'unfreezing').
2   A stage of changing from the present state to a changed state (what Lewin called 'moving').
3   A stage of making the change survive and work (what Lewin called 'refreezing').

In Lewin's view, attention to all three stages is essential. Lewin's theory is frequently considered to be out of date because (a) it appears to assume a more stable world where planned change occurs periodically and linearly rather than discontinuously as in today's world (Burnes, 2004) and (b) in many situations we are forced to change first and think about it afterwards, so moving may precede unfreezing. Accordingly we present four psychological stages of change – denying, dodging, doing and sustaining (Rashford and Coghlan, 1994), which in our experience accommodates both scenarios. In chapter 5 we will show how these stages are enacted in the implementation of change.

First stage: denying

The denial stage begins when the data supporting a change are first brought into the organization, i.e. when disconfirmation first starts. It can be a denial of the need for change in the face of others' assertion of the need to change or a need for change caused by environmental forces. This stage centres on processing information, disputing its value, relevance or timeliness. The change agent may be anywhere in the organization and will meet with denial from above and below. The more unexpected the disconfirming information is, the more likely it is to be denied. The need for change is disputed as denial involves the rejection of the change information as not being relevant or pertinent. If change is being mandated without explanation or because there is no time, then organizational members may comply with the change directive while at the same time denying its relevance.

Resistance to change comprises cognitive and emotional elements that arise from the context of the change or the individual's inability to deal with change. The starting place for dealing with resistance is to consider it as a healthy, self-regulating manifestation which must be respected and taken seriously by managers and consultants. Denial must be treated in this manner. On the cognitive dimension, the substantive issues of why change is needed, the degree of choice which exists about whether to change or not, the nature and strength of the forces driving change, the effect of the change on individuals and teams must be presented in such a manner that the individual can assess the perceived impact of the change in the light of as full information about the change as is possible. On the emotional dimension, listening to fears, empathically understanding different perspectives on the change and creating the facilitative climate whereby the individual can be enabled to acknowledge and come to terms with personal emotional forces inhibiting participation in change is a necessary process for managers and consultants. In short, for movement to occur there has to be sufficient psychological safety whereby the change data can be accepted as valid, relevant and pertinent. In other words, some unfreezing has begun to take place.

At the same time, the acknowledgement of the need for change is somewhat generic. The acknowledgement that change is required is not necessarily internalized immediately. A reluctant acknowledgement shifts the impetus for change to other parts of the system. When this happens the change has shifted to a dodging stage. It must be acknowledged that some may remain in the denial mode and continue to persist in denying that change is needed. For these people the change process may move on without them, and at a later stage they may have to reassess their position or influence management to reassess its position. We refer to these people as 'outliers' and discuss their involvement in the change process in chapter 5.

Second stage: dodging

The dodging stage begins when the accumulated evidence shows that the change is likely to take place. It is acknowledged reluctantly that some change is needed, but that the change is required in another part of the system – 'Others have to change'. There can be a search for countervailing data, which allow the individual or team to avoid or postpone having to change. Individuals and teams can seek ways to avoid or postpone change or remain peripheral to it.

It is at the *dodging* stage when passive-aggressive behaviour is more typical (McIlduff and Coghlan, 2000). Anger is directed at change agents – 'those who are making me change'. If an individual experiences the culture of the organization as not supporting direct expression of anger and opposition, then passive-aggressive behaviours may follow during which time individuals will not participate actively in change programmes. They may physically attend meetings and training events but do not 'participate', and in their passivity communicates unexpressed hostility and opposition. At the same time they vent their opposition and lack of support to peers and friends outside of formal organizational situations. Coghlan and Rashford (1990) pointed to ways in which alienated members engage in distorted and faulty thinking about managerial behaviour. This means that individuals and teams, when they feel under threat, tend to over-generalize, deny the positive, be selective in what they perceive, jump to conclusions and act on the basis of emotional reasoning.

On the cognitive dimension, an individual or team can confuse the issue by presenting the weakness of the approach to the change. There may be a more serious issue that needs to be dealt with first. This attempts to shift the action to a different focus. Another method to subvert is to change the form. If the discussion is on workflow change, change it to personnel. If it is on personnel, change it to bulk capital budget funding or to the expense budget.

The generic approaches to dealing with resistance outlined in the denying section above are also applicable to the *dodging* stage. The issues on the cognitive and emotional dimensions must be dealt with through a process of consultation, listening and serious consideration of the concerns expressed. Movement out of the *dodging* stage comes either when, out of the consultation process, ownership of the need for change is accepted and the changing process can begin, or after some time has elapsed, when others have been implementing the change and the implications and effects of the change are perceived differently and perhaps appreciated or at least perceived less negatively. In terms of the Lewin-Schein model, the elements of disconfirmation, the presence of sufficient guilt or anxiety and the creation of psychological safety are present so unfreezing has occurred.

Third stage: doing

The doing stage is where the need for change has been acknowledged and owned to the degree that explorations of what changes are required, how, where, at what cost and at what cost to whom are undertaken. The doing stage is not comprised of any one action; it is a whole series of actions – diagnosing the forces driving and restraining change, interpreting data, articulating a desired future, having intermediate stages, creating and following a change plan, generating commitment, managing the transition, negotiating and bargaining, implementing, reviewing, and so on (Beckhard and Harris, 1987, Kotter, 1996; Nadler, 1998). It may be spread over a considerable time. As the change process unfolds, issues of where change must occur in the present system, how that change should be made, and what cost must be diagnosed, decided upon and implemented. The change process tests the readiness and capability of the system to change.

Within a complex system, the change process necessitates dealing with controversy and disagreement regarding different diagnoses, negotiation and bargaining within the system and dealing with the conflict that inevitably arises in such a context. Conflict at the doing stage is more focused than at the denial and dodging stages as it occurs within the context of a change plan and in this regard is different from conflict at the dodging stage. The issue is not whether change is required, but what change is required in what parts of the system and affecting what subsystems. Indeed, on particular issues regarding possible solutions to a change problem, there may be a reversal to denial and dodging. Each proposal may initiate its own change stages, so that within the broader change process, a particular proposal may generate denial and dodging and may need to be dealt with in those terms.

There are three directions the *doing* stage can take. One is something of an optimistic view, whereby the change process takes off and it is a matter of jumping on the wagon. A precaution needs to be observed not to change anything that is not germane to the need for change. It is not uncommon to think that because change is taking place, any change can be made. The second direction is a more common one, whereby doing involves negotiation as to what changes take place, how and at what cost. The third direction leads to a sense of futility that while there is a lot of activity, it does not address the real issues. At the moment where action should give a sense of satisfaction, there is an undercurrent that the organization has no identity or is losing its identity or value. It is at this point that the change issue may alter to encompass a more fundamental transformation of the organization. We will take up this point in the following chapter.

Fourth stage: sustaining

As normative behaviour is difficult to change, some reinforcement of changed habits is necessary to ensure change survives and the new state is sustained. The successful completion of this stage is the integration of the change into the habitual patterns of psychology, behaviour and operations (Pascale *et al.*, 2000).

For the individual, the new state must be reinforced by how the change fits the personality and is supported by significant others. This reinforcement constitutes the psychological basis of rewarding the continuance of the change state.

In organizational terms, this stage is best defined as the implementation of operating procedures and is a key stage of any change process. It is the focusing of energy to follow through on programmes and projects. Sometimes new manners of proceeding, new information systems or even new endeavours mark this stage. At this point the organization needs to be attuned to the fact that change is part of life. The organization will have in place the ability to sense changes in the environment and to adapt quickly to them (Schein, 1997). In this respect, sustaining or refreezing does not attempt to create a new stability or close down future change, but maintain an openness to continuous forces for change.

Modern organizations such as complex adaptive systems which are in constant third-order change never go to a sustaining phase but remain in a constant reformulated doing stage.

Organizational learning

The fields of organization development and change and organizational learning are closely related. Both focus on how organizations as collective entities change and learn (Marsick and Watkins, 1999; Weisbord, 2004). Where they differ they differ in emphasis. Organizational learning typically focuses on learning from experience (Dixon, 1994) and on identifying and developing learning capabilities (DiBella, 2001; Shani and Docherty, 2004). What the discussions on organizational learning tend to neglect is that organizational learning is a process of aggregation of learning at the individual, team, interdepartmental group and organizational levels (Coghlan, 1997).

One approach which does explicate interlevel processes is found in Argyris and Schon (1996) who adopt a levels approach when they refer to 'ladders of aggregation' which exist in organizations. In Argyris and Schon's view, the interlevel dynamics may be crucial to organizational learning. They state that learning which takes place in a particular team may be restricted to that team as, for instance, in a change in production-line technology. On the other hand, the introduction of just-in-time paper processing in a bank's division may provoke a change in the norms of how the bank's control system perceives, evaluates and rewards production in all its divisions. In such an instance, what is single-loop learning at one level stimulates double-loop learning at other levels. Indeed, Argyris and Schon highlight the issue of levels of aggregation as one of the important issues in the debate about organizational learning. They pose the following question: At what levels of aggregation – individual, interpersonal, group, intergroup or whole organization – does it make sense to speak of productive organizational learning? Their answer is to place the emphasis firmly on interpersonal inquiry which occurs within what they call 'the constraining or enabling context of an organizational learning system, focusing on how such inquiry interacts with processes described as occurring at higher levels of aggregation' (1996: 200). What this seems to mean is that learning is enabled or inhibited in so far as individuals, whether in teams or across the interdepartmental group, do or do not engage in joint exploration of assumptions and reasoning processes. If these assumptions and reasoning processes are not tested publicly then the result is organizational defensive routines and inhibited learning.

Conclusions

Senior managers, organizational members and ODC consultants need to have some understanding of change and learning in order to work them effectively. In this chapter we have outlined what we consider to be essential core constructs of change. The first is how there are different orders of change for any system, whether individual, team or organizational. We then presented a change process model that is built around how members of organizations respond when mandated to change by their superiors and managers. Finally, we introduced our own research on the psychological reactions to change. In chapters 4 and 5 we will show how these change frameworks work in how change is introduced into and moves through a complex system.

Action research activity 3.1

With respect to change in the organization with which you are familiar:

1   What new understanding have you arrived at by reflecting on the change in terms of orders of change, content and process and how members reacted and responded to the change mandate?
2   How do these theories and frameworks of change help you?

Case: The failed acquisition

When the Dallas-based Compushop was bought by Bell Atlantic in 1987, a basic change process was set in motion. From the Bell Atlantic side this was to acquire a small new computer sales firm. From the Compushop point of view, this was being taken over by a large organization which loomed large on its horizon. Three issues emerged in the implementation of the acquisition. Compushop controlled its own finances in the past as part of its organizational response. Bell Atlantic instituted the requirement that financial statements appear uniform and follow the same methodology as the parent company. This produced a situation in which the microcomputer, a product sold by Compushop, could no longer be used to produce the financials, since it could not accommodate the new programme required to produce the statements. A second issue which emerged dealt with personnel policies. Compushop employed relatively few women and minorities, while Bell Atlantic had a policy that differed substantially in this regard. The third emergent issue was based on values, since the commission practice at Compushop was to pay commission at the time of booking the sale. If for some reason the sale was not completed and the computer returned, the employee was not obligated to return his/her commission. Bell Atlantic challenged this practice. Compushop rebuffed Bell's policy on the grounds that good salesmen would quit.

From the Compushop perspective, these were major changes with a significant loss of control. They lost control on how they would work, who they could hire and how they would be compensated. This produced a significant lack of trust in the change process. Survival anxiety quickly set in and the acquisition was doomed by the failure to address the change process. The change process failed and Bell Atlantic divested Compushop.

Questions for reflection and discussion

1   How do you think the Compushop people perceived the acquisition by Bell Atlantic?
2   Can you apply Lewin's stages of change to this change process?
3   What are the signs of denying and dodging?
4   What could have been done differently?

Chapter 4

The interlevel dynamics of large-system change

In chapter 3 we introduced the subject of change. Now we turn to the question of large-scale and large-system change. What are large-scale and large-system change?

Large-scale organization change

Mohrman *et al.* (1989: 2) define large-scale change as 'lasting change in the character of an organization that significantly alters its performance'. Large-scale change has three dimensions:

1   Deep changes, which entail shifts in members' basic beliefs and values in the way the organization is understood.
2   Pervasive changes, which involve a major proportion of an organization's structures and processes, both formal and informal.
3   Complex change, which refers to the size of the system changed and the size of the change effort necessary to alter the performance of the organization.

So when large-scale change is applied to large systems, then the size of the organization, the depth and pervasiveness of the change come into play. For us, depth and pervasiveness of change in a large system is defined by the integration of change in individual, team, interdepartmental group and organizational behaviour and performance, whether that change be first or second order and involves five strategic foci – framing the corporate picture, naming corporate words, doing corporate analysis, choosing and implementing corporate actions and evaluating corporate outcomes.

Beckhard and Harris (1977: 15) define large-system change as 'a plan defining *what* interventions to make *where*, by *whom* and at what *time* in order to move the system to a state where it can optimally transform need into results in a social environment that nurtures people's worth and dignity'. How do large systems change? What are the kinds of actions that managers need to do in order that organizations move from one state to another? What are the actions that managers and ODC consultants need to do in order to enable organizational members to move change through a system, whether complex or simple? There is a growing consensus borne out of a great deal of research and action as to what leaders need to do. This consensus names a number of key activities that form a generic model of system change (Beckhard and Harris, 1987; Beckhard and Pritchard, 1992; Coghlan and Mc Auliffe, 2003; Kotter, 1996; Kotter and Cohen, 2002; Nadler, 1998; Coghlan and McDonagh, 2001) (Figure 4.1). These activities typically comprise:

1   Determining the need for change.
2   Designing the vision of the desired future state(s) beyond the change.
3   Assessing the present in terms of the future to determine the work to be done.
4   Managing the transition state through the implementation stage.
5   Reinforcing and sustaining the change.

Determining the need for change

The preferred starting place is to inquire into the context for change in the organization, unit or subunit or what Nadler (1998) calls 'recognizing the change imperative'. It may seem obvious that naming the need for change and its causes is essential. The forces for change may be coming from the external environment, such as major shifts in capital markets, global

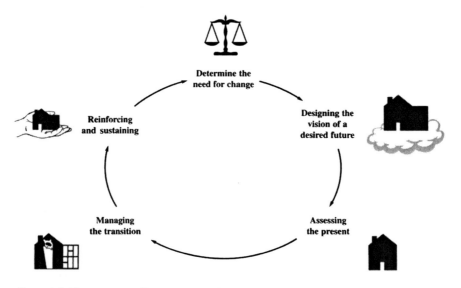

Figure 4.1 The process of large-system change.

market patterns, new competitors who have a new basis for competition, innovations in products and processes, external developments which change the rules of the game, and changes in customer characteristics and demands (Nadler, 1998; Foster and Kaplan, 2001). They may be coming from the internal environment, such as budget overruns, low morale among staff, excessive dysfunctional political inter-group rivalry and so on. The diagnosis of these forces identifies their source, their potency and the nature of the demands they are making on the system. These forces for change have to be assessed so that major change forces are distinguished from the minor ones. Organizational leaders should not be waiting for such forces to become apparent; they need to be actively 'looking beyond the horizon' (Hesselbein *et al.*, 1995; Nadler, 1998).

A second key element is the pressure of time and making the change in a particular window of opportunity. These pressures evolve from the sequencing of events, cycles of events or order of appearance in a market place. Being first makes a lasting impression. In this context the pressure of timing is everything.

A third key element in evaluating the need for change is the degree of choice about whether to change or not. Choices are not absolute. While there may be no control over the external forces demanding change, there is likely to be a great deal of control over how to respond to those forces. In that case there is likely to be a good deal of scope as to what changes, how, and in what time-scale the change can take place. The degree of choice may be mitigated by how quickly competitors respond to driving forces. There needs to be shared diagnosis into how these forces for change are having an impact and what choices exist to confront them.

There are critical interlevel dynamics in the activities of assessing the need for change (Figure 4.2). The change process has to begin somewhere. Who first sees that change is required may be anyone in the organization. As we will discuss in more detail in the following chapter, the gatekeeper, whether it is someone in direct dealing with customers or a high-level executive engaging in economic forecasting who first perceives that need for change, they must have the confidence to take the agenda to those in executive positions and persuade them to adopt his/her insight. If those in the executive positions deny or dodge the relevance of that insight, then the individual may give up or else reconsider how to present the case for change more forcibly. When the senior management group adopts the need for change and begins to act, it has then to win over other teams in the system. Each of these movements – from individual to team to interdepartmental group – is an iterative process. In other words, when the team adopts an individual's position, that adoption reinforces the individual. When other teams adopt a particular team's position, that reinforces that team, and, of course, when customers adopt a new product, that reinforces the organization.

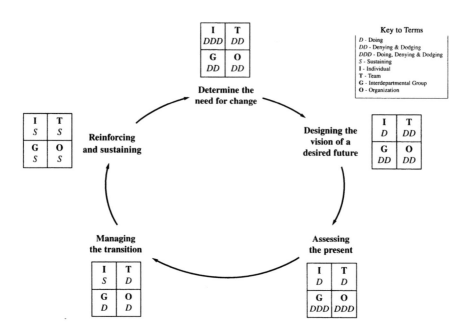

Figure 4.2 Interlevel dynamics of large-system change.

Saint Joseph's University is a comprehensive university of approximately 7,500 students. Located in the competitive northeastern United States, it is one of many private universities competing for the same students. In 1986 a new president came to the university with a desire to overcome issues of stagnated growth and poor economic performance. From the experience of successful graduate programmes in a prior institution, the president opened the discussion for change.

The ODC consultant may be brought in at the point where questions are being asked about how to extend the need-for-change question through the organization. Interventions may attend to how individuals and teams perceive the need for change and what their sources of resistance are. Interventions can focus on how the organization takes in information and address dysfunctions which might occur (Schein, 1997). Examples of dysfunctions around taking in information would be: an absence of structures for sensing changes in the environment, a focus on internal or external data only, and perceptual defences whereby data are distorted, and where different subsystems attend to different data. Critical interventions would focus on building formal sensing structures – planning groups, data-gathering groups, etc. and interfunctional dialogue where assumptions and perceptions of data are shared and heard.

In Saint Joseph's University the initial reactions to the president's change initiative were mixed in the senior management group. New facilities would be required for adult learners. New faculty would require more expense and structural changes as the departments of the university did not have responsibility for graduate programmes. Slowly the senior management group came to embrace the need for change and began a slow implementation. They in turn then met resistance in their departments. Gradually the change was accepted by most of the organization.

Designing the vision of the desired future

Once a sense of the need for change has been established, the most useful focus for attention is to design a desired future state or states. This is like an architect who shows the future picture with vision but leaves room for new ideas or for others' contributions. This process is essentially that of articulating what the organization, unit or subunit would look like after change has taken place. This process is critical as it helps provide focus and energy because it describes the desires for the future in a positive light. It is also positive as it leaves room for additional input. On the other hand, an initial focus on the problematic or imperfect present may over-emphasize negative experiences and generate pessimism. In addition plans that are too grandiose or seen to be out of range can also generate pessimism or apathy. Working at building consensus on a desired future is an important way of harnessing the political elements of the system.

When organizations embark on second-order change they do so in the expectation that there will be a steady state in the new order. This steady state or states may be envisaged in terms of a higher-order operating level (however that may be defined), and can be maintained through iterative corrections. Third-order change emerges when an organization arrives at the new state and is confronted by continuing change. For the most part third-order change does not emerge until second-order change has been embarked upon and cannot be planned for from a first-order platform.

Clearly, the process of defining the future involves interlevel dynamics. If the vision comes from the chief executive, then there are interlevel dynamics from that individual to the senior management group and then to the inter-departmental group and on to the organization. As the CEO takes his/her vision to the senior management group and works at persuading its members to adopt it, the movement is from the individual to the team. If the vision is created by the senior management group, then the process begins with the team and moves to individuals within that team, is reinforced in the group and then goes to the interdepartmental group and on to the organization. So the iteration of issue presentation, perception, assessment of impact and response ebbs and flows from individual to individual, team to team and so on.

Interventions would focus on what the most appropriate way to articulate and communicate vision might be, particularly within the senior management team and between the senior management team and the other teams of the organization (Quirke, 1996).

Returning to the Saint Joseph University case: after several years faculty groups and some administrative groups in the university felt the changes were all top-down and not representative of their own wants and desires for the university. In an attempt to identify a new corporate picture that could gain the support of multiple constituencies, an outside consultancy firm was hired to assist. When the group went away to begin the process, the interlevel level dynamics brought the process to a halt. The conflicts among the senior management group as well as some conflict between the senior management group and the consultants almost destroyed the process. These conflicts focused on whether or not the process could achieve the desired end. Significant progress was made by a combination of confronting the issues between the individuals, and the reduction of the fear on the part of the faculty group that they would not be heard. The president learned which actions of his were contributing to the conflict. As a result, he modified his behaviour, the senior management group and the faculty were able to engage in the process with a new level of openness. A new vision of the university's future that could be embraced by the group emerged.

Assessing the present in terms of the future to determine the work to be done

When the desired future state or states are articulated, the focus is placed on the present reality and questions like 'what is it in the present which is redundant for or a threat to the desired future state that needs changing and what is to be carried forward?' are asked. Because the present is being assessed in the light of the desired future, it is assessing what needs changing and what does not. It may judge that, for the change to take place effectively, a change in current structures, attitudes, roles, policies or activities may be needed. As any change problem is a cluster of possible changes, it may need to group particular problems under common headings, i.e. HRM policies and practices, service delivery, information management, reward systems, organizational structure and design and so on. Then it describes the problem more specifically, and asks, 'Which of these requires priority attention? If A is changed, will a solution to B fall easily into place?' 'What needs to be done first?' This step is about taking a clear comprehensive accurate view of the current state of the organization, involving an organizational diagnosis which names:

- the priorities within the constellation of change problems;
- the relevant subsystems where change is required.

Another element in describing the present is to describe the relevant parts of the organization that will be involved in the change. This description points to the critical people needed for the change to take place. Examples of who needs to be involved might include specific managers, informal leaders, IT specialists and so on. Their readiness and capability for change must be assessed. Readiness points to the motivation and willingness to change, while capability refers to whether they are able, psychologically, technically and otherwise, to change.

At this stage it may be clear whether first- or second-order change is required. As we described in chapter 3, by first-order change is meant an improvement in what the organization currently does or how it does it. By second-order change is meant a system-wide change in the nature of the core assumptions and ways of thinking and acting. The choice of whether to follow a first- or second-order change process may be as much determined by organizational politics or organizational capability as by the issues under consideration. How the key organizational actors interpret the forces for change and how they form their subsequent judgement as to what choices they have are important political dynamics.

Interlevel processes are critical to this step. Assessment of the present may create defensiveness in individuals, teams and between teams. There may be tendencies to attempt to shift blame for change problems from one team onto another. In assessing readiness and capability, a critical aspect may be how teams are capable or ready, or how much capability and readiness there is between teams. This may refer to political dynamics between teams or to issues around such issues as information management or IT compatibility. Relevant subsystems refers to individuals, teams and to the interdepartmental group. In second-order change the assessment of the present inquires into whether the organization has the capability and readiness to make the quantum leap to the unforeseen to future.

Interventions need to focus on dialogue within teams and between teams to agree on criteria for evaluation of the present strengths and weaknesses, with the accompanying focus on reducing the influence of interdepartmental politics, defensive routines and conflict. A particular focus for such intervention might be dialogue between the business functional areas and the IT specialists as to the current and potential role of IT.

To continue with the Saint Joseph's University case: when the small group that had been away for four days returned to campus, the desire was to repeat the process with larger groups of these constituencies. Shared vision exercises carried out in the small group were now repeated with a large group of people from both within and outside the university itself. These groups included more faculty, more administrators, students, parents, donors, alumni and support staff. The outcome of the process with the larger group was very similar to the small group experience. The process itself generated excitement about a possible new future. As people were excited about the new, the fear of letting go of the past decreased. In fact some of the excitement came from regaining some aspects of the past that had been lost. Concerns expressed centred on finding resources to accomplish the new goals. The president had his eyes opened. He was not afraid of the future but was afraid that people would not embrace a graduate programme as part of the university's future. He came to see that people were not only ready to embrace the new order, but had better ideas of how to structure graduate programmes within the current university structure and so helped to ensure its success. This intervention changed the president's thinking and how he acted with faculty teams.

Managing the transition

The transition period is both a period of time and a state of affairs. The critical task is to move from the present to the future and manage the intervening period of transition. This transition state between the present and the future is typically a difficult time because the past is found to be defective and no longer tenable and the new state has not yet come into being. So, in essence, the transition state is somewhat particular, as the old has gone and the new has not yet been realized, and so needs to be seen and managed as such. It is a messy time and state of affairs, where unanticipated events interrupt the formalized plan or its schedule.

As Beckhard and Harris (1987) argue, there are two aspects to managing this transition state. One is having a strategic and operational plan which simply defines the goals, intermediate stages, activities, structures, projects, resources and experiments that will help achieve the desired state(s). As no amount of change can take place without commitment, the second aspect is a commitment plan. The commitment plan focuses on who in the organization must be committed to the change if it is to take place. There may be particular individuals whose support is a prerequisite for the change and a critical mass whose commitment is necessary to provide the energy and support for the change to occur, particularly in second-order change. There are those who contribute new ideas and enhance innovation. The political dynamics of building commitment involves finding areas of agreement and compromise among conflicting views and negotiating cooperation.

Interlevel dynamics are pivotal to the processes of the transition state as individuals and teams address the implications and implementation of the change agenda. As the change agenda affects the work of individuals in what they do and how they do it, individual commitment is essential. Nadler (1998), in his description of the characteristics of how organizations respond to incremental and discontinuous change, notes that in redirecting and over-hauling approaches senior managers are typically replaced, not because of failure to perform but because they don't fit the new situation. Those managers who are flexible to new roles and approaches tend to survive. As the change agenda affects the work of the permanent teams and typically requires the creation of new teams, introducing new members and work in temporary committees or project groups, team commitment is critical to the change process.

In particular temporary task groups which are formed to guide the change process through activities such as steering the process, listening to opinions around the organization, planning and facilitating dialogue meetings and so on are critical. These task forces or project committees need to function well as Level II units and be able to engage in Level III interactions as they work across the different functional and cultural areas of the organization.

In a similar vein, the change agenda involves the interface of multiple teams with respect to information sharing, problem identification and resolution, resource allocation, and collective bargaining. Inter-team dynamics can enable or hinder the successful management of the change process.

Building commitment is essentially an interlevel process. Individuals identify with their teams, profession or occupational community or trade union, so efforts to build commitment involve interventions with teams and across teams, particularly if inter-team relations are likely to have a negative impact on the progress of the change. Strategies to manage resistance and build the commitment of middle managers are particularly important (Flood et al., 2000).

Following on with the Saint Joseph's case: as implementation of the new goals began, groups and individuals within the university were required to change. It became clear that to sustain and reinforce these changes two things needed to occur. First, the changes that were occurring needed to relate directly to what had been the outcome of the group process. Second, the resources used were to help the university make progress towards goals desired by the group.

Three times over the next year group sessions were held that were called 'walk-throughs'. The sessions laid out explicitly what had been set as goals, what had been accomplished and what yet remained to be done. Input from the group was solicited through questions as well as written evaluations. These experiences proved to be very important for the constituent groups to feel connected to change process and remain involved. It gave members an opportunity to see how bigger issues could and would affect them. In fact, the feedback led some things to change before any formal change initiative was begun. The 'walk-throughs' included a wide base of the university's workforce who saw what was coming and began to implement them before they were officially told to do so.

Reinforcing and sustaining

Because change generates so much energy and emotion, there is a danger that both managers and organizational members will relax if the tension of change appears to be over. The personal energy and hard work of senior management in particular tend to go into the earlier stages of getting change in and moving. Yet as Lewin argues, refreezing is as critical as unfreezing and moving, so there is a need to focus on making the change stick, making it work and survive. It is important that senior managers make reinforcing and sustaining part of their personal agendas.

Reinforcement involves consolidation, which Nadler (1998) sees as critical in the period immediately after implementation when the changes have not yet been locked into operational practice. He advises that the focus be placed on middle managers so that they take responsibility for measuring the success of the change, refining it and consolidating it through communication, staffing and HR policies. Measuring the success of the change involves formal evaluation processes. When senior management initiates an evaluation process it needs to be clear what the evaluation is for, what the targets of evaluation are and how the evaluation is to be conducted. In addition, senior managers need to show interest and involvement in the work of middle managers.

Sustaining is a longer-term focus than reinforcement or consolidation as it attends to keeping the momentum going. Processes such as team review meetings, interdepartmental group meetings, review conferences and return visits by external consultants support formal sustaining structures which ground the change, such as restructuring, job and role redesign, performance reviews and reward systems.

As we outlined in the previous chapter, organizations which are in third-order change never go to a sustaining phase but remain in a constant reformulated doing stage.

Review and learning

Review and learning permeate all five activities (Coghlan and Brannick, 2005):

1 Determining the need for change.
2 Designing the vision of the desired future state(s).
3 Assessing the present in terms of the future to determine the work to be done.
4 Managing the transition state through the implementation stage.
5 Reinforcing and sustaining the change.

While reinforcing and sustaining refer to refreezing the change, review and learning refer to the outcome of reflection on the experience of engaging in each of the activities and of the process as a whole. The critical dimension to change is how review is undertaken and managed. Review is essentially reflection on experience and in any such reflection the critical questions are asked, not to evoke guilt or blame, but to generate learning as to what is taking place and what needs to be adjusted. If review is undertaken in this spirit then the likelihood of individual or team defensiveness can be lessened and learning can take place.

As we have detailed already, there are three types of inquiry in review (Fisher *et al.*, 2000) (Figure 4.3). The first inquiry loop focuses on behaviour

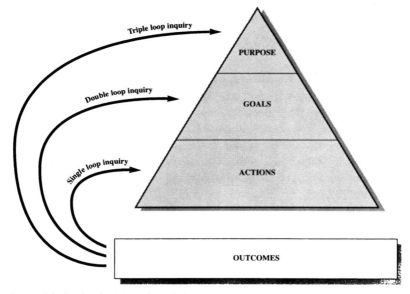

Figure 4.3 Single, double and triple loop inquiry.
(Adapted from the work of Bill Torbert, with permission.)

and actions. How skilful was the organization in each of the five activities and in the overall process of change? Can the critical events be identified? What was learned for future change processes? The second inquiry loop focuses on the strategies underpinning the behaviour and actions. In hindsight do the strategies and plans make sense? From where do they emerge? If skilfully implemented would they stand a chance of being successful? Would the strategies need to be changed to achieve a better outcome? The third inquiry loop focuses on the intentions which the strategies and actions aimed to fulfil. Who are we? Is it what we wanted to be? Given the outcome, how do the original intentions now look? Were they realistic and achievable? Do these intentions need to be adapted, changed or continued?

Perspectives on large-system change

The perspectives of CEO, member, ODC consultant and outcome may be applied to the five activities of large-system change.

CEO

For CEOs the change imperative for first-order or incremental change comes primarily from the non-attainment of targets and market changes (Table 4.1). They design where they want the organization to be, what needs to change, develop and lead a change plan, build commitment, manage the transition and reinforce and sustain momentum. In situations of discontinuous change they intuitively sense a new world coming over the horizon and start designing change towards a future which is difficult to envisage and which may never settle into a steady state.

Member

For members the change imperative questions open up questions of aware-ness of the strategic issues of the organization (Table 4.2). If they have no such knowledge then they question the underlying assumptions of the change, tend to seek people or functions to blame. They typically have no comprehension for the rationale for discontinuous change. Through the change process they participate in the activities of the change process – assess-ment, problem solving, negotiating, adapting roles and behaviour and coping with the uncertainty. They are reinforced in presenting new ideas.

ODC consultants

ODC consultants work with the senior management and members of the organization to facilitate each of the five activities (Table 4.3). They are concerned with content and process issues. Their content concern focuses on

Table 4.1 Change from CEO's perspective

CEO's perspective	1st order/incremental change	2nd–3rd order/ discontinuous change
Determining the need for change	Not meeting goals Market changes	Intuitive sense of a new world Structure of changing market
Designing vision of desired future(s)	New state of operational effectiveness	Vision of new world
Assessing the present in terms of future	What needs to be developed What needs to be cut out What needs to change	What needs to be developed What needs to be cut out What needs to change
Managing the transition state	Implementing change plan Management structures Building commitment	*2nd order* Implementing change plan with no landing point Flexible management structures Building commitment
		3rd order Implementing change plan with no landing point Flexible management structures Building commitment to continuous change
Reinforcing and sustaining	How not to slip back How to sustain momentum	*2nd order* How not to slip back How to sustain momentum
		3rd order How to sustain momentum for continuing change

Table 4.2 Change from member's perspective

Member's perspective	1st order/incremental change	2nd–3rd order/ discontinuous change
Determining the need for change	Awareness of strategic and operational issues	Lack of comprehension
Designing vision of desired future(s)	Future place and role in the organization	Lack of comprehension
Assessing the present in terms of future	Providing feedback Participating in assessment	Comprehending the rationale for radical change

Table 4.2 Continued

Member's perspective	1st order/incremental change	2nd–3rd order/ discontinuous change
Managing the transition state	Participating in change process Adapting to changing organization Coping with uncertainty and stress	*2nd order* Participating in change process Adapting to changing organization Coping with uncertainty and stress *3rd order* Participating in change process Adapting to changing organization Coping with uncertainty and stress
Reinforcing and sustaining	Providing feedback on perceived success of change from operational viewpoint	*2nd order* Finding a place and role in changed organization *3rd order* Finding a place and role in continuously changing organization

Table 4.3 Change from ODC consultant's perspective

ODC consultant's perspective	1st order/incremental change	2nd–3rd order/ discontinuous change
Determining the need for change	Accurate diagnosis Widespread acceptance of need for change	Accurate sensing
Designing vision of desired future(s)	Level of involvement in creating desired future(s)	Buy-in to vision of new world
Assessing the present in terms of future	Assessment of what needs to change Political dynamics of assessment	Assessment of what needs to change
Managing the transition state	Progress of change process Commitment building Problem resolution	*2nd order* Progress of change process Commitment building Problem resolution *3rd order* Progress of change process Commitment building Problem resolution Coping with uncertainty and stress

Table 4.3 Continued

ODC consultant's perspective	1st order/incremental change	2nd–3rd order/ discontinuous change
Reinforcing and sustaining	Reinforcement and sustaining mechanisms in place Continuation after end of consultant contract	*2nd order* Consolidating changed state *3rd order* Remaining flexible for continually changing

the accuracy of the diagnosis and sensing of the need for change, the content of the desired future(s) and of the change plan. Their process concern attends to the involvement of the members of the organization, the progress of the change plan, how commitment is built up and how learning takes place.

Outcomes

The outcomes are that each activity is successful in moving the organization through its change process (Table 4.4).

Table 4.4 Change from outcome perspective

Outcomes	1st order/incremental change	2nd–3rd order/ discontinuous change
Determining the need for change	Accurate diagnosis Widespread acceptance of need for change	Accurate sensing
Designing vision of desired future(s)	Level of involvement in creating desired future(s)	Buy-in to vision of new world
Assessing the present in terms of future	Assessment of what needs to change Political dynamics of assessment	Assessment of what needs to change
Managing the transition state	Successful management of transition Commitment to change Renewed organization	*2nd order* Successful management of transition Commitment to change Renewed organization *3rd order* Successful management of transition Commitment to change Renewed organization

Table 4.4 Continued

Outcomes	1st order/incremental change	2nd–3rd order/ discontinuous change
Reinforcing and sustaining	Change goals achieved Shared learning from experience	2nd order Change goals achieved Shared learning from experience
		3rd order Change goals achieved Shared learning from experience Skills at continual change

Conclusions

In this chapter we have provided the essential structure for large-system change. The five activities (i) determining the need for change, (ii) designing the vision of the desired future state, (iii) assessing the present in terms of the future to determine the work to be done, (iv) managing the transition state through the implementation stage and (v) reinforcing and sustaining the change enable change to enter the system and to become established. The five activities and the management of interlevel dynamics are the essential and critical elements of successful large-system change.

Action research activity 4.1

Review exercise for implementing large-system change

Reflecting on a change process in an organization with which you are familiar, answer the following questions.

Step 1   Determining the need for change:
            What are the external forces driving change?
            What are the internal forces driving change?
            How powerful are these forces?
            What choices do we have?
Step 2   If things keep going the way they are without significant intervention:
            What will be the predicted outcome?
            What is our alternative desired outcome?
Step 3   What is it in the present that we need to change in order to get to our desired future – what is done, how work is done, structures, attitudes, culture . . .?
Step 4   What are the main avenues which will get us from here to there?
            What are the particular projects within those avenues? Long, medium, short term . . .?
            How do we involve the organization in this project?
            Where do we begin?
            What actions do we take to achieve the maximum effect/medium effect/minimum effect?
            How will we manage the transition?
            How do we build commitment?
            Who is/is not ready/capable for change?
            How will we manage resistance?
            Who will let it happen, help it happen, make it happen?
            Do we need additional help – consultants, facilitators . . .?
Step 5   What review procedures do we need to establish?
            How do we articulate and share what we are learning?

Case: Saint Joseph's University

This chapter has contained a series of vignettes on change in Saint Joseph's University. These vignettes build up an accumulated story of large-scale change in this university setting. Taking the elements of the Saint Joseph's University story that are presented under the heading of large-system change:

1   Put yourself into the role of the president, and, drawing on Table 4.1, try to view the change from his perspective.
2   Put yourself into the role of faculty member, and, drawing on Table 4.2, try to view the change from his/her perspective.
3   Put yourself into the role of an ODC consultant, and, drawing on Table 4.3, try to view the change from his/her perspective.
4   Map the large-system change process and, drawing on Table 4.4, assess the strengths and weaknesses of the process of planned change.

The Saint Joseph's University story continues throughout the book, so you can revisit these activities in the light of the information you will receive later in the book.

Chapter 5

Phases and levels of large-system change

In chapter 3, we described individual change in organizations and introduced four psychological reactions to change. Then, in chapter 4, we explored the interlevel processes in large-system change. In putting these two themes together, in this chapter we see how the psychological reactions occur as the change process is initiated and develops within an organization. As the change process moves through an organization, there is a domino effect as the key individual takes the change issue to a team, and the team takes it to the interdepartmental group and so on until the change affects the entire organization, both internally and externally. The change process in a complex system involves individuals and teams, hearing the news of the proposed change, perceiving it, assessing its impact and deciding how to respond. The support of a critical mass is needed for movement to occur and change to take place. This support is built over time and so there is a need to understand how the change process moves through the organization over a time period.

We will now detail how the reactions to change interact with the four levels. Since there are countless activities and interactions in a large system's change process, we have grouped them together to form a seven-phase sequence in order to bring structure to this process (Table 5.1). This approach maps how the change process moves through an organization – across the four levels taking account of how individuals, teams, the interdepartmental group and the organization deny and dodge before doing. While it appears that these phases are linear, they are not. They move iteratively, back and forth in circular loops as the conversations on the change agenda unfold throughout the organization.

It may also appear that these phases form the structure for a social engineering approach through cascading whereby senior management's dictates for change are pushed downwards for compliance through the organization. They indeed may be used in this manner, as we will see in the A&P case in chapter 13. However, we see these phases as a structure for understanding the conversations and interactions necessary for participation in and the internalization of change. The quality of the conversation required is such

Table 5.1 Players in organizational change and the phases of large-system change

Phase	Change gate-keeper	Key individual	Team members	Team outliers	Group members	Group outliers	Organization	Organizational outliers
Ground zero	Denying Dodging							
Change awareness	Doing	Denying Dodging						
Initiation	Doing	Doing	Denying Dodging					
Man-oeuvring	Sustaining	Doing	Doing	Denying Dodging Persistence	Denying Dodging			
Integration	Sustaining	Doing	Doing	Doing Compliance	Doing	Denying Dodging Persistence	Denying Dodging	
Achieve-ment	Sustaining	Sustaining	Doing	Doing	Doing	Doing Compliance	Doing	Denying Dodging
Follow through	New denying	Sustaining	Sustaining	Sustaining	Sustaining	Sustaining	Sustaining	Doing Compliance
Sustaining	New dodging	New denying	Sustaining	Sustaining	Sustaining	Sustaining	Sustaining	Sustaining

that individuals, teams and the interdepartmental group engage in exploring and listening to one another and mutually influencing each other. So individuals and teams are open to influence from one another as the change agenda moves in spiral loops through an organization.

Phase 0 – Ground zero: the need for change enters the organization

Change enters the organization through an individual. The individual goes through his or her own reaction to the need for change by initially denying the validity, relevance and pertinence of the data calling for change. Once it is recognized that the change does apply, the issue of acting on the insight can be dodged and left to others. For change to progress this has to give way to a realization that the information is real and threatening, i.e. the organization may be in peril or lose some opportunity if something is not done. The individual, in this instance, can be anywhere in the organization and is, in effect, performing the 'gatekeeping' role or acting as 'scout' by bringing to the team the special information from the environment it needs to perform its task.

The individual who first perceives the need for change may or may not be a key individual in the organization's hierarchy. He or she may be at the strategic level where the analysis of market trends leads him or her to question how the organization is currently functioning. Or it may be that an individual may be in direct contact with customers or clients and brings feedback to the organization on the organization's product or service as experienced by customers or clients. If that individual is not a key individual then a key individual (manager, team leader) must be approached and persuaded to take on the change issue. The gatekeeper by this point has worked through the denying and dodging phases and is now in the doing phase, while people within the organization to whom the information is being brought are still in the denying phase.

Phase 1 – Change awareness: the key individual denying and dodging

The process from gatekeeper to key individual may have to work through several layers of the organization's hierarchy until it reaches a key individual powerful enough to act on it. At each juncture, the individual presented with the change issue goes through the initial reactions of denying and dodging before reaching the stage of doing and acting on the information. If the key individual is threatened by the change issue or by the gatekeeper's approach, the change process may be blocked and proceed no further. Ownership by the key individual concludes this phase, that is, when the key individual decides to act upon the issue.

It is not unusual for change to enter an organization through the key individual, in meetings with others, such as with other CEOs or presidents, where information is exchanged. This leads to the realization of the need for change. Sometimes the key individual may be meeting with superiors at corporate or a higher level.

Phase 2 – Initiation: the key individual doing and the team denying and dodging

When the key individual has worked through the psychological reactions of denying and dodging regarding the change issue, he or she moves to the doing stage and presents the change data to the appropriate team for consideration and action, emphasizing the necessity for change and beginning to define the dimensions of the change. He or she places an emphasis on the degree of choice and the ultimate control over the change, and why change is necessary at this time. In second-order change the emphasis is on selling a vision of a new order.

The process of denying and dodging is repeated in the team as the individual members deny (believe change is not required) and dodge (believe they do not have to do it now), before entering into the period of doing. The tendency 'to shoot the messenger' who has brought the bad news must be recognized. This phase is concluded when the team, as a team, recognizes the issue as critical and acknowledges the need to do something. Ownership of an articulated issue ends this phase, not just as defined by an individual, but as articulated by the team through consensus. There will be individuals who do not support the change but are not powerful enough to block or stop it.

Phase 3 – Manoeuvring: the key individual and team doing and the interdepartmental group denying and dodging

This phase involves bringing multiple teams together at the interdepartmental group level to confront the issue of the change. Not only does this refer to interactions between the senior management group and other functional teams but also between the temporary task forces and committees set up to guide the change process and functional teams. The process of first denying and then dodging is repeated within the individual teams that make up the interdepartmental group. Each team tends to view the change issue from its own viewpoint and may deny the validity, relevance and pertinence of the change. It will be evident in the organization that at Level III some functions will have to diminish and some will have to grow, e.g. some teams are more critical than others, some activities will be let go and others developed, etc.

The rationale behind the denying may focus on the information system, i.e. that the present form of data gathering is not providing the information that is needed to lead to the change. Denying at the interdepartmental group level typically means the emergence of differing and conflicting interpretations of the data supporting the change. It is argued that the information driving the change is not accurate, reliable and is found to be open to differing interpretations. The political interrelationship between teams may be a factor in denying, as for instance, when one team denies the need for change because the change is being promoted by a rival team.

When the decision support system is questioned the dodging is taking place, as when the coordination of the interdepartmental group is not effective and teams are blaming other teams for inefficiencies. This is when dodging needs to be addressed by internal mapping processes. The interfacing of teams – workflows, information processing – are the most relevant ones for identifying areas of trouble. The critical aspect of evaluating the need for change and getting ownership is to see the problem in a new way. Workflow mapping is a means of extending the boundary of the group's search for information to solve the problem. Each functioning team must become conscious of what other teams do and how what they do interacts with what others do. The dodging stage at this level confronts the assumption that if everyone else did their work, their team would have no problems. This phase ends with agreement on the articulation of the problem and the process steps needed to introduce change. Typically this involves correct identification of the critical people needed to make the change and description of what the new steady state might look like. In second-order change some key people may not yet be part of the organization, so initial consideration of the introduction and integration of new people who have not been part of the process begins.

A significant element of this third phase is the articulation of bargaining outcomes as a prelude to negotiation. In unionized settings when the collective bargaining process between management and unions is undertaken, it can be said that the interdepartmental group is at the doing stage. Collective bargaining negotiates what changes will takes place, how, at what cost and to whose benefit. This phase concludes with ownership and what effect the change will have on the organization's stakeholders, both internal and external.

Denying and dodging are natural reactions to the unexpected news that change is needed. They describe more explicitly the specific reactions in the unfreezing process as experience is disconfirmed and anxiety is felt (see Figure 4.1, p. 59). Because change involves a movement from what is familiar and accepted, it is threatening and stressful. Therefore, the initial reaction to change is that change is not necessary. As we have seen, such a reaction typically shifts to an avoidance or dodging stance. As Schein (2004) points out, the critical issue for movement from dodging to doing is the creation of psychological safety. The doing and changing stages are complementary, as are the refreezing and sustaining stages. Schein's notion of relational refreezing can be understood in terms of the four organizational levels working in harmony to sustain a change.

In our experience there is a danger of regression, particularly at Phases 2 and 3. As the key individual experiences the team's denying and as the team experiences the interdepartmental group's denying, it is often noticed that the individual or the team can lose confidence and slip back into a dodging mode. Not everyone buys into the change agenda. Some choose to remain peripheral to it. It is in this regard that we are introducing the notion of 'outliers'.

Outliers are those individuals who do not buy into the change process in the first round. If the team that is instituting the change is a senior team, some outliers can be managers from areas or departmental groups that have the most to lose from the change itself. It is essential to double back and bring these outliers from denying and dodging into the doing phase. One technique that can be helpful with these outliers is to do a 'walk-through'. This exercise takes all members of the team and presents the findings of the first change with which the interdepartmental group has just dealt. Then the senior management group provides an evaluation of why the steps were chosen and what happened when the change was presented to the interdepartmental group. This is followed by an evaluation of the forces resisting change and the forces supporting change. This dialogue can at times unfreeze members who are outliers or it may uncover a perspective that requires management to step back and rethink its position. In this instance, management may revert to denying and dodging.

The change process is always more difficult in a senior management group. The group member simultaneously reflects his or her own views while being a representative of an interdepartmental group. The presence of a consultant can be significant in confronting outliers and helping the manager and the team process what is occurring, while reinforcing for the senior manager the need for change and the need to remain firm in his or her convictions for change. The purpose of the conversations at this phase is to engage the interdepartmental group in the change process. Through conversation new ideas may emerge and the change agenda may be enlarged and amended to include emerging perspectives and points of view.

Phase 4 – Integration: the key individual, team and interdepartmental group doing, the organization denying and dodging

The organization's adaptive behaviour commences at this point as the organizational change forces its impact on the organization's external functioning and relations. Initially, in this phase, the question is how other organizations and stakeholders will perceive them and the organization if the change is introduced. At this point, assumptions about the interrelatedness of competitive organizations are questioned. At first, such an interrelatedness can be denied and when the denying is accepted, the question of what is the least amount of change acceptable is asked. Accurate competitive analysis leads to ownership of the interlinking of organizations in competitive markets. The open systems planning approach maps the impact of the changed and changing organization on its customers or clients, competitors and the market in general. The organization will be involved in extensive marketing activities in order that the changed organization's products or services will meet customer or clients' needs. Successful change requires an understanding of stakeholder demands and behaviour as well as a proactive stance in their regard.

The senior management group working over time with all of the changes may have overlooked the interdepartmental group outliers. They are the members of the interdepartmental group who are still dubious about the change process. They are not supporting the process, but are mostly very quiet about their disagreement. This is an important check at this point in the process. The solution can be to run a 'walk-through' in which the total interdepartmental group is brought together, placed at working tables, presented with the previous change process and given a chance to evaluate it in small group discussions. When the discussions are finished, input is collected by paper or voice. This can help collect the outliers into the support group of doers or hear their corrective input.

Phase 5 – Achievement: the key individual sustaining, the team, interdepartmental group and organization doing

The key individual goes into a sustaining stage when his energy shifts from initiating the change effort to keeping the organization focused on enacting the change. The energy of the key individual is now refocused to look for ways of sustaining the change. This may involve working with the consultant as to what structures and reward systems may be required to keep the change in place and seeing how other organizations have done it. The focus at this point is on the process of restructuring new functions, setting new norms and making the changed state normative, rather than a focus on the content of the change. These new elements are the part of the change process that must be sustained. Here it is important to determine if any of these critical aspects are not being sustained and, if so, what means are at hand to sustain them. This phase is concluded when the key individual, satisfied that all that can be done has been accomplished, enables the team to own the sustaining issues so he or she can look at new data and other change issues.

Phase 5 deals with the organizational level and the people affected by the change from outside the organization who are now, willingly or not, affected by the change outcome. These people can be suppliers, brokers, customers, the labour market, neighbours or community officials, capital markets and brokers, and any other individual or groups of individuals who relate to and interact with the changed organization.

In Phase 5, we now have, at the organization level, outliers who are a group of people at the edge of the change process still having doubts. It is often helpful to have a follow-up 'walk-through'. The follow-up 'walk-through' enables the outliers to listen to what was intended, what has been accomplished and to look at ways to further enhance the outcome. For some of these, such as customers, the 'walk-through' can be accomplished only through advertising and other forms of communications. Most often, the outliers will consist of people who have the most to lose from the change. When they see the reality of change, their fears will sometimes be reduced or they will be lost to the changed organization.

If the key individual is a creative person and, as such, recognized the need for change in the earlier stages and helped the organization adapt, that same creativity at this point may cause the individual to lose interest in the sustaining process. While progressing to the stage where he or she can see the end point, he or she can lose interest and become bored with getting the organization to sustain the change. Yet, this is a time to show concern and to continue to enable the change process.

Phase 5 is the critical phase in which questions surface of whether or not first- or second-order change is required. The adequacy or inadequacy of the change as perceived and implemented is reviewed in the context of its effects on the long-term perspective of the organization and its ability to engage in continuous change.

Phase 6 – Follow through: the key individual and team sustaining, the interdepartmental group and organization doing

The team goes into the sustaining stage when the process regarding the terminal point of change is defined. The key team defines the end, the phases and the time deadlines, i.e. the who, what, when, and how the change can be sustained. Then it is freed to play an enabling role as the momentum is under way and there is continuity in the entire organization. In high-tech organizations in a web-based world, there may not be time for this phase and there may not be a 'normal' time or period of equilibrium. In many cases the next change initiative has already begun.

If the change process fits the change needs, the organization is free to leave the change mode and move into a more normal state since the momentum is under way and there is continuity in the entire organization. If the change process is not sufficient to meet the change needs, e.g. if there is a lack of satisfaction within the organization or a lack of ownership of the change process, the question of whether a second-order change is required must be asked. It is not uncommon, at this point, for an organization facing second-order change to revert to Phase 2 in which the key individual has to convince the team of the necessity of second-order change and deal with its members' denying and dodging. In second-order change, things are not neat and well defined. Yet the change is played out in a cycle of similar phases: recognition of the change imperative (dodging), developing a shared direction, implementing change (doing) and sustaining (sustaining).

Phase 7 – Sustaining: the key individual, team, interdepartmental group and organization sustaining

The sustaining stage has occurred when there is a new relationship between the organization and peer organizations, when stakeholders come to accept the new relationship and interact with the organization in the new way, and when the structures, reward systems and review processes are in place. In the initial stages of sustaining, a good deal of energy must be devoted to ensuring the change has worked by monitoring feedback, both from within and outside the organization. Feedback is available through attention to each of the four levels. At this point the learning organization makes use of the organization's openness to learning as the ability to change is a confirmation of organizational learning.

After some time, when it is felt that the change is in place and has worked, there is a drop in energy. The organization is moving and it has its own impetus. The organization is fat and happy. Through its normative behaviour it reinforces its culture and thereby sets up the mode for future denying.

As outlined previously, some organizations do not move to sustaining but remain in continuous doing. As we discussed earlier, this may be due to perpetual discontinuous change in the environment where sustaining is a precursor to death (Pascale *et al.*, 2000).

Conclusions

Large systems do not change instantly. Change has to begin somewhere and a movement goes through the organization as those convinced of the need for change engage others and they in turn engage others. The seven phases of change provide a framework for one clear fact of experience which is rarely considered in the change literature, namely, in organizational change, people change at different paces. This is partly as a result of access to information, i.e. the CEO is likely to have a sense of the need for change before others further down the hierarchy because he or she has access to the information. A sales team may be convinced of the need for change from interaction with customers and then have to persuade the top management team to take on the issue. The seven phases framework is built on the sequence that when one party is aware of the need for change and begins initiating change, another party may be caught unaware and typically responds by denying and dodging.

In our consulting and teaching experience, while the seven phases may look linear, they are not. Each phase may comprise multiple loops as interventions are made to build commitment and action and help those who are dubious of the change (whom we have called 'outliers') to move from denying and dodging to doing. That there are individuals and teams in the outlier role provides valuable feedback on the organization's capacity, readiness and willingness to change. The multiple activity loops within each phase depends on management's ability to create minimal survival anxiety and maximum psychological safety. Knowing in advance that denying and dodging are likely to occur provides change leadership with its own psychological safety. These behaviours are common experiences in a change process. Knowing that they are coming is one form of preparation.

While the seven phases may provide a framework for senior management to cascade a change agenda downward through the organization, we caution against this approach. Rather we argue that the seven phases provide a framework for understanding the perspectives and reactions of organizational members (whether as individuals or as teams) as they engage in conversation about what, why and how the organization changes. Each conversation allows for new ideas and new perspectives to emerge. So rather than the seven phases being the vehicle for understanding the process of compliance, they are the vehicle for appreciating the processes of conversation.

Through the seven phases, members of organizations can easily recognize what phase their organization is currently in and identify with the descriptions and issues of each phase. In large organizations, sustaining the change process over a period of time across the four levels requires management and knowledge of the terrain. The seven phases give structure to this process.

Change involves a letting go of familiar and accepted ways of seeing and doing things. It can take a lot for us to acknowledge that change is needed. We will even deny the need for change. Then we dodge it and leave it to others. When that position cannot be sustained, we begin to see what is required, what needs changing, how, when, at what cost, etc. As relevant changes are made, they need to be sustained so that change survives. These seven phases show how members of an organization can be at different stages of the change process because they have access to information others do not have, and describe how in an organization change moves through the key individual, teams and the interdepartmental group towards the entire organization.

The ODC consultant can facilitate the individual manager, the team, the group and the organization to attend to the processes within the change effort and identify and work through the stages and phases of the change. A process consultation approach allows the members of the organization to understand what is going on and to develop the key diagnostic and problem-solving skills to manage change themselves. The ODC consultant collaborates with the members of the organization in designing the particular activities that help deal with the issues of each stage that move the individual, the team, the group and the organization through the change phases.

Action research activity 5.1

Reflecting on a change in progress in an organization with which you are familiar:

1 Review how the change entered the system, with whom, etc.
2 Track how the change moved from that individual to the wider system.
3 Note how individuals/teams and groups initially received and responded to the change agenda.
4 Note how responses changed/did not change over time.
5 Where is the progress of the change now?
6 What now needs to be done?

Case: AT&T Long Lines division

This case is about the Long Lines division of the AT&T Company and how they managed large-scale communications installation projects which extended over long distances and five or more years. It illustrates the phases of change through the four levels with the interventions of a consultant (adapted from Rashford and Coghlan, 1994).

Phase 0 – Ground zero: the problem surfaces

During an executive MBA class on the subject of organizational levels the class was discussing complex change processes in large organizations. One of the students was the vice-president for engineering of a regional division of AT&T. The class discussion centred on large-systems change and the difficulties of detecting errors and correcting them over long periods of time in complex projects. The V-P observed that in his organization it was problematic for him that cost overruns in construction projects that were in progress were causing severe difficulties for the company. Projects would begin with finite funds and at the later stages would end up without the necessary resources to make it possible to finish the projects or enable them to turn over to the operating telephone companies a functioning set of long-distance communications circuits. It was at this stage that the V-P agreed there was a problem. Part of the freedom to admit that a problem existed came from the realization that a solution to the problem was possible. The V-P, as the key individual, moved from denying to dodging at this point.

Phase I – Change awareness

Further discussion led the V-P and Rashford, the professor, to set up a consultation project for a two-year period to study the project management process. The contract was for a process consultation to facilitate the company's staff to analyse the problem and to work with the management team to design a process to solve the problem.

Phase 2 – Initiation: meeting the team and setting the parameters

This phase involved the interdepartmental group leaders admitting in their face-to-face working team that problems existed. The interdepartmental group leaders represented every function of engineering, from current design to installation engineering. The first meeting of the team was most traumatic. The initial reaction was a denial that there was a problem, and if there was, it could be solved without a consultant. The consultant was perceived as extra baggage and tolerated as the V-P's professor. Therefore, he should be endured but largely ignored. The notion that an outsider be brought into the company was itself a sign of failure and not to be admitted.

Overcoming denial

The discussion of the 'problem' soon became technical and the use of jargon and special engineering language proliferated. The consultant who was to participate as a process observer incidentally had a background in military electronics and began participating in the technical discussion. This caught the team by surprise and some of the defences came down. The team slowly accepted the consultant, admitted that there was a problem and began the process of setting out a course of action in which the consultant could play a part. One individual went as far as to suggest that if the consultant had not embarked on a teaching career he might well be working for the company! The rest concurred. The consultant was, at this point, admitted as a fellow technician and not as a process consultant.

The need for focus soon became apparent. The consultant inquired about the most recently completed project and sought to find what could be learned from that project. The discussion focused on the fact that the project had been turned over to a group of operators who were to run the equipment which was providing the communications circuits from point A to point B, and that the people trying to operate it did not have testing equipment. The testing equipment had been part of the project and was necessary for the operations group to work effectively. The money had been spent in cost overruns in the early phases of building linkages between point A and point B so the compensation was not to purchase test equipment.

Overcoming dodging

The discussion grew heated at this point and the people wanted to find somewhere to put the blame. Each area was interrogated to see who was at fault. This went on for some time and the consultant intervened.

He set up a make-believe process in which a culprit was chosen to take the blame. The person was asked to get down on his knees and say 'I am sorry'. The consultant led the way and showed how to adopt the contrite position as it was named. The group was silent and then began to laugh. Soon the pointlessness of blaming became apparent. If one found the culprits and they were punished or shunned, it did not solve the problem or change the situation. The interdepartmental group leadership team, in this way, came to process the situation and initiate and plan for the change process.

Phase 3 – Manoeuvring: getting the interdepartmental group leaders to see the issues and dealing with outliers

This phase began with the defining of the basic problem and an outline issue. A systematic analysis had yet to begin. It is the nature of complex processes that no one individual can see the consequences of their actions, yet each individual can see that this is a process where they stand to lose and the defence mechanisms arise quickly.

The second meeting was set up as an all-day meeting. Each person was to bring a large sheet of paper, or several if they required, creating a chart with all the inputs and outputs from their functional area. Traffic analysis would show their hand-offs to the design engineering group. They, in turn would show their hand-offs to the equipment manufacturers who were not part of the company. The design group would also do the hand-off to the Federal Relations group for getting FCC permission and the frequency allocations. So it would progress until the five years and the full project were detailed. This process took up the entire morning. The team went to lunch and had a drink to celebrate the morning's success. One member decided to continue the celebration in lieu of lunch.

The outlier phenomena: a personal issue sets the interdepartmental group leaders back

After the lunch break the individual who had been celebrating had his area come up for presentation and review. His chart had been rolled up during the morning session and was now revealed to be blank. The individual, in a slurred speech, angrily told the team that the process was useless, that he did not agree with it, never had and that he was the most senior and should know what was best. He stormed out of the room. After the initial awkward silence the remaining team members discussed what was happening. He was a valuable individual, but over the past year had brought much destruction to the team through an abuse of alcohol. His spouse had recently died of cancer and he had begun to drink heavily and to miss work.

It soon became apparent that what the team thought was a team management issue was actually a personal issue. A meeting was held in which the V-P and some other team members who had the required data confronted the individual and enabled him to seek company-assisted help. The project was put on hold. Distinguishing a Level I issue from a Level II or III issue is difficult at best.

Phase 4 – Integration: getting the interdepartmental group leaders involved in the change

The next meeting of the interdepartmental group leadership team took place a month later. The leaders of the teams began to put the internal maps together again. In the process of putting the internal maps on paper and talking about the relationships between different functional areas, some new information emerged. Some of the hand-off processes, reports that were filed and moved to the next group, were done for functions which no longer existed and were not needed. The team receiving the report would file it and do nothing with it even though the team members generating it had spent a large amount of time and money preparing it. At this very preliminary stage of internal mapping, problem areas were soon identified as areas which existed between different subfunctions and the hand-offs between those functions. One group's output became another group's input and the mismatch between those outputs and inputs were very large indeed. The group leadership, reflecting on the internal mapping process, realized the significance of the problem and the extent to which change was required. This analysis only involved the interdepartmental group leaders of Level III. Later meetings with Level II teams brought out that this had been the tip of the iceberg.

Phase 5 – Achievement: an internal mapping process to gather the required information

All the members of the interdepartmental group (numbering about 200) were assembled on a predetermined date, with prior instructions that a detailed list of inputs into their functional areas and outputs to adjacent functional areas be produced for a large display. The flow of each project from start to finish would be explained. This all-day meeting was a complex discussion of detailed inputs and outputs, function-by-function, area-by-area, until at the end of the day complex projects extending over five years were detailed. The group could see them from beginning to end. Looking at the mass of information which occupied three of the four walls of a large auditorium, the group became aware of the incredible complexity – well over 1,200 hand-offs of technical material of engineering design, blueprints, equipment, requests or other significant pieces of data which were required in the process of each project.

At this preliminary stage the group was distinctly aware of the fact that there were two different kinds of projects, and separated one – an upgrade and renewal project – from the second – the installation of an entirely new channel of communication from point A to point B. This analysis and one of the other problem points – i.e. useless information being prepared for reports which were no longer required due to changes in government regulations

– proved significant. This attention to significant irritants was the investment of the subordinate team. They now saw the gain from the change process and bought into it. The recognition of 'useless information' turned out to be a second-order learning moment. In the shift from microwave technology, broadcast from tower to tower, to optic fibre technology, which did not broadcast a signal, these reports were no longer needed and the people preparing them were not needed.

Change of Vice-President

The V-P for Engineering who had started this whole process graduated from the school which had triggered the consulting relationship. He left the company to become president of another communications company operating on the West Coast. Immediately a process to select a successor was initiated within the local company. The person appointed was an engineer by background, who had worked in another division of the organization and so was not privy to the change process in progress in this area into which he was entering. He met the group and consultant and discussed the change project and whether it was valuable or not to continue with it. He also joined the same executive MBA programme in which his predecessor had participated and was exposed to the construct of levels in the classroom discussions. After a lapse of about two months the interdepartmental group was re-assembled and the process was focused on two types of projects – an upgrade renewal project and a new communications channel installation project. These two projects would be examples of the rest of the processes within his division of the company and would be mapped.

Internal mapping with all the interdepartmental group members

The new V-P brought the group together to begin the internal mapping process with two simplified versions of the project which had been delineated at the previous meetings. Once again, a large auditorium with more than 200 people was filled and the process began with input–output maps of each area and each division being juxtaposed with each other area or division in which there were hand-offs. Lines were drawn from one chart to another and the quality of the input–output transactions was discussed. This process took two complete days. A third day was set aside for a discussion of what type of action would be needed and how it would be accomplished.

Phase 6 – Follow through: setting flags and forming correction teams

The action phase took the complex data of the large system and all its interfaces, as played in the mapping function, and began defining problem areas, thus enabling change to take place. After a good deal of discussion with the consultant the group concluded that it needed a way to deal with how certain points seemed more critical than others to some people. A system was set up whereby 'flags' – sets of highlighted markers – could be placed anywhere on the displayed project scheme. When a flag was placed, the person who felt that this was a problem presented what the issue was to the entire group. The group listening to the detailed explanation as to why this was a problem area either agreed or rejected that this was a problem and clarified the issues at stake. Once a flag was placed the group admitted that it was a true dysfunctional point and a fixing team was set up. Any person who had a stake in what was going to be changed in the process of fixing this problem was included on the team. A process flag team leader led the team and a flag solver – the person who had originally placed the flag or had the best description of the dysfunction – was named. It was the flag solver's judgement which would be required for the elimination of the flag. At the end of the third working day, 23 significant flags were located and change teams set up.

Over the next four-month period, flag meetings were held regularly, some weekly and others on a three-weekly basis. These change teams were at different levels of the organization's hierarchy. If a flag was significant enough to cause real disruption in the projects, the change team leader may well have been a vice-president. Others were within functional areas in a division with a group manager leading the team.

At the end of each three-week period an update on the progress of each of the flags was prepared and sent out in written form to the entire group. The top management met weekly and reviewed what was happening in the organization, how the change was progressing and how the change teams were working. Everyone agreed that the process was having a good effect and that change was taking place. In many instances before flags were completed, people realized what was going wrong, came up with detailed solutions and solved the problem without waiting for the entire organization and the next flag meeting.

Phase 7 – Sustaining: burning the flags

At the end of the first four-month period a flag-burning ceremony was held at an assembly of the entire group. Any flag which had been brought to completion was detailed as to how the solution had been found and what action was being taken. The group response was to accept or reject that the flag had been solved. When all parties agreed that a flag was completed, a small paper flag was placed in a fireproof container and burned. The group cheered that change had come into the system.

Overloading

Early on in the change teams it was found that other issues seemed to require attention and were afforded problem-solving time and energy. People saw the opportunity to change the organization and suddenly the change teams found themselves burdened with issues other than the flags on which they were working. Sometimes it was management that added new issues; sometimes it was individuals within the teams. These extraneous, additional incremental-type change processes had to be nipped in the bud and were declared to be outside the realm of the change process.

The sustaining phase of a learning organization was not realized. The organization was restructured and the teams broken up before ongoing learning processes were in place. Later discussions, after several years had passed, revealed that individuals had taken aspects of the flag process into new restructured parts of the organization to overcome problems they found there. The learning that had occurred was by individuals who transferred their experiences to other parts of the organization.

Questions for reflection and discussion

1   How did the change in the case involve all four levels?
2   The project involved face-to-face team interaction in problem identification and solution generation – do you think this changed team behaviour in other functions?
3   The major thrust for change came through the Level III assemblies, where the systemic picture of the projects was displayed in a manner which enabled the different functional teams and areas to grasp the overall picture and understand the linkages between one area and another. What made this effective?
4   The case emphasizes how in a complex change process people are exposed to the change question at different stages and typically respond initially in a denial and dodging mode. Did some of the denial and dodging occur around the consultant?

Case: Saint Joseph's University

The Saint Joseph's University case presented in chapter 4 provides a clear illustration of phases and levels of large-system change in operation. The new president, entering at ground zero, became aware of the need for change and initiated it. He first brought the issues to his senior management groups where he received a mixed reaction (Initiation phase). Some denied the need for change; others dodged by presenting difficulties. New facilities would be required for adult learners. New faculty would require more expense and structural change as the departments of the university did not have responsibility for graduate programmes.

Slowly the senior management group came to embrace the need for change and began implementation (*Manoeuvring*). They in turn then met resistance in their departments. This resistance was not immediate, but evolved over a period of time. After resentment came to a head, a faculty–administrative retreat was planned.

This initial four-day retreat meeting established a forum and process whereby a core group of the university moved to a doing stage and so began a university-wide process of vision generation, which drew in outliers and over several years facilitated the whole university community to buy into change and the university's new mission and identity. The process itself generated excitement about a possible new future. As people were excited about the future, the fear of letting go of the past decreased. In fact some of the excitement came from regaining some aspects of the past that had been lost. As implementation of the new goals began, groups and individuals within the university were required to change. It became clear that to sustain and reinforce these changes two things needed to occur. First, that the changes that were occurring related directly to what had been the outcome of the group process and second that the resources used were helping the university make progress towards goals desired by the group. Three times over the next year, group sessions were held that were called 'walk-throughs'. The sessions laid out explicitly what had been set as goals, what had been accomplished and what yet remained to be done. Input from the group was solicited through questions as well as written evaluation pages on the tables. These experiences were very important for the constituent groups to feel connected to the change process and remain involved. Thus *Integration* was achieved.

Several years passed as Saint Joseph's achieved its goals and surpassed them. Outlying groups of faculty were treated to walk-through experiences to show the attainment of the stated goals. The realization of a new 'Saint Joseph's University' is taking place. Enrolment is up; student qualifications are up and graduate studies are a part of each department. The *Achievement* phase has occurred.

Questions for reflection and discussion

1   How do levels interact with one another in this case?
2   How did management deal with outliers?
3   What is the time frame for change in this university case?
4   Would this be different in other types of organizations, e.g. a high-tech organization?

Part III

The strategy process through interlevel change

Chapter 6

Introduction to strategy and the five strategic foci

In Part II we explored how large-scale, large-system change comprises individual change which contributes to team change (and vice versa), which contributes to interdepartmental group change (and vice versa) in order that the entire organizational system changes. When large-scale change involves the organization's reason for being and what it does, then the interlevel dynamics apply to strategy and are central processes for strategic change.

Introduction to strategy and the use of the five strategic foci

Why do some organizations perform so much better than others? The answer, in great part, is in their strategies – the focus of the following six chapters. Entrepreneurs, as well as leaders of established businesses, develop strategies to seize opportunities in the marketplace in ways that other companies have difficulty matching. This is not just sheer luck as the use of strategic planning is exceedingly visible in the success and failure of organizations.

Strategy is the recognition of opportunity and a plan for seizing it, but it also recognizes and deals with threats to the organization. These opportunities and threats come from external forces – changes in customers' preferences, competitors' actions, technological breakthroughs, government actions such as deregulation, geopolitical shifts, trends in fashions and many other chaotic occurrences. Opportunities also arise from an organization leader's convictions, personal values or a flash of insight on changing times.

We have broken down strategic thinking and acting into five components called foci (Figure 6.1). The term 'focus' implies the clarity and attention that must be given to each of these points in the systematic interaction required to generate and implement a complex and functional strategic plan. Focus is defined as the utilization of all resources, both internal and external, of the organization to develop a key aspect of the planning and implementation processes.

The term 'focus' is used in photography to mean the ability to bring an image into clarity. The photographer accomplishes this by adjusting the

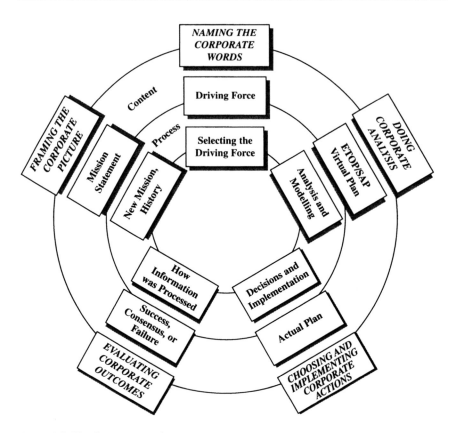

Figure 6.1 The five strategic foci.

lens to obtain the greatest clarity in that part of the image that is the centre of interest. The use of focus is a technique that draws the viewer to the key points of interest in the photograph as determined by the photographer. In strategic thinking and acting a focus occurs when a portion of the whole is clarified in order to attend to it while keeping the whole in perspective. The map of the whole interrelated strategic elements is a nonlinear system similar to a large photograph. A focus is a clarified segment or part that can be attended to in perspective of the whole.

The purpose of the five strategic foci is to define the space in the formulation of and implementation of strategic plans in a complex world by complex organizations. We referred to these spaces as foci not because they are steps in a process but rather five ongoing systematic points of interaction: content, process and culture components which exist within a context in the determination of strategic planning and implementation. Chapter 12 will spell out the interaction among the five foci.

The complex process of generating strategic thinking and acting evolves through the following five foci:

1 Framing the corporate picture.
2 Naming the corporate words.
3 Doing the corporate analysis.
4 Choosing and implementing corporate actions.
5 Evaluating corporate outcomes.

We are applying the template that we introduced in the Overture to each focus. Each focus can be viewed in terms of six components. The content component addresses the tasks and relational issues to be addressed. The process component examines how task and relational issues are implemented and culture explores the hidden collective assumptions that underpin the action of each focus.

The first focus, *framing the corporate picture*, deals with the key individuals and the history of the organization as it comes to affect strategy formulation and implementation. The contents of this focus are on the core mission and its statement of the organization as well as the characteristics of the key players. The process aspect focuses on the construction and involvement of different people and processes and putting together and embracing the corporate mission and its statement.

The second focus, *naming the corporate words*, deals with those operations or functions that had become the lead operations or functions over time. These are most often referred to as driving forces and become the articulation or lived out mission statement of the organization. The process focus of naming the corporate words deals with the power aspects and conflicts as well as successes that come from being the lead function or operation.

The third focus, *doing corporate analysis*, deals with obtaining critical information and the preparation of data into a comprehensive scenario or modelling of alternatives for the organization. The process aspect, of doing corporate analysis, considers whether bias or contamination is introduced into the strategic planning process during this information-gathering focus, whether a comprehensive group of the organization is involved and whether the proper questions are being asked. The analytic process acknowledges the appropriate connectedness of this focus to a previous focus of mission in framing the corporate picture and to the focus of choosing and implementing corporate actions which will of necessity follow.

The fourth focus, *choosing and implementing corporate actions*, deals with the selection and structured implementation of a strategic plan of action with its concurrent implementation plans. The process aspect, of choosing and implementing corporate actions, looks at the bias and influence on the selection process that comes from sources other than the analysis focus.

The fifth focus, *evaluating corporate outcomes*, deals with the acceptance of the choice of criteria in the appropriate review and evaluation of the resulting state of the organization. The process aspect of evaluating corporate outcomes looks at the appropriate and fair evaluation of outcomes. The process aspect of evaluating the organization's outcomes centres on effective avoidance of selective or biased evaluation of outcome states. This refers to possible changes in the mission statement, new driving forces and possibly new methods of analysis in the formulation of ongoing strategic plans.

These spaces are called foci (focus in the singular) in order to avoid the misconception that they are linear steps in a linear process in formulating strategic objectives and then implementing them. The complex processes required to respond to quickly changing environmental issues necessitates the flexible organization must attend to several foci at the same time. The overall strategic process is systematic and dynamic. The model of a living organism comes to mind, being both multitasking and responsive. This is in contrast with trying to come to awareness of the whole all at once or in linear steps. We think there are five distinct points of focus in this reality.

The strategic foci are one part of the picture. The other part of the picture describes how the enactment of the strategic foci link integrally to the interlevel dynamics of planned change. In the following chapters we describe each strategic focus individually and then in chapter 12 show how they are integrated and interdependent. We will use the examples of the ABC insurance company and Saint Joseph's University to illustrate how the strategic foci are applied in action.

Chapter 7

Framing the corporate picture

Framing the corporate picture gets at the heart and soul of an organization. It is the reference for inside and outside the organization to know and understand what the organization is about and why it exists.

The content of framing the corporate picture

Framing the corporate picture is the first strategic focus. This corporate picture is a composite of the history of an organization, its mission, its senior managers, its board of directors and the organization's framing of what it is and what it does. Every organization, no matter how large, has at its root a basic, defined organization from which it started. In long-standing organizations, this originating corporate picture may have developed and changed over time. When organizations merge or have been sold off, it is difficult to reconstruct the corporate picture of these divested major parts. It can be just as difficult for the acquiring organization or the acquired subdivisions to determine the key characteristics that are still important. What appeals to the large conglomerate, e.g. profitability, may not have been the corporate picture of the acquired organization in its independent state. These corporate pictures from the early starting points in an organization's history are important to work out. If these are not acknowledged, they remain as pervasive hidden elements which may compete with the new strategic processes. Wal-Mart is an example of this. The original corporate picture endures to the present day in spite of the tremendous growth and development. The Wal-Mart chain, now one of the largest retail chains in the world, had as its start a single store with a single owner, Sam Walton, and a basic purpose. Walton's single-minded purpose was to bring to small towns a selection of goods at a reasonable price in one location.

The corporate picture is the basic identity of an organization. It consists of at least three components: the original objective of the enterprise in its historical transition over time, the stories and the components provided by the organization's present-day key stakeholders and the ethical imperative to be socially responsible. These components are what give the organization a reason to exist, culture and direction. This sense of direction is the organizational purpose or mission.

The fundamental question, 'What business are we in or what service do we provide?' focuses on the basic identity of an organization. This identity is summarized in the organization's mission statement. The mission statement is a fixed set of expressions, which attempts to convey an organization's spirit or mission in a brief and concise way. It is fixed in that it represents the best expressions in the present time. The critical corporate picture that gives the organization life resides in the minds of the senior executives and other shareholder groups with a stake in the organization. The history and interpreted history of the organization serve as a benchmark for plotting new directions and extending old goals for the people making decisions for the future of the organization. The mission statement can be either successful or unsuccessful in providing a corporate picture both for those inside and outside the organization. The underlying assumptions about the identity of the organization as developed in its tradition are critical powerful forces. These traditions are built on the personalities and successes of the past. Sometimes they are so embedded in the organization that they cannot be seen until some process brings them to light. This is very true in large organizations and those with high turnovers. Sometimes the corporate picture includes the way these traditions govern how the organization operates or whom the organization perceives to be the valued customers. In sharp contrast to Wal-Mart is the history of the Wawa Company, a company whose traditions are deeply rooted in meeting customer need as first a textile company, then a dairy and now a convenience store chain. The contrast to the Wal-Mart example is the change in the type of business at Wawa – Wal-Mart did not change, it just grew in size.

Founded in 1803 in New Jersey as a textile company, the Wawa Company moved into the dairy industry in the early twentieth century. The first Wawa convenience store opened in Folsom, Pennsylvania, in 1964, and the company began expanding into new geographic territories and experimenting with several new offerings, including fresh meat, two fast-food stores, and even hydroponic tomatoes.

Today Wawa operates more than 530 stores in five states and employs over 13,000 associates. Wawa's business is built on a foundation of trust and strong corporate values, and is led by a management team dedicated to the consumer, focused on people and unrelenting in its approach to service. Dick Wood, the company's current president and chief executive officer, speaks passionately about the need to make consumers think of Wawa as their store of choice. This commitment to the consumer is reflected in a company statement – Wawa will stop at nothing to deliver the best in the industry, which brings our customers back to visit us day after day – and in its stated 'core purpose' (to simplify customers' daily lives) and 'core values' (value people, delight customers, embrace change, do the right thing, do things right, have a passion for winning). This basic vision is the point of continuity from the textile organization, through the dairy to the convenience store chain of today.

With annual sales of more than US$1.7 billion, the company regularly shows up in the top third of Forbes magazine's annual 500 Top Private Companies feature. The dairy itself generates sales of more than US$70 million a year, and processes more than 100 million fluid quarts annually.

Wawa today sits at a crossroads in the company's history. The opportunity to go public is a viable business alternative, especially if the company continues to pursue a path as a gasoline retailer. The ability to expand through the acquisition of existing resources or the construction of new resources would be greatly aided by a public offering to raise capital. This will necessitate a new corporate picture.

Culture is partially shaped by the persuasive power that mission statements have or do not have. When the mission statement clearly articulates the commonly held perception of an organization's core mission, people feel involved and important. This is vital in forming an accepted corporate culture. When mission statements are posted around an organization and are perceived by staff to be largely untrue or far from reality, this creates a corporate picture which differs from the one created by senior management and contributes to an adverse corporate culture.

The process of framing the corporate picture

The process whereby identity is articulated normally comes through a study of the history of the organization and the formulation of its contemporary mission statement. Framing the corporate picture can be achieved through two approaches. The first approach deals with a review of the historic timeline of the organization where leaders and members are involved in a process to discern in the historic timeline elements that have endured. These consist of values, beliefs and practices that remain for the organization. This approach can be used either to produce a new corporate picture or reinforce present identity. The second approach, detailed in the A&P case in chapter 13, deals with the formation of a corporate picture, in which there is involvement of senior leaders only. Although this leads to a speedier process in framing the corporate picture, the process of communicating the corporate picture to the organization's membership is much more difficult. The choice between these approaches is based on the need for involvement. High involvement to embrace the mission and carry it out requires early involvement in framing the corporate picture.

The key process is reaching consensus between constituent groups as to how the corporate picture is framed and the mission perceived. An organization's board, chief executive, senior management group and members are the central stakeholders in formulating organizational identity and mission.

The role of the CEO, and of all senior leadership for that matter, is to own and embrace the process and to show leadership and interest in it. Without this interest and involvement, neither of the approaches will work. Interest and enthusiasm are essential elements in this regard. Conversely, experience shows that lack of vision and committed leadership in the process by the CEO dooms the framing of the corporate picture to failure. Concomitant with this vision is the ethical stance of the CEO. Leadership on social responsibility, personal and corporate ethics are major factors in how the organization's members act ethically and are part of the corporate picture.

The role of the member should also not be underestimated in the effective framing of the corporate picture. The involvement of members in carrying out the mission is much less likely without their participation in framing the corporate picture. Participation for a member consists in sharing of individual historical antidotes relating to the corporate history. The members' contribution to the debate in the formation of the statement used to frame the corporate picture is equally important. Unfortunately, this membership input is often forgotten in many organizations.

The most important group in ratifying the mission of an organization is the board of directors. How the board performs this task is critical to its success. Sometimes the board accepts and ratifies the mission statement prepared by the organization. Other times the board places its imprint on the mission statement by adding components of its own. This is a legitimate role of the board, which has policy responsibility for an organization. Even though the board provides important input, this must not be done at the cost of suppressing input from the rest of the organization.

The contrast to the formal and large organization approach to framing the corporate picture is the new entrepreneurial organization where the founder brings the vision and forms the corporate picture.

VerticalNet had its origins in 1995 when Mike McNulty the trade publishing salesman for trade journals came up with the idea that the time had come to move trade publishing for industries such as those selling pumps and valves to the Internet. Mike Hagan, his friend, left Merrill Lynch and joined him in this new venture. The initial momentum was helped when they raised

US$7 million of new capital from the Internet capital group of Wayne P.A. and another US$9 million from other firms. With this money McNulty and Hagan and set up offices in Horsham, PA. The location was chosen because it was close to b2b publications that were based in Philadelphia, New York and Boston. They started putting together sites on the web for the industrial communities in these vertical markets surrounding particular industries with focused interest.

In the early days at VerticalNet, very little time was spent in formulating a mission statement. But clearly a corporate picture emerged. The picture was clear enough to attract investors and emerged from a clear vision of the purpose of VerticalNet. The focus was on the users in the formation of these vertical communities on the Internet. The uniqueness came from a different approach. Most Internet entrepreneurs had attempted to use the web to replace the traditional marketplace with their Internet marketplace. McNulty, who knew the industrial trade sector of the market as a salesman, had the vision to realize that in the world of purchasing agents everybody knew one another and had relationships through trade shows and business dealings. McNulty saw it as a world in which they needed to supplement these relationships, not try to replace them. VerticalNet became a member of this marketplace and did not try to replace it.

About a year later, as VerticalNet grew rapidly, Hagan and McNulty realized that they needed some more experience and help, and they hired Mark Walsh. As a new CEO, Walsh had been running AOL Enterprise, the b2b division of America Online. In the Internet world, Walsh was well known and his reputation was respected.

The corporate picture framed by VerticalNet was unique and respected the new environment in which they found themselves. Since McNulty knew the environment very well from his previous work, it was easy to adapt to those needs. The understanding of who they were and whom they served made a difference to their success versus those Internet companies that failed.

ODC consultants' role in framing the corporate picture

ODC consultants are useful in helping organizations frame their corporate picture. With their skill at process they can facilitate the dialogue needed to articulate mission. From a collection of process designs by Napier *et al.* (1999), the following five activities are well suited to help frame a corporate picture:

1   *Shared history exercise.* This activity creates a common ground experience for participants regarding their organization's history. A large sheet of paper on a wall is utilized in this exercise. A timeline is drawn reflecting the significant events in the history of the organization. Participants share their perspectives and insights regarding their history. This enables everyone to see the significant choices that have been made and reveals the values the organization has held over time. This helps develop a shared perspective and deep appreciation of the uniqueness of the organization. This helps people forge new directions and creates enthusiasm for tackling the future. The historical values that are revealed contribute to the corporate picture.

2   *Stargazing exercise.* The key to this design is to select a quality group of 'stargazers' as panel members whose purpose is to help participants broaden their perspective, deepen their knowledge and stimulate their thinking. Stargazers are individuals who tend to have a future focus, a broad perspective or a deep knowledge about a particular subject. They should be individuals who have a reputation for creativity, clear thinking, credibility and autonomy. The panel members can be individuals within the organization, complete outsiders or a combination of both. After opening remarks, each panel member meets with small groups of participants (10–20 people). They spend some time in each group sharing their expertise and answering questions. Every 20 minutes, the panel members rotate to a new group and the process continues until they have interacted with all the small groups. It creates energy, enthusiasm and real participation of all who are involved. After the small groups have interacted with the panel members, they organize themselves and make strong recommendations that help form the corporate picture.

3   *Heroic journey.* In some sense the strategic planning process is a journey into the unknown. It takes real courage and discipline to ask the tough questions, define the core principles of an organization, and take risks in the decisions that are made. This activity is a powerful design. The participants are asked to reflect on heroic experiences in their own lives. These are shared with the group. The participants then develop a heroic code for the organization. Participants find three of the heroic statements that they can all agree upon. The summary of these statements becomes a basis for the values or principles to guide the organization. They provide the heroic vision of the corporate picture.

4   *Creating a vision statement.* The purpose of this activity is to create a shared picture of the future for an organization or group. The design starts with each individual taking 10–15 minutes to write five or six statements that best describe what he or she would like to see in the vision statement of the organization. These individual statements are then shared in small groups (4–8 people). Each group seeks common ground first, around the strategic themes for the future. After common

ground has been established, groups can include 'gentle agreement' statements. These are statements that are accepted by all members of the group. These individual statements are then shared in small groups (4–8 people). Each group first identifies all the ideas that are held in common. After common ground has been established, groups can also include 'gentle agreement' statements. These are individual statements that each group member can agree to because it is worthy of their commitment. The ultimate goal is to have a 50–75 word statement written on a flipchart that is the formation of a vision statement or corporate picture.

5 *Scenario planning exercise.* This design first pioneered by Shell Oil Co. anticipates a range of different possible futures and frames each with a strategic vision with an understanding of what actions will be best under each possibility. The goal of the design is to find a series of trends that the group can verify, which will impact the organization's future. How each trend exerts influence is then discussed. The group then spends time looking at what the corporate picture would look like to deal with each scenario. This design works well with a small group of 10–12 and is suited for a senior management group in working out a corporate picture. This dovetails with the scenario-building activity outlined in doing the corporate analysis in chapter 9.

Interlevel dynamics in framing the corporate picture

Framing the corporate picture is a process necessitated by changing environmental conditions, changing strategic advantages, changing expectations from outside shareholder groups and by interactions among the key participants within the organization. The process of changing an organization's corporate picture necessitates a clear sense of why change is needed, a formulation of what the new corporate picture would ideally look like and building support for change through the transition from the old to the new one (Nadler, 1998). Changing the corporate picture is a large-scale change as described by Mohrman *et al.* (1989), as it constitutes deep changes which entail shifts in members' basic beliefs and values in the way the organization is understood and effects pervasive changes throughout the organization.

Listed below are seven interaction scenarios, which can challenge an organization's current corporate picture:

1 The interaction between the CEO and external information source.
2 The CEO with the senior management group.
3 Relations of both the CEO and senior management group with the interdepartmental group level.
4 The circumstance when no single CEO exists and the mission comes from multiple sources.

5   The context of a merger or acquisition when all parties are required to understand and manage new relationships as the total organization merges into or is acquired by another.
6   The integration of the board's changes to the corporate picture with the CEO and senior management.
7   The integration of outside influences, such as financial analysts, with the CEO and CFO.

The CEO and external information sources deals with the interactions that occur when a CEO meets other CEOs or information sources of trade or professional organizations. A CEO's relationships with these competing organizations and trade groups or associations are key to finding information on benchmarks, industry trends or economic conditions that are in play at any time. The CEO should also be attuned to issues relating to corporate social responsibility which may surface through external relationships.

The CEO is often the conduit of disconfirming information. It is difficult to accept and process information within an organization when it comes from outside. This occurs through the previously mentioned association with other CEOs, in relations with customers, in the application of intuitive dreaming of the next plateau, or in contact with other organizations, as we saw with Mark Walsh in VerticalNet. In the process of examining and evaluating new information or ideas, the CEO moves a stage ahead of everyone else in the organization. He or she is past denial of the disconfirming information and ready to begin an organizational change process. The converse is also true and will have the same results. This occurs when others bring the disconfirming information into the organization and the CEO is in denial of it and not ready for change. In both of these situations, the process questions become: how are information, the time for reflection and ownership handled?

If the new information and the conclusions drawn from it are thrust on the organization or the CEO, while little reaction may be observed, a large effect can be set in motion to deny later participation because of the lack of ownership in the early definitional stage. Any negative information that disconfirms a central belief of an organization will produce denial when it is first presented. This was explained in chapter 5 when we discussed how change moves through an organization. Disconfirming information will either contribute to a corporate picture that has no reality or to a hung process that will not frame a corporate picture that can provide an energizing mission statement.

The CEO with the senior management group is the next interlevel relationship for the process of framing the corporate picture. Here the critical issue deals with how the senior team processes the elements of the new corporate picture. Each senior manager leading a functional area looks at these elements with different amounts of threat. The threat comes from having to embrace change in his/her functional area. The reverse is also true.

A senior management group with new ideas can threaten the CEO who does not want the organization to change. The amount of threat is related to the amount of change required in accepting and implementing the new corporate picture. As new ideas are used to frame a new corporate picture, they are being assessed by the interdepartmental leaders on the effects that the change will have for their members. In this scenario, individual issues deal with the change in role and identity of the team members as well as the CEO. As a new corporate picture emerges, individual roles change and some are eliminated. Team issues relate to the new determination of priorities and task assignments. A new corporate picture forces the senior management group to set new priorities and allocate work to the divisions and departments in a different way. Interdepartmental issues centre on the new allocation of resources and information flow required in carrying out the new corporate picture. The CEO should also inquire into and receive reports on issues that reflect corporate social responsibility, particularly to be able to recognize unethical behaviour that may be occurring across the organization.

The senior management group is quite different from other face-to-face working teams and plays the pivotal role in this dealing with framing the corporate picture. In the prevalent working team, each member participates in a role for and by himself/herself to accomplish team and organizational goals. In the senior management group each line member represents a functioning interdepartmental group; hence the actions of the group affect the entire organization.

When in the interdepartmental group a function is threatened, the respective officer-team member acts many times in a defensive way on behalf of his or her own functional area constituency. As mentioned before, the reverse can be true when a CEO is threatened by change suggested by his/her management group.

Relations of both the CEO and senior management group with the interdepartmental group level involve the process behaviour around the corporate picture between the Level II senior management group and the Level III interdepartmental group. This aspect is most often overlooked because many senior managers believe that working groups do not need to be brought into the discussion until it is time to implement the new corporate picture. This, however, is too late in the process if participation and commitment are needed. The Level III interactions with Level I produce a most challenging task if an organization is to be successful in achieving its goal of enabling divisional human capital in the organization. When people are changed in function or role, this affects their Level I matching needs with an organization. The interdepartmental functional change (Level III) produces an effect in Level I with a new required role or functional change for the individuals within the functional area. The challenge comes from the need to work with both individuals (Level I) and teams (Level II) in the allocation of work and priorities generated through the new or changed mission within the interdepartmental groups (Level III). The need to accept change comes from the shift in resource reallocation and the adoption of new information systems required for the new or changed mission. Also implicit is the effect on individuals (Level I) if the new mission brings about a change in self-esteem, job design or internal motivation. While the completion of this complex interaction in working out a new corporate picture with its resultant required behavioural changes occurs throughout all of the focuses in the strategy/change process, it is here that perceptions of the organization are formed. Perceptions last a long time.

The circumstance when no CEO exists and the mission comes from other sources is the fourth scenario for interlevel relationships. Sometimes in not-for-profit organizations the response to multiple boards of directors and complex relations with sponsoring organizations makes framing the corporate picture very difficult. The following case of Wills Eye Hospital is an example of such an occurrence.

Wills Eye Hospital is an institution of national renown in the field of ophthalmology. Throughout a decade of great change in healthcare, creative innovations by Wills management allowed the institution to consistently maintain an operating profit through programmes of diversification into other medical specialties. In addition to ophthalmology, Wills moved into the areas of hand surgery, geriatric psychiatry and neurosurgery.

During the 1990s, the general philosophy was to bring more patients to the hospital on an inpatient basis to increase revenues. Such an aggressive policy, however, was unlikely to succeed in the future since the continual move to outpatient care reduced the need for inpatient care.

With this in mind, Wills' core mission could move in several directions. First, it could pursue an aggressive programme specifically designed to elevate the reputation of Wills' stature as the premier ophthalmology programme in the United States. Second, it could pursue an outpatient surgery network. Third, it could continue to diversify into other medical specialties in order 'not to put all of one's eggs into one basket'.

Since three constituent groups with competing interests administer Wills Eye Hospital, it was difficult to find agreement on a mission statement. The first group, composed of the Board of City Trusts, desired to be true to the intent of the original financial gift which was service to the indigent. The second group, the management group, desired to operate a financially viable institution. The third group, the medical staff, desired that it be a centre of world-renowned ophthalmology. These three groups, by nature, were at odds to accomplish a single purpose. Here the interests of the initial charter, financial savings, and excellent patient care and research (which led to increased spending) competed against one another. In addition, there were no physicians on the Board of City Trusts and no one person as overall CEO. Recently, Wills Eye Hospital sold its major facility to another medical institute and, thereby, relinquished its inpatient business. It has moved to a central facility that enables it to do outpatient work and research and provides a place to train residents. It continues to build a network of outlying centres as well. The new situation does not require maintaining the overhead of eight floors of a hospital. Nor do other specialties come into play in the new situation.

The Wills Eye Hospital case illustrates the point that mission statements are not necessarily the first element in proposing a new strategy. Circumstances, the environment and history influence the mission statement. The case also illustrates the difficulty in getting a total organizational buy-in to a complex mission statement when different segments have different missions. Framing the corporate picture proved very difficult when no one could get the groups to work together to frame a single mission statement.

Mergers and acquisitions is the fifth scenario, which is likely to impact the focus of framing the corporate picture. In this scenario, what was at one time a Level IV organization becomes a Level III interdepartmental group in a larger organization. This is a 'demotion' in emotional terms from the point of view of the organization that is the merged one.

Integration of the board's changes to the corporate picture with the CEO and senior management. The board of the directors, the board of management or the board of trustees is the group that has the power of authority in most organizations. In dealing with mission statements or corporate pictures, most boards let management construct the statement and then ratify it. In those cases where the board takes an active role in the design of the mission statement, this input tends to happen after the members and senior management group have generated a statement. In discussing the statement for approval at the board meeting it is tempting to adapt or change this phrase or word. This can often be done without the benefit of a facilitator or reflection on the part of the board. The rewritten mission statement is then approved. When this happens the changes have to be processed by the CEO, who can feel undercut in the process, and the senior management group that must explain the changes to people who had contributed to the original statement and now see a different one coming from the board. The board also has the responsibility for ensuring the organization's ethical behaviour in the marketplace.

The better approach with a board in framing the corporate picture is to open the organization's process to board members and have them experience the dialogue and the interaction with the organization's members. When they are part of the process and understand the deliberation that has gone into it they will have less will to change it later on when it is their duty to ratify it. External groups and organizations have input that need to be integrated into framing the corporate picture. Financial analysts may seek definitive statements in the corporate picture, such as levels of profitability or particular markets. While these do not have direct input, what is excluded from a mission statement may raise serious questions. Private universities in the United States cannot be controlled by external groups and still receive federal funding. Yet the corporate picture can be representative of the values and beliefs of the founding institution. In other types of organizations, such as public trust, donor requests must be accounted for in the corporate picture for legal reasons.

Conclusions

In this chapter we have described the first focus, framing the corporate picture, and shown how it deals with the key individuals and the history of the organization as it comes to affect strategy formulation and implementation. The contents of this focus are on the core mission and its statement of the organization as well as the characteristics of the key players. The process aspect focuses on the construction and involvement of different people and processes and putting together and embracing the corporate mission and its statement.

Table 7.1 summarizes the central issues regarding the first strategic focus – framing the corporate picture – which is detailed in this chapter.

The perspective of organizational leaders, whether the CEO, board of directors, members of a senior management group or divisional heads is that the corporate picture enables an organization to move in a proactive,

Table 7.1 Framing the corporate picture

	TASK	RELATIONAL
Content	What business are we in? Core mission Corporate social responsibility	Differing view of key strategists and stakeholders
Process	History search Examine mission statement Stargazing	Building consensus Agreeing to differ
Culture	Traditions of the organization Build ethical culture	Power of key statements

ethical and adaptive manner to meet future challenges. The perspective of an organization's members is whether or not they fit into the corporate picture and whether they have a role. The ODC consultants' perspective is whether the organization has a clear and jointly owned picture of itself. The outcome of framing the corporate picture is that the organization has a clear identity to present to the external world: a picture which is clear and owned within the organization as well as enhances and energizes the other four strategic foci.

Figure 7.1 provides a structure for inquiring into how the corporate picture is framed. The three inquiry loops begin from the outcomes of framing the corporate picture and move inquiring about actions taken, goals set and ultimate purpose.

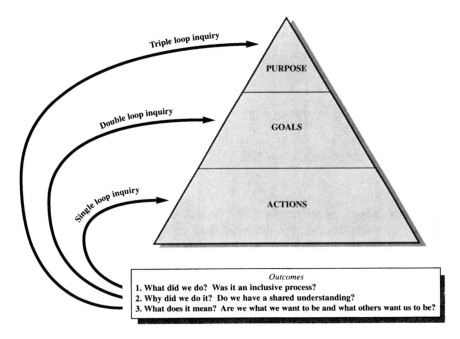

Figure 7.1 Single, double and triple loop inquiry.

Action research activity 7.1

Below you will find a blank table. In relation to an organization with which you are familiar, fill in the boxes with what you see as the important content, process and cultural issues in task and relational terms in framing the corporate picture. Discuss this with your team or better still, copy the blank form and have each team member fill in the blanks prior to your discussion.

	TASK	RELATIONAL
Content		
Process		
Culture		

Action research activity 7.2

Leaders

Corporate leaders, whether the CEO or members of senior management group or divisional heads, may consider the following questions:

1   Given the goals and modicum of excellence that we have achieved, how do we now get to the next level of goals and excellence?
2   How do we enrol others in partnership to achieve this?
3   What is our shared history? What does it tell us?
4   Who are the stargazers that can give us input for a new future?
5   What are our criteria and standards of corporate social responsibility?

Organizational members

Organizational members may ask the following questions:

1   Do I know what the organization's mission is?
2   Does the stated mission fit my experience of working in this organization?
3   How can I adapt my work to fit the mission?
4   Can I take the risk required to trust in a new future?

ODC consultants

ODC consultants may pose the following questions:

1 Does the organization have a clear picture of itself?
2 Is this picture jointly owned?
3 What group experience designs can I use to help in the determination of the corporate picture?

Outcomes

1 Does the stated corporate picture reflect the reality of the key activities of the organization?
2 Were any parts of the mission statement disregarded or set aside in the final assembly of the statement itself?
3 Were there previous corporate pictures, such as those of sub divisions that were purchased, not taken into account in the final corporate picture?
4 Does the organization exhibit ethical behaviour?

Case: ABC Insurance Company

The ABC case begins in the mid-1990s. Privately held by a foundation, ABC was an insurance organization dealing directly with workmen's compensation. The organization had a long history and functioned as a closely held private company. This is in sharp contrast to the corporate picture of 2003 in which ABC is a public traded company.

ABC's present policy is to provide specialty risk products and services in the insurance and reinsurance spectrum. It maintains a staff with a high level of expertise. ABC's policy is to continue to achieve their high rating and positive standing with the rating agencies. Its policy for providing capital is to combine capital from all companies and provide it to the businesses that have the ability of making quality returns.

The strategic stance of the company is to earn a profit and create value for its stakeholders, grow the size of the company and to communicate properly with analysts. It has and will raise premiums when the market allows and it will continue to tackle the challenges of being a public company. Its goals, policy and strategies fit with what the organization says it wants to be. ABC wants to be a company that has market growth and improve return on equity. For the fiscal year ended 31 December 2001, revenue rose 29 per cent. Net income quadrupled. The results reflect the higher premiums it has earned with lower interest expense and increased tax benefits.

Leadership roles have changed dramatically. Before becoming public the senior management group focused its attention within the business. In the public company the CEO and senior management group are oriented to the outside financial and customer markets. The roles of lower echelons are dramatically different as well. In the old situation job security, working in a familiar world, was all part of the private culture. In the new culture everyone has to be responsive to the needs of changing marketplace as well as the constant review by financial analysts. The pace of life has picked up considerably at ABC. Not everyone has responded to this change. Outcome expectations have changed radically. In the old private organization service and even philanthropy were key values in the expected outcomes. In the new public organization earnings on stock shares and growth are expected outcomes.

The move from private to public

The change to going public was ongoing for approximately eight years. This was triggered in 1996 as a significant loss became evident at one of the operating subsidiaries. It was while the organization was engaged in doing the analysis to consider a change in the corporate direction that the loss was recognized. The need for large-scale change was seen by the CEO who had the ability to look over the horizon and see a world that did not yet exist. The need for change on a large scale was triggered by small-scale changes that could not be explained away. The eventual new CEO, a member of the senior management group, saw the need for change and had initiated the analysis required to make the decision.

Questions for reflection and discussion

1   Why did a loss in a subsidiary company lead to the move to becoming a public company?
2   How does becoming a public company mean a change in the corporate picture?
3   What would you think are the implications across the four organizational levels for this change?

Case: Saint Joseph's University

The mission of Saint Joseph's University traces its origins through the 450-year tradition of Jesuit education as well as 150 years as a Jesuit college in the Philadelphia, PA area. Traditionally Saint Joseph's University has been centred on undergraduate education. The university prides itself on small class size and a high student–professor interaction. The commitment to graduate and lifelong learning programmes in most of its history is through a part-time evening division. This, in effect, generated two Saint Josephs which had persisted from the turn-of-the-century until about 1986.

The new president of 1 July 1986 started to work at changing the corporate picture by making the graduate and evening programmes part of the mainstream university. This second stream of the university was primarily taught up to this time by part-time faculty, and responsibility for the credibility of the programmes resided with the evening division coordinator. The faculty had no sense of ownership of this graduate programme and in truth many did not want to teach in it.

Adding to this concern on the part of the faculty was a perception that people were not being listened to and challenges to the new status were perceived to be rebuffed. A group of the faculty met some staff and formed a committee to confront the situation. Its suggestion was that an external ODC consultant would be helpful. A number of consultants were reviewed. One consultant team with acceptable stature for both faculty and administration was found to work with them to resolve the situation.

The president and the senior management group then agreed with the plan to obtain an outside consultant team. The senior management group and the consultant team went away for a four-day retreat meeting. Creating a vision statement and a shared scenario exercise were used as the processes to arrive at some understanding of the issues that could be shared in common. Several times during these days of discussion the tension between some members of the senior management group spilled out and caused concern in the larger group. These tensions provided a block to engagement in the exercises and to exploring a new corporate picture. The energies of both the senior management group and the faculty-administration group were being directed towards the internal conflict rather than their vision for the future. When the conflict was resolved, the exercises were resumed and a new corporate picture was framed.

Questions for reflection and discussion

1   What triggered the change in Saint Joseph's University's corporate picture?
2   How was the process for framing a new corporate picture structured?
3   How do organizational levels and interlevel dynamics help understand what took place and why?
4   What levels were evident in the four-day retreat meeting?
5   What role would you think the ODC consultants played?

Chapter 8

Naming the corporate wor〔

The second functional focus is the determination of corporate words through driving forces. Corporate words in this context are different from the 'words' used in the mission statement. The mission statement, while it uses words, is a fixed set of expressions that attempt to contain the spirit or mission of an organization in a brief, concise way. The concept of corporate words has a more dynamic nature. It is the tactical application of the mission statement. Tactical in the sense that it represents the forces or drives interpreting the mission statement. An organization's effort is directed toward the products and services generated by the organization divided by geographic markets or market segments or customer groups that are served. While an organization's resources and capabilities, plans, structure, decision making and problem solving are important activities, they are ultimately directed toward producing products or services for diverse markets. Thus, the basic fundamental strategic question is, 'What should the scope of our products and services or markets be?'

A driving force is defined as the primary determinant of the scope of future products, services and markets. Tregoe and Zimmerman (1980) have defined nine basic strategic areas or driving forces. They are grouped into three categories: products/markets, capabilities and results (Table 8.1). In general the products and markets category is most often associated with flexible organizations that are customer- and market-oriented and respond quickly to the needs of the customers. Capability-centred companies are most often inward focused with advantages of skills, products, methods or resources that give them advantage. Results-associated companies are often conglomerates or large complex organizations with many divisions or sub-units.

The products and markets category is expanded further into two sub areas – products offered and market needs. The capabilities category is expanded into five different sub areas: technology, production capability, method of sales, method of distribution and natural resources. Results as a category is divided into two sub areas: size and growth and return or profit. Tregoe and Zimmerman postulate that an organization has only one driving force. They hold this to be the case because it is the precondition or assumption

Table 8.1 Driving forces

Categories	Driving forces
Products/markets	Products offered
	Market needs
Capabilities	Technology
	Production capability
	Method of sales
	Method of distribution
	Natural resources
Results	Size and growth
	Return or profitability

Adapted from Tregoe and Zimmerman (1980)

that underlies the forming of the corporate strategy and implementing the corporate plan. While it can be understood there is only one main driving force, the total organization may not agree with it and other factions can vie for the role of main driving force.

The articulation of the organization's driving force goes to the heart of asking the question: what ultimately drives the organization? Is it engineering? Is it sales? Is it that the organization maintains a great distribution system? Can it be that profitability drives how the future is approached? It is not always easy to sort out the driving force and sometimes two competing forces can survive for a time together.

Mosaico S.A. is a company established in Chile in 1990, devoted to the production of plumbing products. Mosaico has its headquarters in Santiago and its production operations in China, with approximately 200 employees, who manufacture more than 800 products under two brands for different markets.

The CEO, Horacio Pavez, says that in the beginning, he started his operations with sales of wooden toys made in China. Through this he developed contacts in China for production and importation of toys for the Chilean market. Later on, with these established contacts and having experience in the processes and the regulations of offshore businesses, he decided to evolve the business toward more lucrative plumbing products but distributed through the same hardware channels as the toys.

After being a sales and marketing company in the import business, Mosaico needed a shift in its corporate words. Seeing the possibilities and advantages of a global operation, Pavez decided in 1994 to change the business by developing his own production and assembly of plumbing products in China. The plumbing fixture market in Chile was dominated by a local company which manufactured in Chile. In order to overtake his competitor Pavez would have to have a better and cheaper product. To this end he established his own production operations in Hong Kong through a branch company Plumbtech Industries Limited, with a manufacturing plant in Guangzhou, China, taking advantage of the quality production advantages of the area.

Pavez shifted from a sales and marketing driving force to a production driving force. He did this by a distinct shift in thinking and approach. He hired engineers and plant managers. He added skills not present in the company before. He determined that by doing this he could move to the top market share position in Chile and successfully overtake a major Chilean company with its production in Chile. He focused the company on quality production run by managers and engineers from Chile in China. This shift in driving forces achieved its goal and today Mosaico is the leader in the marketplace in Chile and is moving to dominate Latin America.

The power and priorities of stakeholder groups in the selection of the driving force are significant. When a driving force favours one part of the organization, this can cause friction. A common example occurs where engineering or any other function is 'king' in a functionally driven organization. At Hallmark Cards, quality is the driving force. The corporate slogan 'if you care enough to send the very best' stressed quality. In most people's eyes at Hallmark, production was king. The quality of the printing was synonymous with quality products. In discussions on artistic merit, if the card could not be printed in a quality manner as designed, quite often a change in artistic design occurred. This is not to say that there was no artistic component, nor even that it was not strong, but how the product was made, that is printed, was key to its quality.

This relative power derived from the unstated driving force may be formal or informal: formal in that there is a clear articulated hierarchy of functions within the organization and informal in that individuals or functions may manage to build powerful positions which are resented and not discussed formally.

The process of naming the corporate words

An organization's driving force is identified and selected through an examination of the organization's traditional strengths and functions. How the inputs of key stakeholder groups are received and processed, how decisions are made and conflict managed are critical in the process of selection of the driving force and have the potential for inter-group conflict. At Hallmark

Cards when discussions were held between the artistic and production components, often the production control won.

Roles in determining driving forces

The role of the CEO in determining the strategic direction is taken up in each focus. In discussing the driving force the CEO role is very important. Many organizations do not deliberately choose a driving force, for them the past functional role of the chief executive is the driving force. There are three factors that play into this. It is the past functional job experience of the CEO, where they are in the CEO life cycles and critical events that affect the organization as perceived by the CEO.

CEO job experience

For example, each CEO will have come to the chief executive role from within an interdepartmental group, either within the same organization or from another organization. Return on investment will be a key driving force for a CEO whose background is finance. Similarly design will be key for a CEO from an engineering background, production for a CEO from production and so on. This will be especially true with new or young entrepreneurs who have designed the business and been involved in all aspects. Howard Head is a good example of this involvement. He was a design engineer and production specialist, and when he tried to run the company he could not move away from his own expertise. This made it especially hard for him to let others run these aspects of the ski company (Rashford and Coghlan, 1994).

CEO life cycles

Donald Hambrick and Gregory Fukutomi (1991) of Columbia University have studied the seasons of CEOs and their life cycles. The first phase begins as a response to a mandate. This occurs when the new CEO embarks on his or her tenure with a commitment to a particular paradigm – a model based on personal assumptions about how the organization ought to be structured and managed. This model is fuelled, of course, by the CEO's toolkit – the knowledge base and experience that he or she brings to the job.

Next is *the experimentation phase*, where the CEO's commitment to his or her original paradigm varies depending on the success or failure in the initial stage. This is when the CEO's knowledge of his/her task required by the job is moderate, interest is high and power is somewhat increased. The CEO's information continues to flow from numerous sources, but becomes increasingly filtered by the time it reaches him or her.

The third phase, to a great extent, is the CEO's *defining phase*. It is characterized by the CEO's level of commitment to his/her paradigm. At this point, the CEO's task knowledge is stronger, rate of learning declines, interest remains moderately high, and information comes from fewer and somewhat filtered sources. Here, the CEO's power is moderate and continues to grow.

The fourth is a *convergence phase* as a CEO pursues a series of incremental actions to reinforce the major changes that have resulted from his/her commitment to a certain paradigm. By this time, a strong task knowledge has grown, interest is starting to diminish, and information is highly filtered and from even fewer sources. The CEO's power is strong and ever increasing.

In the final stage, which is defined as *dysfunction*, the CEO's effectiveness is seriously diminishing. The CEO's commitment to a given paradigm is hardened and any interest in experimentation seriously weakened. As specific tasks become habitual, the CEO's interest in them wanes considerably. At this stage, the CEO depends only on a very few, highly filtered sources of information. As the CEO's interest ebbs, his/her energy for risk and dramatic changes all but vanishes. Paradoxically, the CEO's power and ability to lead are at an all-time high.

The CEO and critical events

Triggering events that start a change in driving forces can occur from critical events that arise and face every CEO. They are the recent issues, most often in the form of a threat that needs solutions and that takes the CEO's time and need attention. When these events run in over time, such as tight capital markets, new competitive products or customer-based change, they have to be addressed. Most CEOs react by using the greatest strengths in an organization to address the issue. If the strength does not exist in the organization it must be developed from within or hired in to counter the threat or take advantage of the new opportunity. This can cause a change in the driving force of an organization.

With regard to the driving force in phase one the CEO most often brings it with him or her. In internally focused organizations it is the functional role that the CEO knows best and most likely the reason for his or her choice as CEO. In results-directed organizations with profitability as the driving force, the critical profitability criterion is likely to be the one for selecting a CEO with financial experience. In phase two of the CEO lifecycle, it is often reformulated. CEOs with operations skills types can shift to profitability or the opposite in financial types selected as CEO. With either type leader this may be put off until phase three. In phases four or five there normally is no change in the driving force.

Role of the members

There is a real lobby in most organizations, subtle or not, for the driving force role. Each Level III group or interdepartmental unit wants to take the lead. If not addressed, it remains as a subtle force pushing behind the scenes. This is most apparent in organizations that are internal focused because of internal strengths. If, on the other hand, the organization is externally driven or results driven, there is less appeal for Level III groups to jockey for power.

Role of the ODC consultants

There are consultants that work with organizations to help them determine their driving forces. They are content specialists. There is also a role for ODC consultants as they can be useful in the emergent driving force situation where the perceived power is lost by one group and won by another. When an organization moves from an engineering driving force to a sales driving force, information and resource flows change. If this is missed and not reflected on, dysfunctions will follow. ODC consultants can work with the manager to address the Level III issues of information flow and inter-group politics.

Interlevel issues in determining driving forces

Naming the corporate words is a process necessitated by changing environmental conditions, changing strategic advantages, changing functions from mergers or acquisitions by outside shareholder groups, and interactions or changes among the key participants within the organization. The process of changing an organization's corporate words necessitates a clear sense of why change is needed, a formulation of what the new corporate picture would ideally look like and building support for change through the transition from the old to the new one (Nadler, 1998). Changing the corporate words is also a large-scale change as described by Mohrman *et al.* (1989), as it constitutes a deep change which entails shifts in members' basic beliefs and values in the way the organization is understood and effects pervasive changes throughout the organization.

Listed below are four interaction scenarios, which can challenge an organization's current corporate words:

1   Interdepartmental nature of a driving force.
2   Key individuals and their respective interdepartmental groups.
3   Team issues in the senior management group with an origin in the driving force choice.
4   Level IV or organizational issues around naming the driving force.

Interdepartmental nature of a driving force

Driving forces are by their nature interdepartmental. If the driving force in an organization is designated as engineering, then the key interdepartmental group is engineering. In the same way, if design and production are the key words of the organization, then the interdepartmental group which has priority is production. Therefore driving forces are directed at the key interdepartmental group and give it priority within the organization.

Senior individuals and their respective interdepartmental group

In understanding the interdepartmental group (Level III), relationships and the functional teams' level (Level II), with the senior individuals (Level I) who lead these teams, the driving force provides a key element for one team. As was pointed out earlier, the discipline or field in the career path of the CEO can provide a bias toward that discipline as the driving force. This especially becomes true with change of CEOs from different disciplines.

Team issues in the senior management group with an origin in the driving force choice

Team-level issues within the senior management group are sources of conflict as senior management group members represent the different constituencies within the organization, which are potentially vying to be the organization's driving force. The tension arises when team members are caught between supporting the team effort of the company and representing the needs of their functioning group. Most often this comes into the forefront when there's a redefinition of the key driving force and a restatement of the corporate words.

Level IV or organizational issues around naming and changing the driving force

The subtlest interlevel conflicts arise between Levels III and IV around naming the corporate words. The change of a lead group or function provides a shift in perceived power or influence. In this shift there are winners and losers. This changes the overall organization climate when some people no longer feel appreciated and others feel more important. The rest of the organization gets uncomfortable with this submerged conflict. The best way to address the issue is to discuss the change, the reasons for it and the natural resentment which can occur. It is also an occasion to stress the importance of support people in an organization.

Conclusions

In this chapter we described the second focus, naming the corporate words, and how this deals with those operations or functions that had become the lead operations or functions over time. These are most often referred to as driving forces and become the articulation or lived out mission statement of the organization. The process focus of naming the corporate words deals with the power aspects and conflicts as well as successes that come from the lead function or operation.

Table 8.2 outlines the task and relational issues of naming the corporate words.

The perspective of organizational leaders on naming the corporate words is that the driving force be the appropriate one, that it represents balance and functionality within the organization and that it enables the organization to fulfil its corporate picture.

The perspective of members is to want to be part of the mainstream of the organization and to contribute to the organization's thrust. If particular members are not part of the driving force then they need to know how they relate and contribute directly to it.

The ODC consultant keeps an eye on whether there is congruence between the organization's espoused driving force and the one that actually has priority. Is the driving force that is espoused within the organization the same one that is perceived externally by customers and other stakeholders?

Figure 8.1 provides a structure for inquiring into the outcome of naming corporate worlds. The three inquiry loops begin from the outcomes of choosing a driving force and move inquiring about actions taken, goals set and ultimate purpose.

The most favourable outcome of the process of naming the corporate words is that the driving force is congruent with the corporate picture, that it is not perceived as a force which excludes people and functions within the organization, but as one that enhances participation and contribution rather than curtailing it.

Table 8.2 Naming the corporate words

	TASK	RELATIONAL
Content	Driving force CEO lifecycles	Priority of functions Are we marketing or engineering or . . .?
Process	Look at past decision processes	Stakeholder input both internal and external
Culture	Unexamined driving forces	Relative power of stakeholder groups

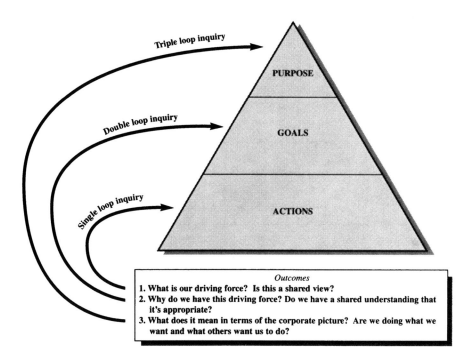

Figure 8.1 Single, double and triple loop inquiry.

Action research activity 8.1

Below find a blank table. In relation to an organization with which you are familiar, fill in the boxes with what you see as the important content, process and cultural issues in task and relational terms for your organization with regard to naming the corporate words. Discuss this with your team or, better still, copy the blank form and get them to fill in the blanks prior to your discussion.

	TASK	RELATIONAL
Content		
Process		
Culture		

Action research activity 8.2

In relation to an organization with which you are familiar, reflect on the following perspectives and try to answer the questions.

Leaders

Senior organizational leaders may pose the following questions:

1   Given the corporate picture we have selected, is the driving force correct and appropriate?
2   How do we in the senior management group work together to select and implement the driving force?

Members

Non-executive members may pose the following questions:

1   How do I relate to the driving force of the organization?
2   Do I agree with it and am I part of it or in support of it?

ODC consultants

ODC consultants may pose the following questions:

1   Is there congruence between the espoused driving force and the one that actually operates?
2   How does the senior management group process work to be an effective working team on selecting and using the driving force?
3   How does the organization as a whole manage interfunctional cooperation and rivalry and conflict?

Outcomes

1   Does naming the corporate words enhance the productivity of the organization?
2   Does the process of naming the corporate words get in the way or help organization productivity?

Case: ABC Insurance Company

Continuing with the ABC case from chapter 7, there were a number of outcomes from this private–public transformation. The non-existence of a dedicated corporate finance department independent of the operating subsidiaries prior to the earnings charge made it difficult to fully evaluate the company's success or failure to meet goals. In addition, at the operational level, informal relationships developed between the newly formed corporate area and certain members within the operating companies along relationships that remained from the old structure.

The foundation needed to be laid in 1996–1997 for the ultimate public offering that took place in 2001. This is a clear demonstration that the CEO had a clear vision of what the company would be and a plan for that eventuality. During this time resistance to the vision of the company remained at many hierarchical levels. The question 'where do I fit within the organization?' was being asked not only by the employees of the operating subsidiary that had experienced significant management turnover because of the loss, but also by the new employees that were hired to fill some of the corporate roles. Resistance occurred with employees of the operating subsidiary who were not open to working with the new corporate employees.

Between the 1996 and 2001, ABC continued to develop its corporate finance operation and furthered the private to public transition, filing with the SEC and listing on NASDAQ in 1998. The transition was slower than the CEO would have liked and was reflective of the hesitancy that remained with some of the older officers and directors of a company that had been private for approximately 80–90 years. A public stock offering was finally completed in 2001, and this marked a more significant commitment to the public arena. The offering came complete with the rigours of reporting results in a public environment and the accompanying expectations developed by outside investors. During this time, the company started up a new subsidiary to focus on a niche market.

During this phase the CEO's vision from the early 1990s of transition to a public company was more fully attained via the public offering. The rigours of being a public company were somewhat greater than the CEO had initially anticipated and discipline was required to maintain a long-term perspective in the face of a number of short-term requirements, including the road show with the financial analysts in New York that preceded the offering. The new driving force was financial.

During this period, some of the issues of how people felt toward the ABC company during the private to public transition had been worked out. The emphasis turned to developing strong relationships with the subsidiaries, as the corporate finance department began to work with the operating subsidiaries and the subsidiaries began to explore how they could fit into the overall structure and what changes and resources were necessary to support the move to a public environment. Certain concrete examples would include the need to perform the monthly close at a quicker pace and to deliver an enhanced analysis package to anticipate and answer analysts' questions.

Questions for reflection and discussion

1   Given a change from private to public ownership, what change in naming the corporate words would you expect in such a setting? Does ABC match your expectation?
2   What department had the new role of being the driving force?
3   What steps should ABC be taking to integrate this change?

Case: Diaz Steel Group

The Diaz Group, Inc. (DGI) is a privately owned holding company for several subsidiaries, one of which is ABC Tolerance Rings. ABC Tolerance Rings serves a number of industries as a marketing arm of British Tolerance Rings, a UK engineering company. Each of these two companies has a long, rich history and a strong footing in South America through Chile.

ABC Tolerance Rings is in the business of selling tolerance rings, which are corrugated metals strips that act as frictional fasteners by acting on principles of spring and friction. Tolerance ring technology competes favourably with other methods of fastening, including epoxy and set screws. Customers for tolerance rings include manufacturers of automobiles, home appliances, power tools, electric motors and computer disk drives, as well as many other mechanical products. The tolerance ring is a versatile item, since it is both tough and delicate. For example, a tolerance ring can be used as an anti-theft device on a steering column in an automobile, or as a miniature ball bearing in a computer disk drive.

The company has been in business since 1961 and is optimistic about growth potential because there are proven applications for markets that have not yet been fully tapped. The challenge for ABC Tolerance Rings is to double sales in the next five years. It primarily acts to market and sell products manufactured by the UK-based British Tolerance Rings, although they both produce or source items in alternative ways. With an expertise in engineering, British Tolerance Rings is well-suited to address engineering issues, while ABC Tolerance Rings focuses on market expansion in Latin America. Chile is an effective base of operations because of its recent growth and stability.

A single, identifiable driving force is the required outcome of the corporate picture and is needed to execute the plan to double sales. At present the driving force is in engineering, not in marketing/sales. The organization's history is one of engineering a solution by finding a manufacturer for the customers' specifications that ABC designs or manufactures itself. In the day-to-day work of the organization such a driving force no longer meets their sales plan.

For the tolerance ring business, Mr Diaz the CEO expressed the importance to ABC Tolerance Rings that it should function exclusively as a marketing arm of British Tolerance Rings. Mr Diaz also explained that his employees had, for years, devoted the majority of their time to providing engineering solutions. The present sales people, engineers by profession, do not share Mr Diaz's view – many in fact openly say they are not marketing or sales people but engineering people.

Questions for reflection and discussion

1   Where does the need for this change arise?
2   What needs to happen to get this change in driving force to take place?
3   What are the interlevel issues and how would you contribute to enabling this change to take place?

Chapter 9

Doing corporate analysis

The third strategic focus, doing the corporate analysis, is the foundation for the focus on choice of alternatives, and it can be the foundation for the focus on framing the corporate picture. While the generation of alternatives or scenarios provides direction, it is not itself the choice. This is a critical stage in strategy formation and the method chosen to do the analysis determines the structure of the answers and affects the outcome. This is the essence of the content and process of engaging in the task of doing the corporate analysis. In relational terms across the four levels, the task of doing an analysis involves the complex involvement of senior management and organizational members in technical analytic activities that are also highly political. In this chapter we first describe the technicalities of doing analysis and then we explore the organizational processes by which the technical elements are done and the role they play in the change process.

The content of doing the corporate analysis

The standard analytic process focuses mainly on the internal and external environments as they affect the organization. The analysis of customers, suppliers or other outside elements is treated insofar as they relate to the organization itself. Since the late 1970s, the range of strategic analysis concepts (such as SWOT analysis, portfolio analysis, the five forces framework and experience curves) are standard in the management arsenal.

The process of doing the corporate analysis

There are essentially four approaches to the technical tasks of doing the corporate analysis:

1   Standard analytic process.
2   Standard analytic process with consideration of the competition.
3   Proactive analytic process with scenarios.
4   Analytic process using models and game theory.

Standard analytic process

The elements of this approach to analysis are illustrated in Figure 9.1. The factors, seen on the left side of the figure, normally comprise the elements of the environmental threats and opportunities profile (ETOP). They are: economic (including government and legal), marketing, competitive, supplier and technological.

The first, the economic factors, sets the overall milieu in which the organization is functioning. The economic analysis includes but is not limited to such things as growth of the economy, consumers' ability to afford products and services, exchange rates in international organizations, economic constraints on consumers or suppliers, the cost of borrowing money, equity returns against savings returns, etc. A component of the economic factors is the government and legal environment. This category includes things such as

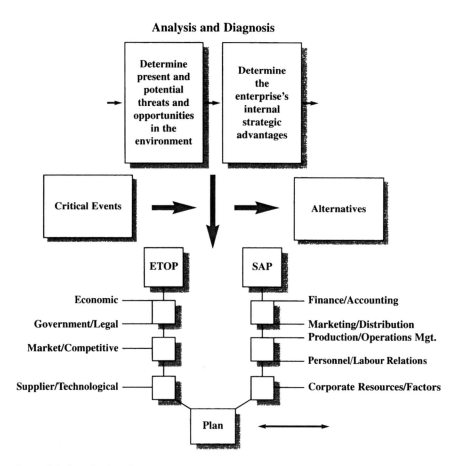

Figure 9.1 Standard analytic process.

laws that govern operations and products, international trade agreements, tariffs and other restricting devices, requirements for services provided, service and product liability questions, issues concerning patents and equality employment legislation, etc. e-business and new approaches to commerce are impacted by these regulations as well as government regulations of stocks and bonds.

The next factors are the market competitive ones. This is consideration of the competitors and how they affect results. Market share by product or service, product innovation, product packaging, market presentation and advertising are analysed at this stage. Important to this type of analysis is the trend over time, i.e. are the market and the share declining or growing? This is analysed by each product or service in isolation and then in the aggregate. The organizational life cycle should be a background to the alternatives that are developed at this stage. The presence of the organization in its external environment and its ability to be a player are accounted for in this phase of the analysis.

The next factors deal with the suppliers and technological changes in the environment or on the horizon that could affect production. This would seem at first to apply only to a production organization where the technological know-how and source of materials are essential. The aircraft, auto and electronic components in the computer industry are classic examples where this information and analysis are critical. Yet the supply chain can affect every organization. Medical supplies to hospitals, books and food service to universities are but some examples. Critical cost changes can produce dramatic effects on service pricing. In most situations the supplier has a great hold over the end producer of the products or services. Sometimes the reverse is true when one end producer is the sole buyer of the supplier's product.

Suppliers are not alone in having effects on service organizations. Technological factors can also have a strong effect. Medical organizations are a good example where new technology is an advantage in gaining patients and providing better care. This is very true with new radiological procedures. Each hospital or clinic needs to have the latest MRI scanner to serve patients. Hospitals also have learned how important the physician supply of patient referrals is to their census. This has caused new hospital physician alliances and has introduced competition in medical care in both the USA and Europe.

When Christian Haub became president of A&P and had total control, he began the process of analysis to determine where the company was and where it should go. As Haub describes: 'the group sat down in April and May and set out criteria for the analysis. The auditors provided the results of their internal audit and we put together analysis for the external environment. In order to enhance the outside information we engaged investment bankers to help us get competitive data, most which was publicly available, to determine the critical benchmarks in terms of sales, growth, profitability, return on capital, financial comparisons and market share.'

It is interesting to note reliance on outside analysts, because Haub felt the internal people were too close to the issue to be able to clearly and accurately do the analysis that was required. The result of the analysis made it clear that the company had to change fundamentally. It was mostly Haub's own vision that provided the clarity to see the present methods would not work. The end product of the analysis was to begin forming a new corporate picture.

Strategic advantage profile

The focus of analysis now turns inward and deals with the strategic advantage profile (SAP) located on the right side of Figure 9.1. Some of the internal factors have a counterpart in the external analysis with a resultant relationship. Economic condition relates to finance and supplier/technological relates to production. These relationships should be kept in mind. The factors involved in this internal analysis are: finance and accounting marketing and distribution, production and operations management, personnel and labour relations, and corporate resources. Corporate resources is the catchall of other factors that should be looked at and analysed but that do not have a specific category.

The first factors are the finance and accounting factors. Here consideration is made of the major financial ratios. Some of the important financial ratios in this area are: rate of return, debt to equity, inventory turnover, sales turnover, equity to sales and sustainable growth rate. The comparison to industry norms on earnings, net worth and inventory turns is also critical. Cash management and other financial procedures are processed in this analysis.

Sustainable growth rate is also a crucial analysis tool for new or smaller organizations. This ratio determines if a firm can continue to grow by its ability to generate and keep adding equity in order to increase production. This ratio is most important to small organizations that tend to be under capitalized. Acquiring external equity funds in small firms can dilute the ownership. Most entrepreneurs do not want their ownership diluted. The accounting analysis consists of determining whether there are an effective budget and plans in place, and suitable controls used in the implementation of the budget. The accounting report, 10K, etc. are all part of the analysis at this point.

The next part of the analysis is marketing and distribution. The key questions here deal with market share. How firm is this share? Is the share diversified between different products? What is happening to prices and margins in the markets? Grid analysis for products is a useful analytical tool, if appropriate. The distribution system, which can be a driving force as we have already seen, is a part of the analysis of an organization's efficiencies. The type of distribution systems used can directly affect the success of an organization. Many firms use the distribution system as their critical advantage. One such company is Wal-Mart. Wal-Mart is effective in getting large amounts of goods sent from its manufacturers to its outlets/distribution sites. In doing distribution in a 'just in time' method to the point-of-sale they achieve a great cost advantage over competitors.

The analysis of production and operations management provides new processes, savings and faster production yet is often overlooked in importance in the analysis focus. This is an opportunity to analyse whether the production process is correct and if it offers any strategic advantages by using the 'power alley' concept, found in manufacturing. The 'power alley concept' maintains that the more common processes that can be found and maximized, the greater the cost savings will be. You can gain a market advantage as seen in the example of the Black & Decker Company. It did not invent the weed-eater but by analysis of available processes and building a product with no additional production or engineering costs Black & Decker introduced the Weed Wacker. This product competed and won against a new product from a new company. Having the production required for the new product and using its own distribution system to sell this product it was possible to do a national rollout and win on price. Additional savings were obtained because Black & Decker did no marketing. Through these savings, Black & Decker were able to profitably produce and sell more product than its competitor because of its production analysis, and strong name. When customers came to buy a 'Weed Eater', Black & Decker, with a better name, had its 'Weed Wacker' on sale at a lesser price.

The production and control analysis can provide other sources of advantage. Take, for example, the Hallmark Card organization, which through large-scale printing and a high quality control, can produce high-quality products at low cost. This enables Hallmark to price in a higher margin or compete on cost. It does both under different names with quality under the Hallmark label and cost under the Ambassador line.

Included in the analysis are personnel and labour relations. It is at this point that the amount of turnover among employees and senior executives is analysed and is compared to the rest of the industry. Also the labour relations climate in which the firm or organization operates is analysed.

Corporate resources and other factors are also analysed in the SAP. An organization has a life cycle. An organization has its birth; it has a place within an industry. There are critical people who founded and influenced the organization and they are important to note. The development of the goals and products over the years and what the organization has learned from

vital as well. How an organization has gone through past change
; its ability to support future changes. The organizational life cycle in
ance is internal-looking and deals with the ability of an organization
to change. This analysis is used in the case of acquisitions to determine the
price paid for goodwill. That is the value the long-standing organization
gives to its products and services.

A critical aspect in today's organization is the determination of the
quality of the management information systems (MIS) or information and
communication technology (ICT) aspects of the firm or organization. The
information system and the technology required to operate it are critical
to the real-time understanding of the factors affecting an organization.
The analysis aims to see if the information system works and does what it
is designed to do: assist in the decision-makers' processes. The question is
twofold: is the information valid and is appropriate information being used
in the decision process?

It should be noted that the 'Balanced ScoreCard' approach to strategic
management by Robert Kaplan and David Norton (1996) is implicit in the
five foci approach used here. The balanced scorecard approach uses four
areas of measurement for successful strategic management:

1   Customer perspective.
2   Financial perspective.
3   Internal business process perspective.
4   The learning and growth perspective.

Each of these perspectives has four components: objectives, measures, targets
and initiatives. The basic assumption that there is nothing that can't be
measured is valid for making a difference in the greater strategic picture.

In the five strategic foci approach, two of the four perspectives are here in
the analysis chapter and two follow in later foci. The customer perspective
is a major part of the external analysis with its objectives, measures and
initiatives. The financial perspective is a major part of the internal analysis
with its objectives, measures and initiatives. The basic steps of the balanced
scorecard for these two aspects occur in this focus.

Standard analytic process with consideration of the competition

Many times the senior individuals play on both sides of the line as they move
from one organization in the same industry to another. Trade shows and
industry or sector associations are another venue in which the strategic players are known to each other and learn how each one will act in competitive
situations. Organizations want to analyse the uncertainty of a wider environment, and then with such knowledge situate their own plans with those of

the competition (Figure 9.2). This process is often used in the acquisition process. When internal growth cannot keep up with expectations, organizations turn to acquisition to meet goals. This is especially attractive with a large cash-in-hand position. The analysis with the competitor becomes particularly important, as the competitor is the potential acquired object. If a potential purchase is contemplated, then more information is shared across organization boundaries in preparation for the buyout.

Proactive analytic process through scenarios

The process of action and reaction becomes a closed system when organizations within the same industry closely interact with one another (Figure 9.3). A consensus of sorts is effectively built among organizations and critical moves of the senior players in an entire industry can be anticipated. The input required to achieve this close interaction is intelligence on the competitors. This intelligence is of two kinds. The first kind is accurate knowledge from public documents on competitors and general overall figures for an industry. The second kind is good intuitive approximation from past experience extrapolated into the future. The likely scenarios are most effective with a wide range of inputs from everyone with knowledge of the competitors or industry from within the organization. Good scenarios lead to the formulation of models.

Analytic process using models and game theory

Building a simulation model of the organization in its environment provides an ongoing process of analysis, done continuously in real time (Figure 9.4). Appendix 2 provides guidelines on how to use models. The use of such a model creates a virtual plan. In this virtual reality a computer simulation is used to model the competitive universe. By putting on the computer hood one can 'fly a plane' or 'walk on the moon' provided the reality is accurate in its computer presentation. Analysis using a virtual plan allows a model of the business environment with a comprehensive systems approach, documenting all the key relationships then modifying them by added to the equation time delays between actions and reactions as well as economic consequences.

Game theory can be introduced at this juncture. By playing the 'what if' games, with win and lose as well as probability attached, the analysis shows how the bottom line is affected. In other words, a virtual plan calculates the risk and rewards of each scenario and predicts the financial consequences of the alternative. Game theory adds to the analysis the 'win' or 'lose' probabilities and simulates real outcomes. Both of these work best at the edge of chaos and are structured guesses at the reduction of the unknowns. This model incorporates the resultant actions and the expected reaction from competitors. Initially, the perceived information from the competitors

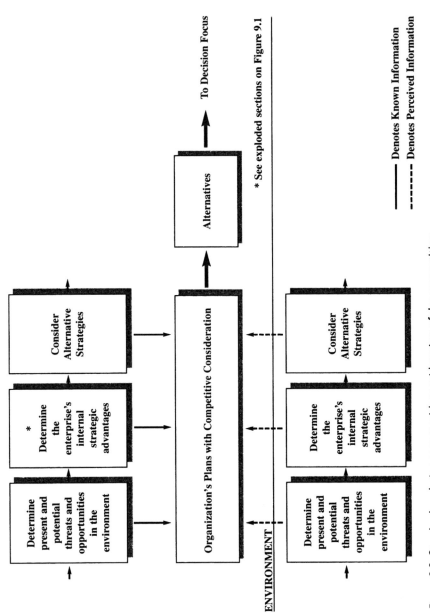

Determine present and potential threats and opportunities in the environment

*
Determine the enterprise's internal strategic advantages

Consider Alternative Strategies

Organization's Plans with Competitive Consideration

Alternatives

To Decision Focus

Determine present and potential threats and opportunities in the environment

Determine the enterprise's internal strategic advantages

Consider Alternative Strategies

ENVIRONMENT

* See exploded sections on Figure 9.1

——— Denotes Known Information
- - - - Denotes Perceived Information

Figure 9.2 Standard analytic process with consideration of the competition.

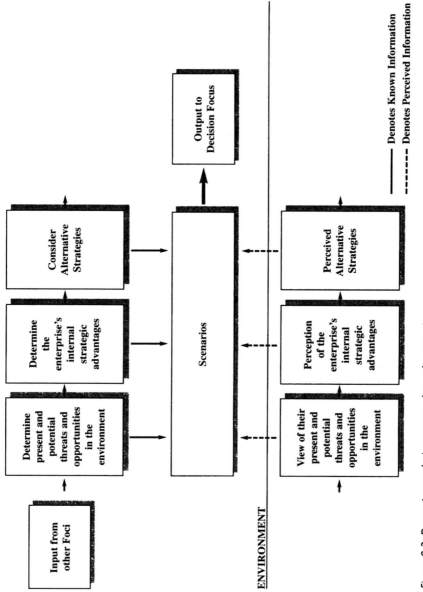

Figure 9.3 Proactive analytic process through scenarios.

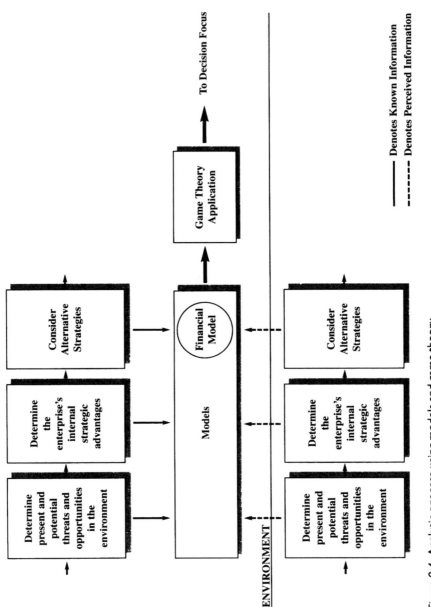

Figure 9.4 Analytic process using models and game theory.

is unclear, or less reliable, because the information is perceptual. However, with experience, a firm's process of guessing what will occur checked against the reality of what did occur in the competition can over time come close to simulating reality. This produces a model that can be used in real time.

A large university in the northeast part of the United States began a process of modelling in 1985. The key variables, such as enrolment, departmental budgets charges for depreciation, potential tuition increases and a myriad of other important data points were put together in the model. The model continues in use over the next 15 years. With each annual iteration, the model became more accurate and had applications in more ways. When the question arose to self-operate the telephone system or submit it out for bid, the model showed self-operation integrated with information technology would not only save money but make money. If the decision was made with confidence, it was due to the model. The predicted result was met within 1 per cent. Other significant issues provided the same economies using the model.

A suburban water company in a large metropolitan area established a model for its own use. It modelled the timing and methods of reading meters with labour and fixed costs as well. The model was successful in predicting when to change from labour-intensive meter reading to electronic encoded reading. The model was also successful in determining when to acquire water companies in other areas.

In both of these vignettes the organizations are leagues ahead of their competition. Both organizations have flexibility and confidence in the decisions they make in highly competitive environments. It has been the experience of both organizations that the models take time to work and be of value. It is also the experience of both organizations that when they do work and are reliable they provide an incredible competitive advantage.

Summary of the process steps of analysis

The process steps are analysis through the four approaches: the standard analytic process, the standard analytic process with consideration of the competitors, proactive analytic scenarios and modelling and analytic game theory. All of the approaches to analysis presume the basic ETOP and SAP on which everything else takes place. Each organization runs this task process in its own unique way. Most common is the practice of an organization using ETOP and SAP analyses to make minor corrections.

The more difficult task of strategic planning is to find discontinuous change. This is addressed using the complex adaptive system approach of the living world as a model. Pascale *et al.* (2000) argue that for an entity to qualify as a complex adaptive system (third-order change), first it must be comprised of many agents acting in parallel. It is not hierarchical control. Second, it continuously shuffles these building blocks and generates multiple levels of organization structure. This is subject to the second law of thermodynamics, exhibiting the winding down over time unless replenished with energy in this sense; complex adaptive systems are vulnerable to death. A distinguishing characteristic of all complex adaptive systems is to display a capability for pattern recognition and to employ this to anticipate the future and learn to recognize the anticipation of seasonal change. This is the ability of an organization to look at a process of analysis that does not follow directly from the processes at hand or from past experience. The discontinuous change is a second-order change and the analysis that sets up looking for such a change, by its nature, questions the status quo. The use of executive intuition in sensing a new and discontinuous direction and desired corporate outcomes is part of this function. Christian Haub makes such a choice in the A&P case.

Roles in doing corporate analysis

CEO and senior management roles

The role of the CEO in the process of doing corporate analysis begins by setting up the criteria for analysis as well as having clear ownership of the process. Showing this interest is important for the outcome. The second role of the CEO is to be open to the outcome of the analysis focus. This means putting aside preconceived notions of what 'should' be the output of the analysis. Doing the corporate analysis is an ongoing process. The difficulty that a CEO has is not to lose interest in the routine outputs and as a result not look for discontinuity.

Corporate leaders, whether the CEO or members of senior management group or divisional heads, are constantly monitoring whether correct and useful information is being gathered and whether its assessment is intuitively right. They are comparing the organization's analysis with industry and competitors' benchmarks.

In terms of a broader picture, senior management needs to come to the analysis focus with the possibility that discontinuous change could be needed. This openness to the possibility of discontinuous change often occurs without direct information that can be tested for accuracy. It is possible that the critical information for a decision on discontinuous change is information that is absent or null. This intuitive guess opens the door for research and analysis. How the analysis is performed affects outcome. The dynamics of the committees and task forces which analyse the organization's ETOP and SAP are critical in order that the organization formulate proposals for strategic direction or pass the information to the senior managers who do the selection of alternative scenarios. This is seen in the change in recent years at VerticalNet.

VerticalNet illustrates the need of using different processes at different times so it could adapt to the chaotic Internet environment. In the early years of the organization, the standard analytical process was used (Figure 9.1). In later years proactive scenarios were used (Figure 9.3). In the early growth years, the strategic planning process focused only on the marketplace. The standard analysis process on the marketplace faced one critical flaw. It researched and understood the background and wants of the individual specialists who made up their multiple communities of supporters and users. The fact that it understood the marketplace was clear from their success. Experience shows its revenues increased from US$965,000 for the first six months ending June 1998 to US$5.5 million for the six months ending June 1999. The analysis showed that it had maintained 9 per cent of the advertisers who started with it in the 1998 period. The analysis focused on the external environment and not the internal strategic advantages. The real failure in terms of analysis was a failure to control expenses. As of June 1999 accumulated deficit totalled US$31.7 million – almost US$7 million of which had been incurred in the three months ending June 1999. VerticalNet shifted to the standard analytic process with consideration of the competition, but against its own and its competitors' increased expenses.

Most corporate directions of Internet companies were still chained to the purchasing of market share and not profitability. The disaster of this approach would only be seen in 2002. The questions not asked in the research and analysis were: who were the actual subscribers in the vertical communities, who were the real customers they were supporting? The largest segment of the support communities not attended to was the wider universe of people in individual organizations that were authorized to make individual purchases. On the manufacturing side, many managers not in the community controlled the different lines of products for sale and were not in the electronic Internet exchange. No one seemed to evaluate the readiness of the internal software systems of these users to be integrated to each other within the buyers' community and then integrated to the Internet and then from the Internet to the internal manufacturers' community of users. This failure more than any other, the failure of the analysis of the user groups, led to the failure to grow by VerticalNet and its competitors. This was a process failure, as well as a failure to look at the right analytic content.

Member roles

The members' roles are multiple in this focus. There is the necessity for members to be involved to build a model if one is used. The choice of criteria and measurements that reflect the reality in each aspect of the organization's function falls to members throughout the organization. The critical testing of reliability and validity of the research analysis by each factor falls to members and in itself is a reason for inclusion.

Role of the ODC consultant

ODC consultants perform a dual role in the focus of doing the corporate analysis. They ensure that the technicalities are performed accurately by asking questions: Is there completeness in data gathering? Is information openly shared and jointly owned? What happens to negative feedback? Is process critiqued and reviewed? These are the hard questions for organizations to ask themselves. This is a valuable role for the ODC consultant. In the heat of the discussion on alternative scenarios quite often the process issues get lost. Without an ODC consultant, less invested in the outcome, these questions do not get asked. Another valuable role of the ODC consultants is to provide a process for developing scenarios. They also ensure that the interlevel dynamics which we will discuss in the following section are being managed properly.

Interlevel dynamics in doing the corporate analysis

Doing the corporate analysis is a process necessitated by changing internal or external conditions, obtaining strategic advantages, changing functions from mergers or acquisitions by outside shareholder groups, and decisions by or changes among the senior leaders within the organization. Listed below are five interaction scenarios that can challenge how the organization does its analysis.

1   Cultural issues in how the analysis is performed.
2   Key roles played in analysis by interdepartmental groups.
3   Disagreement in facing discontinuous change by senior management group.
4   Degree of change affects degree of conflict experienced by interdepartmental groups.
5   Relationship to model, if one is used, has associated interlevel conflict.

Cultural issues in how the analysis is performed

There are cultural issues in how an organization engages in analysis. Each functional area has to examine its own analysis and process its own functionality as well as how the interdepartmental group's function affects others and its output. Each functional area is a subculture that exists in an organization, where functional groups have developed their own traditions, language and basic assumptions which provide a self-contained subsystem. The ability to self-correct and to hear critical comments forces new relations from this 'content' area. So each functional level is offering its view of the whole from the perspective of its own subculture in the interdepartmental group activity. How these analyses or 'views' interrelate or are accepted are critical, as most often in integrating multiple functions the cross-links between functions are the sources of trouble. The analysis within functions is most often correct. The workflow or process flow between functions is one such source of trouble.

Key roles played in analysis by interdepartmental group

Determining the corporate directions is the most complex of the foci. Doing the corporate analysis requires both looking inside and outside of the organization. The interlevel aspects of this focus as a result is complex.

The senior management group plays a central role

The CEO plays a key role. Each of the units in the interdepartmental group normally has some analytic expertise. The finance department also plays a central role, as financial data are critical in this analysis. There are also contributions from the IT area that must be considered.

Disagreement in facing discontinuous change by the senior management group

The senior management group usually determines the potential threats and opportunities in the environment. In its work with counterparts or even competitors at national meetings, an intuitive insight gives the group a starting point for this analysis. Whenever intuition comes into play it is easy for disagreement to arise. The CEO can see it one way and others see it quite differently. The resolution of these conflicts is then offered to the research team for analysis. Due to internal competition between functional areas, the senior management group may well be in conflict and has to resolve it.

Degree of change affects degree of conflict experienced by the interdepartmental group

The amount of interlevel conflict will be directly related to the degree of change required by the organization. In those changes which are incremental, conflict may be minimal, and disagreements revolve around performance. In those changes that are disjointed, the disagreement about a new environment can be quite severe. These conflicts are between Level II and Level III, and between Level I and Level II and Level III.

Relationship to model, if one is used, has associated interlevel conflict

If a financial model is used in determining the corporate direction, this whole process of interlevel conflict becomes more complex. In forming a model, the cooperation of all is required. There must be a common view of the operation of the organization both internally and externally for a model to be designed. Once designed, the model has to be honestly adjusted for reality. This requires cooperation between Level I in the CEO, Level II in the senior management group and Level III in the interdepartmental group.

Conclusions

The analysis on which a strategic plan rests is its foundation. If the foundation is poor, strategy likewise will be poor. The focus on doing the corporate analysis is an intricate mix of task and relational and content and process elements operating together to open the organization's leadership to new possibilities, even discontinuous ones. For organizations to respond quickly, this analysis focus must be second nature and habitual. In environments, as summarized by chaos, quick, efficient, inclusive and responsive analysis is critical. Intuition comes into play on how the choices are made on what to analyse.

Table 9.1 outlines the task and relational issues of doing corporate analysis.

The leaders' perspectives on the activity of determining the corporate direction through analysis focuses on (a) the quality, comprehensiveness and relevance of the information gathered, (b) whether it appears to be intuitively right and (c) whether benchmarks with competitors can be made.

Members are concerned with why they are doing the analysis, what its relevance is and how it is congruent with their own understanding of the situation. A process concern is the role of disagreement and whether members feel free to challenge the analysis.

ODC consultants focus on the completeness of the data gathering, whether it is openly shared and jointly owned, and whether alternative views and

Table 9.1 Doing corporate analysis

	TASK	RELATIONAL
Content	ETOP and SAP analysis Virtual plan	Link (or not) those analysed with those doing the analysis
Process	Analysis Modelling Intuition	How planning committees and task forces are chosen and their effect on outcome
Culture	Sense of confidence in the analysis; either true or false way of proceeding	Divisional cultures, market segments or operations as a whole

negative feedback are encouraged. They work at enabling review and critiques of processes and at facilitating shared understanding of the workflow process across the multiple functions of the interdepartmental group.

The outcomes of determining the corporate direction is that there is organizational learning about what needs to be changed in the organization.

Action research activity 9.1

Below find a blank table. In relation to an organization with which you are familiar, fill in the boxes with what you see as the important content, process and cultural issues in task and relational terms for your organization with regard to determining the corporate direction through analysis. Discuss this with your team or, better still, copy the blank form and get them to fill in the blanks prior to your discussion.

	TASK	RELATIONAL
Content		
Process		
Culture		

Action research activity 9.2

In relation to an organization with which you are familiar, reflect on the following perspectives and try to answer the questions.

Leaders

Leaders may pose the following questions:

1   Is the proper information being gathered?
2   Is assessment of the information intuitively right?
3   Are benchmarks available?
4   What are our competitors' benchmarks?

Organizational members

Non-executive members may pose the following questions:

1   What are the reasons for doing the analysis?
2   How does my part of the analysis fit?
3   How do I relate to other areas or people to make a complete analysis of my area?
4   Will this information change my work situation?

ODC consultants

ODC consultants may pose the following questions:

1   Is there completeness in data gathering?
2   Is information openly shared and jointly owned?
3   What happens to negative feedback?
4   Is process critiqued and reviewed?

Outcomes

1   Is the analysis authentic?
2   Are there flaws in the information?
3   Does the analysis show up an agenda for change?

Case: VerticalNet

VerticalNet is an example of the use of standard analytic process with competitors. This process utilizes the internal and analytic process on itself and on the competitor and then makes a decision on an acquisition. This comparison is centred on the question of compatibility. VerticalNet, a dotcom company, found itself in this situation in the 1999–2000 time frame. Just as important as internal organic growth, VerticalNet was extremely aggressive in terms of external growth through acquisitions. As one of the darlings of NASDAQ, VerticalNet's stock was as high as US$297 a share and Hagan noted that the company 'used their stock as a (strategic) weapon'. In analysing the competition, the price of the stocks was compared and became a factor in choosing which organizations to acquire. Among their key acquisitions were: Safety On-Line, an on-line occupational health and safety community; ElectricNet, an on-line electric power industry; LabX.com, a scientific laboratory equipment e-commerce site; and Real World Electronics, an electronics exchange.

VerticalNet's model sought to provide richness within a specific industry and only achieved reach through the expansion of the industries in which it served. As such, each of VerticalNet's communities featured its own version of distinctive branding, lending to the air of focus that was necessary to achieve the trust of the individuals within the industry that the site served. This approach was validated by industry experts as well as by the influx of capital to fund new competitors, such as Fobchemicals.com and Promedix.com.

VerticalNet's 'formula for successful on-line communities' included the analysis of 'content, community and commerce'. Content factor was achieved by offering a variety of news and other information, including white papers, coordinated by respected industry insiders that served as managing editors, not unlike a standard print trade publication. Each acquisition was analysed for the content it could provide. The community analysis involved a number of beneficial components, including discussion fora, career information and events. This analysis scaled each acquisition target for its contributions area and added this to the contribution the acquisition made to VerticalNet. Commerce factor analysis included on-line auctions and transactions and it too was scaled and combined with the other factors in order to make the final decision on acquisition. Like many new media companies, VerticalNet's primary revenue source was advertising, including the development of storefronts or web pages within the vertical trade communities that highlighted the advertiser and provided links to the advertiser's web site.

VerticalNet's valuation, however, like that of other b2b Internet companies, was based less on the current revenue mix and more on the company's potential to deliver enormous transaction-related revenue in the future. This drove the analysis towards potential growth rather than present revenue. It also provided a structural problem of how to structure these acquisitions.

The information age organization does not abandon traditional strategic design principles, but instead builds upon and redefines them, very quickly for the most part. The structural design of these acquired companies was consistent with VerticalNet's main purposes. It resembled a galaxy system, with all its 'suns and planets' all apparently operating by themselves, but every one of them perfectly interconnected to the total system and all of them both self-sufficient and mutually dependent on each other. All the sub-systems were inherently attracted to their mass centre, but were also continually trying to escape from this attraction. As Walsh noted when reflecting upon his experience with America Online and its ability to defeat superior technologies with a simplistic approach, 'being simple . . . is always a winning strategy'. This analogy of clusters of stellar systems simplistically sums up this structure. While this structure can sometimes resemble the accepted strategic business unit (SBU) model, it differs fundamentally from that design in both structure and the interconnection process.

Questions for reflection and discussion

1   Through your analysis, which acquired companies seem more congruent with VerticalNet's culture and corporate self-image?
2   In the simplest definition of their business, VerticalNet sees itself as a 'market maker' that links buyers and sellers. Is it a natural evolution for it to increase its transactional revenue, moving away from its reliance on advertising into more of an e-commerce revenue model?
3   How do interlevels bring an understanding of this case?

Case: ABC Insurance Company

The second significant event to affect the ABC company began to unfold as a result of the tragedy of September 11th, 2001. The events of 9/11 at the World Trade Center changed the basis of analysis for every insurance organization in the world. While the impact of the event on the company was modest in relation to the overall impact on the industry, it did coincide adversely with certain other events. A new debt facility that was scheduled to close shortly after September 11th was put on hold as banks worldwide tightened credit. The method of calculating risk had changed. The following year analysis showed that a new operating subsidiary disclosed significant losses and a decision was made to shut it down. The negative potential implication of these activities, along with a market opportunity for increased growth, gave rise to concerns within the rating agency environment that capital adequacy may be overly stressed at the current level of growth if the debt facility, cancelled after September 11th, was not completed by the following year end. The change that took place this time, while abrupt, was not discontinuous. It was more in line with a redirecting of new benchmarks of success. The 'crisis' was identified by the corporate entity and, while it coincided with changes in certain key managers, the scale of the upheaval was nowhere near as significant as the earlier changes that accompanied the first significant event of going public.

From the perspective of the CEO and senior management, this new challenge led to the need to refocus the organization on profitability. The decision to discontinue the new operating subsidiary was an affirmation of management's commitment to profitability and to remain focused. The groundwork that was laid in 1996 provided a better platform from which management could analyse the situation and respond in an expedient fashion.

Questions for reflection and discussion

1   What changes brought about the change in analysis? Were these internal or external or both?
2   How does the analysis process change without an effect on other foci?
3   What interlevel conflicts are likely to be caused?

Chapter 10

Choosing and implementing corporate actions

The fourth strategic focus is choosing and implementing corporate actions. The issues requiring a decision by an organization can arise from three sources. They are the outcomes, the scenarios or decision matrix derived in the focus on determining the corporate direction through analysis (chapter 9). Second, they arise from critical events that require decision responses occurring on a regular basis in most organizations. Third, they come from the need to respond to threatening situations that face the organization. In the case of critical events or a response to threats, when time permits, they are analysed in the previous focus with a set of alternatives and then are processed in this focus. Decisions and implementation need to comply with the organization's ethical norms for corporate social responsibility. In this chapter, the decision process, both who and how, and the implementation process are presented and followed by discussion of interlevel interactions.

The content of the choice process

The input scenarios or decision matrix derived in the focus on corporate analysis can carry a bias with them. When the CEO or senior management group is invested in the analysis process, this can have both a positive and negative effect. It is positive in so far as it helps in the selection process because people have been engaged in the analysis. It is negative in so far as it pre-empts their freedom to choose equally among all of the alternatives. When a significant investment of monies and time has been spent on analysis, it is very clear that a decision of some sort is required to complete the process. In this situation, not to decide is not acceptable because of how much investment has been made in the analysis.

The few issues that require a decision without analysis come to the CEO with a critical time limitation. Some of these are decided in combination with the senior management group, while the CEO alone decides others. These issues arise from changes in existing plans, unforeseen changes in the environment or customer base, or threatening elements from within or outside the organization. One such example is the Wawa case when Dick

Wood had set a goal for a margin of profitability on gasoline. The change in the world oil marketplace, causing the changing prices at the retail level, made it impossible to achieve this margin. To accept this as a loss just to encourage customers to come to the stores was not enough. He wanted to determine what approach would return the margin to its original goal. Then he had to decide how to do it. This is an example of a critical event triggering a new round of analysis and decision-making.

The content of this focus, as we have stated is: a set of input scenarios or alternatives, the decision made, the ethical norms and the steps to implement them. Each one is critical for the selection and implementation of corporate actions. Each of these components, the alternative set, the decision process and implementation directive forms a part of the whole. The alternative set, scenarios or alternative matrix needs to be pared down to one or two as a first step. This determines how many alternatives from which to choose. If only one remains, it will be necessary to obtain one more to enable a choice. If there is only one alternative, then there is no choice or a decision has been made by default. Neither of these conditions is desirable.

The content of implementation

Implementation has two major aspects. They are: setting implementation criteria and delineating implementation processes. First, we look at criteria. Criteria need to be agreed upon by the CEO, the senior management and be directly tied to the analysis. The criteria resulting from the analysis are such things as: the financial ratios, the level of anticipated success, turnover, ethics and all the other elements anticipated in the analysis phase that must be stated as goals that can be measured.

Additional criteria can come from benchmarks from comparative organizations or even from the industry-measured averages. It is important to tie the criteria to precise goals with a clear agreement of what constitutes success. The CEO is critical in setting up these criteria because of the interaction with counterpart CEOs who are providing a good sense of the competition. Organizations that are innovators have to determine these criteria internally.

Implementation processes directly depend on the type of decision. Implementation of the new corporate picture requires a new organization. The development of a new organizational skill requires at least restructuring. Other more basic changes, i.e. new products or services, will require new goals and new criteria.

The implementation directive, i.e. the detail of how to implement, can often be neglected in the name of speedy decisions. The implementation details are necessary for the completion of this focus. The complexity of these details varies directly with the type of change that has been decided.

Incremental change requires less in the way of implementation. On the other hand, discontinuous change can require restructuring or reformulating the organization which requires great detail as well as large-scale change (chapter 5).

The strategic option carries some implementation detail from the analysis focus that is imbedded in the scenarios. Some evaluation goals are brought forward as well. Who decides and who is involved in the role of decision-making discussed above becomes critical in the implementation. If people do not own a part in the decision, they will not own a part in the implementation.

Returning to the balanced scorecard approach (Kaplan and Norton, 1996) presented in chapter 9, the internal business perspective of Kaplan and Norton is imbedded in this focus. A major part of the implementation aspect of this focus is the processes and measures required. Both mission-oriented processes and customer-oriented processes occur here in this focus.

Some cautions

Alternative strategies have to be reduced to two choices. How this is done can determine the choice. A quick reduction of alternatives to one favourite alternative backs into the decision process by making a decision which is not a real choice. It lacks the comparison of a pro–con dialogue between two good choices. Yet this is a common enough default process often resulting in nobody feeling good about the decision. The more people who are tied to a particular alternative in the decision process, the more difficult it is to pare down the alternative matrix. When the CEO is engaged in this by him or herself, the intuition and a gut sense form a big part of the selection process. When the senior management group works together to pare down the decision matrix, some members find it difficult not to protect their own turf. This influences the decision choices they would like to keep on the table. Is also illustrates the driving force effect on the reduction of alternatives (chapter 8).

The reduction of alternatives has a direct connection with the corporate picture (chapter 7). How does each alternative fit the corporate picture? Some alternatives may be eliminated because they do not fit within the corporate picture. The corporate words have an impact as well. Does one alternative fit the driving force of the organization better than any other? The remaining criteria tend to be outcome-oriented. Which one will increase market share? Which one increases return on investment? Which one meets shareholder acceptance? Which one fits customer needs the best? Sometimes a decision tree is constructed with each path given a value on a set of criteria. The process works best if it is selected before the decision point. How the decision is made can and does have outcome implications.

The process of choosing and implementing corporate actions

Who makes the decision? Who owns it? These questions are at the heart of strategic choice. The variations of decision are not as straightforward as we might want to believe. How this process is perceived by members has important outcome effects.

The CEO taking sole responsibility for making the decision

The CEO making the decision alone is quite common in start-up organizations, family-owned organizations, or in those facing a crucial life or death situation. The obvious advantage is that the process is quick but will not have input other than that developed by one individual. The risk is concentrated in one person and responsibility unquestioned.

The CEO making the decision with consensus of the senior management team, but still keeping sole responsibility, is an approach seen in larger more complex organizations that work well as a team and have multiple interdependencies. The advantage is that the approach can be carried out quickly and has more inputs than the CEO alone. Yet the risk is concentrated in one person and responsibility is focused. Wawa is a good example of this approach. Dick Wood made the decision after general agreement was reached in the senior management group. He discussed the issues to get all of the input before making the decision. This reinforced the core mission of an organization that was caring of the customer, by his caring to hear input of the senior management group on his own decisions.

A strong CEO in a large organization typically has the CEO making the decision with consultation. This consultation can be either internal or external and sometimes both. This approach is quick, in that the CEO controls timing and input is selected by expertise. This expert input can be of the content or process variety. The disadvantage is that the decision can be perceived as a 'fiat' from on high and support may not be forthcoming in carrying out the decision.

The senior management group sharing responsibility with the CEO in making the decisions

The senior management group making the decision with the CEO and sharing responsibility for the decision is often seen in larger organizations with strong senior management groups. While this is not the quickest approach, it does provide support from the functional areas of the organization, which having taken part in the decision will be more inclined to execute it. A variation of this approach is open discussion of all decision matters with senior management. The discussion is held open until dissent is removed and then the decision is made by the functional member of senior management when the decision is in their own area. This does delay decisions and needs a process facilitator to make sure the senior group does not prevaricate and decisions are put off. The Saint Joseph's University senior management group, during the time of the case presented, was functioning with shared responsibility. The senior management group heard input from all others in the group before making the decisions that affected their functional area. This flowed from a larger inclusive planning process of the university's constituent groups. By sharing the discussion, senior management could convey to the constituent groups why and how the decision was made. Senior management making the decision after consultation is most often used in a large organization with a strong senior management group and input is sought from those with expertise. This can be internal and be in the form of input from the analysis focus by the people who did the analysis. It can be external in the use of consultants in setting the context and process for a complex decision. The advantage in this approach is the use of multiple inputs and a wide perspective. The process can be time consuming and frustrating if the analysis is too far removed from the decision, allowing things to change in the interval. VerticalNet used this approach for the decisions in acquiring new companies. The senior managers in each vertical network were involved in what could be purchased and what could add overall strength to each area of company business.

The senior management group making the decision with consensus is the most highly process-oriented decision methodology and most often seen in large organizations with a strong sense of involving everyone in the analysis and decision-making. Such an organization is involved in high technology, aerospace or other technical and scientific fields. The distinct advantage of this operation is the commitment of each member of the organization involved in execution of the decision. The disadvantage is that a consensus is hard to achieve in a short period of time, and most often requires an internal process consultant. Organizational examples of this decision process are rare.

Mental processes in decision-making

There are two mental processes used in making decisions. The first is an analytical process sometimes referred to as 'playing it by the numbers'. The second is an intuitive approach, referred to as 'using a gut feeling'. Both approaches can be used alone or are used together. Christian Haub at A&P can be seen to have used both. He had a good gut feeling of what can be transplanted from Canada to the USA and then ran the numbers to assure himself and the board that it would work.

Analysis after intuition is the decision process that uses intuition to set the stage and analysis to work out the details. The advantage of this approach is a reduction in work because only the best choices are processed. Using analysis alone has the disadvantage of too much detail work and lack of focus. Intuition alone has the advantage of being quick, but the disadvantage of not having good detail. Probably the most common approach is the use of intuition after the analysis has been done. The decision is not made on the basis of the numbers alone, but by using intuition to consider the best fit for the organization, the situation and the organization's ability to implement. Decision speed is important when environmental conditions affecting a whole industry sector are faced by individual organizations. How they react can provide a competitive advantage. The CEO who is quick to react to a situation that affects the total industry is the one who stands to gain the competitive advantage. The use of the focus in this way is to provide a decisive quick response.

Interlevel dynamics in choosing and implementing corporate actions

As decision-making lies with senior management, the interlevel dynamics of this focus concentrates on the CEO, the senior management group and the board of directors.

A central aspect of this process is the political and competitive dynamics in the interdepartmental group as different alternatives have different supporters. There is likely to be a perceived winners' and losers' arena. Hence an important covert agenda is how individuals' and teams' attitudes and inferences are privately held and so the issues pertaining to the planning process, which people think to be incorrect, never surface or are discussed (Argyris, 1985). This becomes the hidden area of what is not chosen or discussed openly within the organization.

Role of the CEO

The role of the final decision-maker resides with the CEO. Most CEOs bring an outside perspective, in the form of a gatekeeper role, by looking at the competition through exchanges with other CEOs. The CEO also is most often the one to see problem areas that are internal to the organization when they are cross-functional. This comes from having an overall view of the organization. Both of these roles give the CEO a unique perspective in decision-making.

The Level I aspects of these two perspectives are profound. CEOs bring with themselves their career paths and anchors. Both of these tools provide team members, board members and OCD consultants with insights into the CEO. There is a clear relationship between anchors and decision process and career path and the view taken in a gatekeeper role.

Another role the CEO brings to the decision process is that of closure. In most organizations, the CEO is expected to have the final word. In this role, expectation is the perception that a decision is not final until the CEO has acted on it. CEOs who like to take high risks often reject closure on the grounds of wanting to wait to find a better solution. CEOs who like closure can often be rushed to conclusions in order to be finished with the decision. CEOs in their decision role also interface with senior management groups. When this interface is prolonged and the differences between alternatives ambiguous at best, the CEO can get trapped into deciding along the lines of his or her own past career experience.

Sometimes when the CEO makes the decision alone, his or her involvement in the analysis phase becomes critical. When he/she is required to make a final decision on a process of which they have not been part, the outcome can be unexpected.

Role of the board of directors

The CEO may have closure and final say in most organizations, but all of this is subject to ratification by the board of directors. Normal procedures involve operating responsibility for the CEO and senior management and policy responsibility for the board of directors. This interaction can be easy or difficult depending on the personalities, temperament and history of the participants. When the board becomes an operating board, there is a distinct role change by members. They become a second senior management group. The career background and the 'expertise' brought to the board become the members' portfolios, i.e. the bankers become finance officers, the accountants become controllers, CEOs become alternate CEOs, while marketing take on the marketing and sales roles. In most situations the board acts like another senior management group. When this is the case all of the issues attributed to senior management apply to boards functioning in this way.

Interlevel role of the senior management group

Senior management group members have different levels of involvement on different scenarios or in different alternatives sets. With the responsibility for functional areas, senior team members can find it difficult to separate the corporate good from their functional perspectives. The role of being defender of a particular function, when that function is under attack/is up for change, conflicts with the role of being open to the greater good. Often, conversations on quality of analysis will have occurred with some of their subordinates who worked on the decision matrix. In critical events, sometimes the solution comes to the CEO from one of the senior group members because the solution that solves the problem lies within that senior member's area.

Interlevel role of the members

The role of the members of the organization varies greatly by type of decision, time allotted for making the decision or even the magnitude of the decision. In general most of the members do not have a role in the analysis or the decision. Some members of the organization do have a role in the analysis, but not in the decision. In more complex organizations, those who worked on the analysis phase are given the chance to have input into the final decision.

Members can have four distinct roles in the decision process. They can be aware of decision processes going on in the organization, but are not involved. They can be involved in one phase of analysis, but not involved in decisions. They can be involved in the analysis and the decision. Of course, the total non-role is not to be involved or even aware that a decision process is going on.

On the question of member involvement, the more collaboration that occurs in the decision, the more involved participation is in the implementation. Repeated non-involvement will generate a culture of defensive routines. On the other hand, the higher the number of people in the collaboration of the choice, the more difficult it is in limiting the alternative sets. Over time this generates an open, non-defensive routine culture in an organization. Yet the external analysis must weigh heavy in the choice process. It is the customers, clients and financial markets in same external environment that help decide if the organization succeeds or fails.

Role of the ODC consultant

The role of ODC consultant in this focus is mostly a process role, rather than a content one. To engage in content at this point would be to have a direct input in the decision. The appropriate process role of an ODC consultant is to keep the process on track, free from bias, and to engage the proper people and not to engage in the actual decision process itself. The ODC consultant role at Saint Joseph's University was of this nature. Hired to start an inclusive planning process, the ODC consultant remained and provided a process consultant role throughout all of the process including decision and implementation. Sometimes, the ODC consultant role is assigned to a member of the organization. While this is a difficult role to perform from within, it can be very helpful.

Process of implementation

Once the strategy decision is made, leadership, policy and organizational implementation follow. The final step in this focus is the directive of implementation in the setting of evaluation criteria. Once the decision is made, leadership implementation consists of putting together a brief on why and how the decision was made and the steps needed to implement the decision. This is usually provided to anyone needed in implementation. Work commences on policies and plans of what needs to be done. This has traditionally been a motivational component of getting the chosen strategy to be accepted.

Implementation of decisions has traditionally been a group of action policies and procedures that break down the strategy into subsets or goals that, when accomplished, serve to provide a path for the organization to achieve the end determined as correct by the strategy. This is the Taylor-like process of dividing the overall work into smaller pieces of work. When they are integrated, those subsections, united with some other subsections, form a coherent goal of this strategy for the organization. Data systems control this interaction in large organizations.

The extent of the decision drives the organization to be restructured, if it needs it. A major change in a major organization requires extensive work of job change, location change and, in some cases, change in purpose to enable implementation of the decision. By the time an organization has been reorganized, it will have moved into the evaluation focus of the strategic plan. The more encompassing the change required to enable new functions, the greater the need for restructuring.

Conclusions

In this chapter we have described the fourth focus, choosing and implementing corporate actions, which deals with the selection and structured implementation of a strategic plan of action with its concurrent implementation plans. The process aspect, of choosing and implementing corporate actions, looks at the bias and influence on the selection process that comes from sources other than the analysis focus.

Table 10.1 outlines the task and relational issues when choosing and implementing corporate actions.

The leader's perspective on choosing and implementing corporate action is that the action desired and planned takes place and that there is congruence between the corporate picture, the corporate words, the analysis and the action. Members need to know how their own micro-level action contributes to the macro-level situation and whether senior management cares about their contribution. ODC consultants look for a basic honesty in evaluating

Table 10.1 Choosing and implementing corporate actions

	TASK	RELATIONAL
Content	Actual plan alternatives	Ownership of plans
Process	Decision-making Implementation processes	Political dynamics of choice and implementation
Culture	Meaning of plans to organization	Defensive and non-defensive routines

action and minimal defensive routines. They watch for continuing resistance and dysfunction. The outcomes of choosing and implementing corporate actions are coherent, coordinated and owned actions that are congruent with the corporate picture, the corporate words and the analysis in which survival and productivity are achieved.

Action research activity 10.1

Below find a blank table. In relation to an organization with which you are familiar, fill in the boxes with what you see as the important content, process and cultural issues in task and relational terms for that organization in choosing and implementing corporate outcomes. Discuss this with your team or, better still, copy the blank form and get them to fill in the blanks prior to your discussion.

	TASK	RELATIONAL
Content		
Process		
Culture		

Action research activity 10.2

In relation to an organization with which you are familiar, reflect on the following perspectives and try to answer the questions.

Leaders

Corporate leaders, whether the CEO or members of senior management group or divisional heads may consider the following questions:

1   Is the planned and desired action taking place?
2   Is the action ensuring the organization's survival?
3   What has slipped between the picture, the words, the analysis and the action?
4   Are the actions ethical?

Members

Non-executive members may consider the following questions:

1   Are the actions realistic?
2   Do I feel part of the decision?
3   Do I feel part of the change?

ODC consultants

ODC consultants may pose the following questions:

1   Is there consistency of effort across the organization?
2   Is there dysfunction in the action?
3   Are there people distressed and fighting the action?

Outcomes

1   Is there a plan for implementation?
2   Are there criteria for evaluation?
3   Is the implementation sufficient to accomplish actions needed?

Case: ABC Insurance Company

How did ABC make the decision to go public? The movement toward a decision was mostly reactive, with turnover at many of the essential leadership positions and the creation of a separate, dedicated corporate finance department. The CEO John Smith had the vision but needed a triggering event to make it happen. Before the loss against earnings that triggered the change, the corporate finance functions had been performed by management of the operating subsidiary that had taken the loss. The loss was quite significant and all management efforts were employed to satisfy regulatory and rating agency concerns as to the size of the earnings charge and to the company's capital adequacy following the charge. The end result was to spur forward the overriding need to become a public company. The challenges the company faced highlighted the difficulties private companies face when needing to raise additional capital quickly and efficiently.

The earnings charge created the sense of urgency needed to unfreeze the organization and the senior management group. This was the opening John Smith wanted to start ABC down the path of transition to a public company. He envisioned this transition some time earlier and now saw the chance to implement it.

At the early stages of the change process, significant turnover took place within the senior management of the operating subsidiary. It took some time for these changes to filter down to the other hierarchical levels of the organization.

Questions for reflection and discussion

1   Who made the decision?
2   How was the decision made?
3   What were the triggers that promoted the decision to be made at this time?
4   How do interlevel dynamics help you understand the organizational issues that ABC faced in the sources for and implementation of the decision?

Case: Saint Joseph's University

At the end of March, 2004, the Institutional Planning Committee (IPC) issued a progress report to inform the university community about the status of its efforts to draft a new strategic plan for Saint Joseph's: Plan 2010: The Path to Preeminence. What follows is an update on the drafting of Plan 2010 and its supplemental documents, a new process for all divisions to better participate in long-term strategic planning, as well as projected changes in the annual budgeting cycle for fiscal year 2006.

During the latter part of the spring semester and earlier that summer, IPC engaged various constituencies at the university in discussing the seven initiatives that would constitute the heart of the new strategic plan. The seven initiatives were originally forwarded to the IPC by the President after consultation with the senior management group. During June and July, the IPC Drafting Committee reviewed input gathered at these community sessions, incorporating it into further revisions of the initiatives and other sections of the projected plan.

The Drafting Committee had also been reviewing recommendations developed through the Middle States process (the university's accreditation agency) to ensure that all were represented in the new plan. The committee also reviewed and revised the SWOT analysis, which would constitute another part of the plan. Finally, the enrolment profile discussed by the community earlier in the spring went through another revision and provided the basis for a five-year enrolment management plan.

Plan 2010 was supported with more detailed five-year plans designed to make the goals of the overall strategic plan operational. The following five-year corollary plans were put in place: a capital plan, an enrolment management plan, a financial plan, a comprehensive campaign plan, a diversity plan and an assessment plan. A draft of the five-year capital plan was completed by the vice presidents and senior management group. The enrolment management plan was drafted and reviewed by a new enrolment management task force when it was completed. The Budget Advisory Committee (BAC) worked on the financial plan. The Development Office drafted the comprehensive fund-raising plan and the IPC Drafting Committee put together the diversity plan based on the Report of the Diversity Commission in 2000 and the International Education Task Force Report of 2003. An assessment plan for the university was developed.

Five-year divisional plans

A subsequent step in the new planning process was the creation of five-year plans for all divisions of the university. In academic affairs, for example, this meant that each of the colleges would have its own five-year plan, based on Plan 2010 and its corollary documents. Next, each department would draft a multi-year plan (three- or five-year) based on both the university's strategic plan and the respective college plan. These plans would then be the basis for requests for resources from the budget advisory committee for each ensuing fiscal year.

Questions for reflection and discussion

1   How do organizational levels and interlevel dynamics frame your understanding of how Saint Joseph's University went about choosing and implementing its corporate actions?
2   Does this process of choosing and implementing show openness for all constituents to have input?
3   Would other organizations have the time required to approach the implementation process in this manner?
4   How could this process be improved?

ting corporate outcomes

[handwritten marginalia: fast/growth stop and evaluate where you really at]

The fifth strategic focus is evaluating measured outcomes of corporate actions. This functional focus is concerned with the evaluation and organizational learning component of strategic management. The evaluating corporate outcomes focus has three aspects:

1 Content of the evaluation methodology.
2 The process of evaluating.
3 Utilization of the output.

The content of evaluation methodology

The evaluation methodology starts with a set of expectations and assumptions about the future goals and structure of the organization. Key questions on the content are straightforward, such as have we achieved the preset targets? Have we made our marketing goals? Key process questions that have to be asked in this focus are as follows: Are the significant criteria set before starting the evaluation? Can the criteria be applied in an open and equal way for everyone in the organization? The evaluation takes place by a careful review of the set goals, over a set time frame. Incremental deviations are evaluated for impact and meaning. Large deviations are studied for their relevance as to internal or external factors being the contributing cause.

The intuition that comes into play then forms the second-order change questions. Has the paradigm shifted? Is there a change larger than the original analysis dealt with taking place? The question of second-order change is also clarified by the outcome of the process review of each focus. If more than one focus is found to be contributing to the failure to reach strategic goals, it is very likely that a second-order change is required.

Evaluation as a process occurs within every set of actions that are tracked and reviewed. Each of the four other foci contains an internal review process, which evaluates this within each focus. The evaluation within this functional focus differs from the others in that it not only has outcome evaluation, but also the evaluation of the effectiveness of the total strategic plan which may provide clues for a possible second-order change.

Outcomes evaluation: origins of the criteria

The evaluation criteria are first outlined in the focus on analysis and selected and spelled out for implementation in the focus on decision. They are now evaluated in this focus. The criteria used are applicable to incremental or discontinuous outcomes depending on which choice was made. A common failure is not to do any evaluation at all. This set of criteria and their outcomes directly relate to the ETOP and SAP of the analysis focus (covered in chapter 9). In addition to the inside criteria, judgement is made from external comparisons to the organization as well.

Criteria from outside sources

Every organization is evaluated by critical outside sources. Owners or shareholders evaluate for-profit organizations on a continuous basis. One evaluation criterion for publicly traded companies is their stock price. This constant evaluation comes from the outside world of stock analysts, stock traders and the general public. This evaluation is not always based on company performance. Market conditions, world issues and availability of funds to invest can all affect stock price. Nonetheless, this is an important factor as it determines the availability of funds to develop and grow as an organization. Responding to these evaluations and making them part of the ongoing outcome evaluation process is a part of this focus. How outsiders perceive the change is important input for the continued evaluation of the strategic plan, as well as important input for the next round. To look at outside input as a threat rather than an opportunity can be a mistake.

New relationships and changes in existing ones are important aspects of evaluating corporate outcomes. Some measure of the degree of customer satisfaction and employee motivation can be a significant contribution to the evaluation. Customer satisfaction leads to sales and success for the organization. The level of employee satisfaction provides a key element of the 'climate' aspect of the organization. It is important to realize that this is one step beyond the measurement of an effective plan. This is the determination of the characteristics of what makes a successful organization and what has contributed to the success for giving the organization a sense of purpose and a positive climate. A more complex set of criteria looks at what unstated attitudes are underlying selected criteria. What climate will be produced by these outcomes? Is this the climate that is appropriate for the organization? Customers are also part of this factor in that they hold unstated opinions and feelings on the outcomes. This can be a very difficult area to get in touch with for most organizations. New people who come to work in an organization are resources for this questioning before they are crafted into the culture of how reality works in the organization.

> As we saw earlier, Subsole, the Chilean fruit company, adopted the strict standard that is required for the UK market, called EUREPGAP, specifically designed by the main British supermarkets.
>
> Subsole not only decided to adopt that GAP standard but also find a company in Chile that could certify with international validity that their growers meet the standard and that way introduce the standard in Chile. They used one of the partners of the company as the pilot, who was the first grower to be certified in Chile with EUREPGAP.
>
> The process of evaluation of their own set criteria, generated by meeting the outside source criteria of EUREPGAP and certified by another organization, becomes a significant strategic advantage. The company considers this as an opportunity to differentiate itself from the rest of the competition, and has agreed from the CEO downward that they adopt this strategy.

Evaluation with consequences for the other foci: looking at the bigger picture

The second-level evaluation process focuses on larger issues. It evaluates the contributions from each of the other foci in order to make the determination if second- and third-order change is required. This process consists of the reviewing of the contributions or lack thereof from the other four foci; that is, framing the corporate picture, naming the corporate words, doing corporate analysis and choosing and implementing corporate actions to the overall strategic plan as it was carried out or was attempted to be carried out. This evaluation reviews the interrelationships of the foci.

The basic first-order questions have been discussed above. These are the most often asked questions, even on a daily basis. They are the first-order feedback answering the question: did we do what we said we would do? The second-order questions are more complex. They're less frequently asked. Have we made the appropriate choices? Were the key people involved in the decisions that should have been? These questions send us back to the focus on choosing and implementing. Did we use the appropriate analytic tools? Was the analysis broad enough and inclusive enough? These questions send us back to the focus on analysis. The least frequently asked questions concerning driving forces regarding the corporate picture are the most difficult to ask. Does our major effort constitute our driving force? Do we know who we are? Is there broad understanding of what we are? Are we continuing to learn? (Figure 11.1)

These evaluation questions are a different magnitude at each of three orders. Operational issues and the resulting adjustments constitute continuous change. Organizations deal with these on a regular basis. Even adjusting the choice methodology and methods of an analysis can at times be incremental. Change required in adjusting driving forces or adjusting a corporate picture is discontinuous change requiring much greater effort. Since these questions are not asked every day, when should they be asked? When operational goals are not met or shifting analysis methodology doesn't seem to help, it is then that the questions need to be asked. In many high-tech organizations existing at the edge of chaos, the time span for asking these questions may be short. The need to morph into a new reality can occur in a month or a few weeks, due to the volatility of the environment. The continual third-order question is, can we reassemble ourselves and still function over an extended period of time on a regular and repeated basis?

Evaluation focus: differing roles in finding discrepancies

CEO

The source of the discrepancy of expected and found results is important information. If the outcomes do not match expectations from the analysis outcome then the corrections are incremental and should be easy to make. The CEO's role is to stay attuned and to determine the scale and sources of the discrepancy. Senior management's role is to find the source of the discrepancy and correct it without finger pointing. Members need to find correct information and communicate it to senior management. The consultant's role is to maintain objectivity and facilitate the listening process without finger pointing. VerticalNet used this approach in choosing new companies to acquire. Mike Hagan had the final say on what would be acquired. He looked at the results of the company to be acquired and evaluated the results as if the company was his own organization. The closer the companies were to the expected results, the higher they were on the desirable acquisitions list.

If the outcomes do not match those expected, and a solution requires a new critical skill to be developed by the organization, then the corporate words focus needs to be revisited and a structural change implemented. The CEO's role is to embrace the perceived need and lead in setting up a process to determine a new critical skill for the organization. Senior management's role is to look at the need of the total organization and enable the individuals in their own functions to work through their own denying and dodging in the face of change.

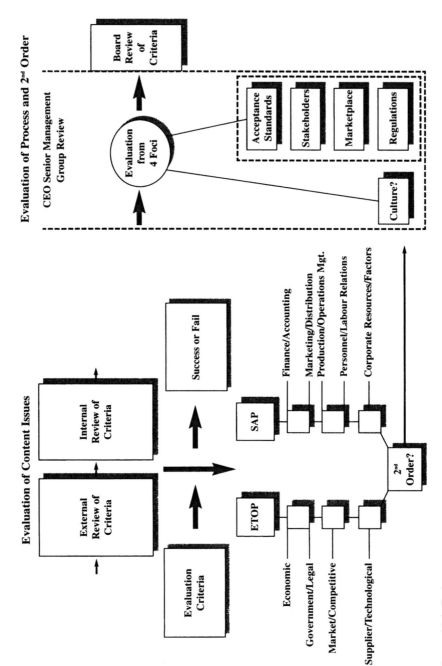

Figure 11.1 Evaluation process.

Members

Members' roles can run the gamut from minor adjustment in the work methods to the need to look elsewhere for employment. Another alternative is to find a new role in a changing and developing organization. For members who love a challenge, this is difficult but exciting. Their own career change models the change in the organization, including the transition state on the way to a desired future.

ODC consultants

The key role for a consultant is to help manage the transition period. If the desired future is not clearly articulated, then the transition period may be difficult. The consultant can assist in clarifying future goals and in helping to establish new functional groups and a new senior management group when it is required.

If the outcomes do not match those expected and a solution requires a new organization, then the corporate picture needs to be revisited and a new organization developed. The CEO's role is to think and lead outside of the box. One solution could well be a different organization and a different CEO. This type of thinking is not something done with ease. Senior management's role is to avoid panic and start a process, if possible, to generate a new organization from the ashes of the old. Members' roles may well be to look elsewhere. The consultant role here is to help develop a transition process.

If the outcomes cannot be measured, then the decision and implementation focus needs to be revisited. The solution in this case can be as simple as a new measurement process or resetting goals that can be measured. The CEO's role in this endeavour is to ensure that the change is not a cover-up for a missed goal. Changing the criteria is not recommended, but changing measurement techniques to obtain the needed information is important to an organization. Senior management's role is not to get lost in the detail but to agree on the new techniques. Members need to buy into a new process. The consultants' role is to provide a bridge to the new process.

The process of evaluating

The implementation process requires a clear understanding from all who have input on how information is processed. In cases of large-system change, non-measurable criteria are brought into play. These need to be articulated and agreed on by everyone. The reason for this has been discussed in phases and levels of change in large systems (chapter 5).

The evaluation process involves review of outcomes and processes and then interpretation. Some of the key questions that need to be asked are as follows: Was there data contamination? Do all the affected people embrace the review process and accept the evaluation of outcome success or failure? Do we feel that the right questions were asked? Are there some larger issues that need to be addressed?

Utilization of the output

Utilization of the output should be articulated as well. This implies that there exists a clear set of steps that would be pursued if different aspects of the strategic plan did not come into existence. These are often referred to as fallback plans. It is easier to get agreement on these plans before they are needed rather than afterwards. Some sketch, even if it is a rough sketch, should be given on how results will be used. Will results cause second-order change? Will the people engaged in the change have an opportunity to have a place in the new situations?

Interlevel dynamics in the evaluation of outcomes

The task of evaluating corporate outcomes includes all four of the levels. Individuals from all over the organization are involved in the evaluation. Teams, especially the senior management group, are involved as well. The implementation of this focus is centred on Level III, consisting of how different functional areas are involved in evaluating and how much time and energy is given to it. This is where the win–lose behaviours are most evident and contribute, in a large way, to the culture of the organization. The evaluation in terms of outcome states contrasted with the competitors is Level IV. Do the people most affected by the outcomes, customers, suppliers, etc., agree with our assessment of the success or failure of the plan?

Board's interaction with the CEO

The board in its totality acts at Level IV. It is responsible for the organization's choices as a total organization. From this one view the board can disagree with the CEO and senior management. These disagreements, while painful, are essential for a strong organization. Sometimes these divergent viewpoints can produce a change of the CEO. If the board functions as it should, it forms the conscience of the organization. Board members need the skill to confront in dialogue the CEO when the situation requires it. This usually occurs through the executive committee to the CEO, or through the chairman to the CEO.

The CEO's interaction with the senior management group

It is important to make a distinction between the evaluations of the individual functions within the strategy and the overall success of the strategy. Sometimes individual functional goals are successful, but the overall strategic goals are not achieved. The interlevel challenges arise in this evaluation of outcomes perceptions between Level I (the CEO) and Level II (the senior management group). A major point of conflict can be between the interdepartmental group (Level III), the senior management group (Level II) and the CEO (Level I). Each of these will be addressed in turn.

The evaluation of the corporate outcomes most often resides with the senior management group and the CEO. This evaluation is prepared for them by the internal review team; the financial criteria by the internal audit team from within the organization and additionally financial and control audit by the outside auditors. Sometimes key pieces of information come from customers or other unique individuals. Ultimately the people that look at and evaluate this information are the board of directors. Another group brought into the loop is the financial analysts' group representing capital market interests. Most organizations have, or purchase, outside analyst reports on themselves and their competitors. These documents are semi-public: investors and others can purchase them. Because they can have such wide access, they must be considered in fact public documents. This source of information provides knowledge to competitors as well as customers and friends, while introducing the larger system in which the organization operates into the mix.

Evaluation of both outside and inside reviews provides the grist of the interlevel interaction between the senior management group and the CEO. This discussion focuses on the nuances of how the data are formed into information. The senior management group views the data from its interdepartmental perspective, as it represents that perspective on the senior management group, while the CEO looks at the data most often from the total organization's point of view, or even from an outside point of view. Another aspect of the interaction of the CEO (Levels I and IV) with the senior management group (Levels II and III) is the determination of the presence of missed criteria. Both the CEO and the senior management group (Level IV) can disagree with the outside sources.

In the final analysis, these are examined for range of deviations from the expected. When there are deviations, it is critical to find out what went wrong. Are they due to poor outcomes, wrong strategy or the use of an incorrect model?

Level II interaction with Level III

The Level II with Level III interaction is more often spent in evaluating the incremental deviations from goals. This questioning can be a way of testing the validity of the information. In this situation it is not uncommon for teams or groups to experience the typical finger pointing between departments and functions. Some of this frustration can be avoided if the goals are quantified in detail and agreed upon in the corporate decision focus. As we discussed earlier, we know that denial is the first reaction to the possibility of change and that it then shifts to dodging, which at this point can take the form of blaming.

Returning to the balanced scorecard approach (Kaplan and Norton, 1996) presented in chapter 9, the learning and growth perspective is part of the evaluations focus. In our view the learning and growth has three orders of change questions to be answered and goes beyond the balanced scorecard approach. It looks at the continuous adjustments to meet targets, discontinuous adjustments to ask what do we want to be and opens the possibility of self reconfiguring to adapt and learn.

Conclusions

The continuous evaluation of the strategic goals is often a weak link in the strategic process. Many organizations do not evaluate multiple year goals or look at the larger context. The five strategic foci enable this to be done as the evaluation criteria are set early in the process. The larger involvement of the organization members also provides a gauge on progress, as the goals are corporately owned, not held only by a select few, who could forget or leave their position or even leave the organization. If the ownership for change is owned by only a few, it runs a serious risk of failure.

Table 11.1 outlines the task and relational issues in evaluating corporate outcomes.

Leaders' perspectives on evaluation are whether outcomes are measurable and whether they reflect expectations and plans. Good outcomes need to be celebrated.

Members' concerns are with the role of evaluation in relation to their own micro-level work and how evaluation affects their work in the longer term.

Table 11.1 Evaluating corporate outcomes

	TASK	RELATIONAL
Content	Consensus on what is successful or not Consensus on what needs to be changed	Satisfied customers Motivated workforce New relationships
Process	How information is collected How model was constructed How changes were made	How involved people are in the evaluation How honest people feel
Culture	What was evaluated and what was not questioned What new culture is forming	Protect turf, lack of openness Sense of fairness Sense of success and achievement

ODC consultants focus on whether evaluation takes place, whether it is before during or after, whether it is celebrated and whether the evaluation brings change.

The result of evaluating corporate outcomes is organizational learning and an input into a repetitive change cycle, which leads to increased profitability and integration of the strategy process of the corporate picture, the corporate words, the corporate direction and action.

Figure 11.2 provides a structure for inquiring into how inquiry into corporate outcomes may be undertaken. The three inquiry loops begin from the corporate outcomes and move to inquiring about actions taken, analysis done, choices made and goals set and ultimately to corporate words and corporate picture.

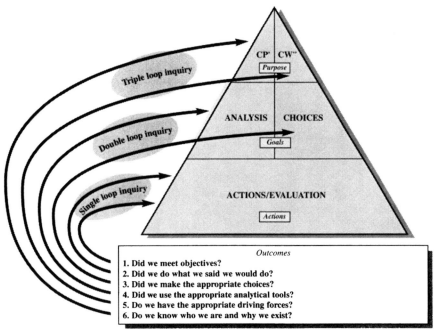

Figure 11.2 Cross foci evaluation feedback questions.

Action research activity 11.1

Below find a blank table. In relation to an organization with which you are familiar, fill in the boxes with what you see as the important content, process and cultural issues in task and relational terms for that organization in evaluating corporate outcomes. Discuss this with your team or, better still, copy the blank form and get them to fill in the blanks prior to your discussion.

	TASK	RELATIONAL
Content		
Process		
Culture		

Action research activity 11.2

In relation to an organization with which you are familiar, reflect on the following perspectives and try to answer the questions.

Leaders

Corporate leaders, whether the CEO or members of senior management group or divisional heads may consider the following questions:

1　Are the outcomes measurable and reflective of plans and expectations?
2　Are they accurate?
3　Is the action ensuring the organization's survival?
4　Do we celebrate the outcomes?

Members

Non-executive members may pose the following questions:

1　Do I agree with the evaluation?
2　Do I concur with the evaluation process?
3　Do I have a place in the new organization?

ODC consultants

ODC consultants may pose the following questions:

1　Do they evaluate?
2　Is evaluation leading to change?
3　Do they celebrate?

Outcomes

1　Is the organization disposed toward change?
2　Has the change met the criteria that were stipulated in the beginning?
3　Is further change required?
4　How have stakeholder groups reacted to the change?

Case: ABC Insurance Company

The change to a public structure that took place in ABC throughout the late 1990s was really a shift in the culture of the company. The success of that change was the movement from an internally focused company to one that was more in tune with the industry and expectations of the investment community. The deep culture change to a public structure has been slow, but success can be measured by the public stock offering in 2001, an event that would not have occurred under the prior culture. While the changes did not prevent the second significant event that took place in correlation with September 11th, it did provide a strategic and tactical framework from which the company could respond in a more organized fashion. The informal relationships among the corporate area and the operating units still played a significant part in the response. While extremely beneficial, the next step will need to be a continuation on the evolution of the company's culture such that the operating units can function in unison across all levels rather than via informal relationships. This evaluation of the success of the transformation is measured in the success of the new organization with its customer base and with its analyst base. Interestingly, this success has been hampered by conflicts that either developed as a result of going public or during the period following the first event when the different operating subsidiaries and the corporate entity were struggling to determine their roles. The CEO's role throughout this process was to champion the private to public transition.

Evaluating the overriding change from public to private, it could be viewed as a first-order change, internally focused, where the corporate picture moved to an unresolved corporate picture of a public company with the corporate words still evolving into a new driving force. The change is not complete because the cultural shift has, even now, not been fully completed, with vestiges of the private structure remaining. As an example, up until the mid-1990s the then two primary operating subsidiaries were allowed to operate in an autonomous manner, with independent IT, operational and financial departments. With the exception of the earnings charge in 1996 at one of the subsidiaries, this approach was largely successful in fostering an entrepreneurial spirit at the operating companies. The corporate entity that was established as a result of the first significant event had direct control over mostly financial issues, and even then often had no real explicit authority, but rather had to develop personal relationships with team members from the operating subsidiaries in order to be truly effective. While the corporate function has made much progress, the company maintains a high level of autonomy and still does not have a centralized IT or operations department.

The crucial challenge for the CEO at ABC is to maintain the entrepreneurial spirit of the operating subsidiaries while leveraging the benefits of integration. The CEO has been aware of this issue. Furthermore, the CEO has recognized the need of the operating subsidiaries to have the flexibility to make sound operating decisions, even when they do not coincide with the expectation of the stock analyst community.

The broader vision of the CEO is being accomplished. The groundwork has been established to more quickly identify and respond to corporate issues and challenges. What has been discovered in the corporate evaluation focus is that the business model employed at the two successful subsidiaries may not be applicable in all situations, and the recognition of this fact resulted in a redirecting of the company back to its core values and identity. The challenge is to again determine how to proceed in light of this fact.

Questions for reflection and discussion

1 Does this outcome require a new corporate picture?
2 How much is riding on the CEO?
3 If results are not as expected, will ownership of the change evaporate?
4 Do you think that ABC understands the difference between first- and second-order change?
5 What is the role of ODC consultants in this focus?

Case: Exportadora Subsole S.A.

Exportadora Subsole S.A. is a Chilean fruit export company that specializes in the trade of fruits with North America, Europe and Asia. The company started in 1991 as an association of growers that decided to join forces to export Chilean fresh fruit. It started mainly with table grapes and slowly opened itself to other types of fruit. Currently it exports four types of products: grapes, avocados, Kiwi fruit and citrus fruit (Naval and Clementine) from Copiapó valley in the north of Chile to the Santa Cruz area in the centre south.

It has grown to export annually some 5,800,000 boxes with a FOB value of US$55 million, representing a 20 per cent annual increase in sales. Subsole has faced turbulent times, but has managed to overcome all of the obstacles to keep up continuous growth. The core business is as a trading company, a middle man that brings together growers (some of whom are owners in the company) and the international fruit buyers in North America, Europe and Asia. Its mission is to offer healthy, fresh and on-time fruit to the North American, European and Asian markets.

The company is one of the few that export fresh fruit from Chile to the UK market, which has the most complicated requirements because of very strong regulations in terms of food handling conditions and fruit growing requirements. If a company is able to satisfy the UK market, it can satisfy any other market. The UK is considered to be the benchmark for what is required in that market.

The current trend is for higher security around all food products, and fresh fruit is a food product that is vulnerable, so the agriculture industry must adapt itself to compete by meeting these requirements. The growers must make expensive changes to meet these standards. Some growers and even some associations, competitors to Subsole, think that if they ignore these changes they will not serve the UK market.

That challenge is one of the biggest in the industry, requiring the adoption of rigid standards of Good Agriculture Practices (GAP) that presently are not homogenous across all the importing countries.

After a long analysis and discussion, because of its special relations with the UK market, because it determined how to make it financially possible through loan programmes and because it wanted a leadership position, Subsole adopted the strict standard that is widely accepted for the UK market, EUREPGAP, specifically designed by the major British supermarkets. Subsole not only decided to adopt that GAP standard but also decided to find a company in Chile that could certify with international validity in order that their growers could meet the standard, and that way introduce the standard in Chile. They used one of the partners of the company as the pilot, who was the first grower to be certified in Chile with EUREPGAP.

The process of evaluation of its own criteria, by meeting the EUREPGAP standard and being certified by an outside organization, became a significant strategic advantage. The company now considers it has an opportunity to differentiate itself from the rest of the competition, and has agreed from the CEO downward to adopt this strategy. To this end, the company has agreed to pay the growers during the first year for the changes that are required to meet the standards. During the second and third years they will provide loans to the growers for the further adaptations required by the farmers to meet the standards.

Subsole has set itself apart by its evaluation process in maintaining the quality of the fruit produced by its growers. Taking a threat to the industry and turning it into an advantage is a courageous decision. All indications show that this decision will provide an advantage for the company strong enough to enable the 20 per cent annual growth that it has enjoyed in the past to continue in the near future.

Questions for reflection and discussion

1   How often would the evaluation process of strategic action itself become a strategic advantage?
2   How can the evaluation focus be turned into an advantage?
3   What is the purpose of providing loans to the growers?
4   How is this converting a threat to an advantage?

Chapter 12

The relationships between the five strategic foci

In chapter 6 we introduced the five strategic foci and drew on photography to describe a focus as bringing an image into clarity and so adjusting the lens to obtain the greatest clarity for that part of the picture of greatest interest. The use of focus is a technique that draws the viewer to the key points of interest in the photograph as determined by the photographer. In strategic thinking and acting a focus occurs when a portion of the whole is clarified in order to attend to it while keeping the entire strategic map in perspective. The constellation of the whole interrelated strategic elements is a non-linear system similar to a galaxy. A focus is a clarified segment or part that can be attended to in perspective of the whole. We also pointed out that the five strategic foci should not be viewed as linear steps (Figure 6.1, p. 100). In chapters 7–11 we described each focus in detail and provided applications in case examples. Table 12.1 summarizes the main questions arising from the four perspectives – leader, member, ODC consultant and outcome. In this chapter we stand back and reflect on the five foci and how they interrelate in a systemic manner.

The five strategic foci in strategy formation and implementation are part of a very complex whole. While it is important to understand each focus it is also important to understand the relationships between the foci. The process issues that arise between the five focus points can distort the strategic outcomes, as we will see.

Relationship between corporate picture and corporate words

The corporate picture deals with the key individuals and the history of the organization as it comes to affect strategy formulation and implementation. The content of this focus is the core mission and its statement of the organization, including an ethical statement, as well as the characteristics of the key players. The process aspect focuses on the construction and involvement of different people and processes and putting together and embracing the corporate mission and its statement. Naming the corporate words highlights

Table 12.1 Summary of functional foci from four perspectives

	Corporate picture	Corporate words	Corporate analysis	Implementation	Corporate outcomes
Leader	From where we are now, how do we get to the next level of success? How do I get others to participate to reach the next level of success?	Is the driving force appropriate? Does it enable the organization to achieve its picture?	Is the proper information being gathered? Are assessment and information intuitively correct? Are there benchmarks available? What are the benchmarks of the competition?	Is the action I wanted happening? What has slipped between the picture, words, direction and action? Is the action ensuring sustainability of the organization and true to identity? Do we do what we say we do?	Are the outcomes memorable and reflective of expectations? Do we celebrate? Do we evaluate?
Member	Do I have a role in the future of this organization? Will I fit?	Am I part of the mainstream? Do I contribute? Can I identify with the driving force?	Why am I doing this analysis? Is it relevant? Is it congruent with my understanding of the situation? What happens if I disagree?	Does my small part have a role in the bigger picture? Does anyone care about my actions?	Do we have an evaluation process? Does anyone listen or care? Does my piece fit? Is there life after evaluation?
ODC consultant	Do they have a picture? Is it jointly owned?	Is there congruence between the espoused driving force and the one in action?	Is there competent data-gathering? Is it jointly owned, openly shared? Is negative feedback encouraged? Is process critiqued and revised?	Is there a basic honesty in assessing actions? Is there unified effort across the organization? Are there people distressed and fighting the action? Is there dysfunction?	Do they evaluate? Do they celebrate? Does evaluation happen before, during, after? Does evaluation bring change?
Outcome	Is the stated identity perceived by the outside world?	Is the driving force congruent with the picture?	Is organizational learning the basis of what needs to be changed? Is there structured implementation and process implementation?	Is the coherent, coordinated, owned action congruent with the corporate picture, words and direction?	Is there productivity and achievement? Is there organizational learning?

those operations or functions that are the lead operations or functions over time. These driving forces give a unique and special aspect to an organization, separating it from its competitors. These driving forces are central to the articulation, or lived out mission statement, of the organization.

There is a close relationship between corporate picture and corporate words that centres on the lived out skills of the corporate words as an articulation of the core mission. The reverse can also be true if an organization develops a new critical skill: this can force a review and change in the core mission. If the corporate words are new to the organization, it will pull at changing the core mission. A new core mission will threaten the existing corporate words by threatening the existing critical skills. This latter shift is important to anticipate at it affects the functional or Level III of an organization. A lead division losing its place because of the need and development of new skills is a major process issue.

Relationship between corporate words and corporate analysis

Naming the corporate words, as we saw above, deals with those operations or functions that had become the lead operations or functions over time. These are the driving forces and become the articulation, or lived out mission statement of the organization. Doing the corporate analysis deals with the obtaining of critical information and the preparation of these data into a comprehensive scenario or modelling of alternatives for the organization. The relationship here is that in most organizations the managers and analysts preparing the data in the corporate analysis are some of the people with the critical skills in the corporate words.

The interest in self-preservation is key to understanding this interaction. The managers in the lead or critical skill, the driving force, protect that status and may be unable to be totally objective in doing the analysis. Often these distortions are not at all obvious and not detected. This can be further complicated if the critical skill is the one held by the CEO, for example the engineer who is CEO in an engineering company, or a CEO who came out of manufacturing in a company where manufacturing skill is the driving force.

Relationship between corporate analysis and corporate decision and implementation

As seen above, doing corporate analysis deals with obtaining critical information and the preparation of data into a comprehensive scenario or modelling of alternatives for the organization. The focus, choosing and implementing corporate actions, deals with the selection and structured implementation of a strategic plan of action with its concurrent implementation plans. The relationship is close as the alternative set and how it is formed can be a factor in the decision process. If the alternatives are pared down to one or a small number that eliminate choices, this has a significant effect on the outcome, Sometimes the need to keep the analysis separate from the decision process is not understood. Forming an open and comprehensive set of alternatives is the basis of making an informed decision. By not looking at enough alternatives or even possibilities reduces the chance of a best decision.

Relationship between corporate decision and corporate evaluation

Choosing and implementing corporate actions deals with the selection and structured implementation of a strategic plan of action with its concurrent implementation plans. Evaluating corporate outcomes deals with the acceptance of the criteria for evaluation and the appropriate review of the resulting state of the organization. The relationship here is that the outcome measured should be the outcome desired in the decision process. This relationship fails in either of two ways: if the original criteria are not evaluated, or if new criteria are generated not related to the original decision.

New criteria for evaluation can be generated if these are more detailed, or adapted to better means of capturing the data required. Sometimes the evaluation process is difficult or cumbersome and is aborted. Monitoring of goals is a critical part of any change process. It is used to make sure that the correct end was achieved and also to make sure the new change behaviour remains in place to become the norm.

Relationship between corporate evaluation and corporate picture

Evaluating corporate outcomes deals with the acceptance of the criteria for evaluation and the appropriate review of the resulting state of the organization. The corporate picture is the core mission and its statement of the organization. The relationship is closest when the evaluation criteria are such that a new core mission or a new critical skill is part of the evaluation. In these situations the organization is in evolution and a new organization is being developed. During such an evolution the tension is the greatest. The basis for the new corporate picture is in the evaluation criteria of the corporate evaluation. This is the linkage for the ethical and social responsibility audit as part of the evaluation to be fed back into the verified corporate picture.

It should be noted that the first two foci, framing and naming, are actually transformational activities, in that, together, they set the foundation for the later activities (Figure 12.1). They are also the first two foci that must be addressed, and addressed well, when a new direction is sought. The remaining

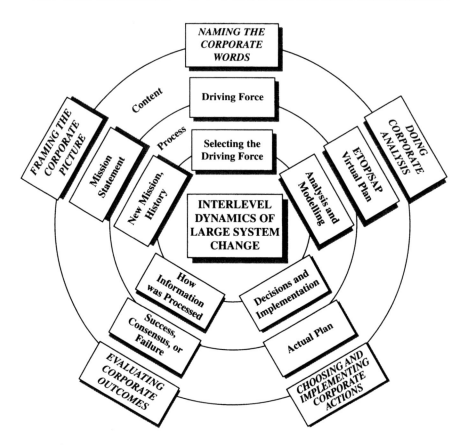

Figure 12.1 Interlevel dynamics of large system change within the five strategic foci.

three foci, doing, choosing and evaluating, are collectively understood as incremental activities that build on the foundation and influence the direction set by the transformational activities. As incremental activities, they are no less important than the transformational activities of framing and naming, as their successful implementation and execution are essential to the near-term success and long-term survival of the organization.

Strategic foci and large-system change

We have presented large-scale change in a large system in terms of two interlocking processes.

1   The process of change in a large system involves moving from a perceived need for change, through articulating an envisioned future, through assessing the present to determine what needs to change and

getting to the envisioned future by implementing change and m.
the transition.

2   The process of change in a large system involves interlevel dynamics .
that large-scale organizational change comprises individual, team and
interdepartmental group change respectively and that how change is
introduced and implemented through the system is a complex movement
from individual to team, team to team in the interdepartmental group
and to the organization's external stakeholders over time in iterations
where the movements are circular with each iteration being a cause and
effect of another.

Each of the five strategic foci entail interlevel dynamics of change as an
organization seeks to frame its corporate picture, name its corporate words,
do its analysis, choose and implement corporate actions and evaluate outcomes (Figure 12.2). Such dynamics can be viewed from different perspectives, whether one is a senior manager, a non-executive member, an ODC
consultant or a student viewing the outcomes.

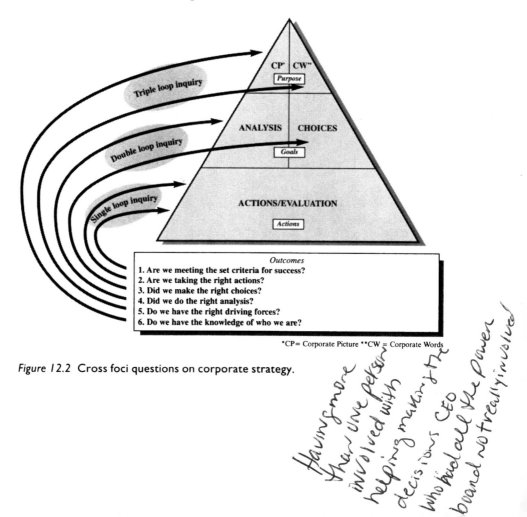

Figure 12.2 Cross foci questions on corporate strategy.

Part IV

Integration

Chapter 13

The Great Atlantic and Pacific Tea Company case

CEO different & Styles

This case is a comprehensive look at the Great Atlantic and Pacific Tea Company (A&P) during the first ten years of Christian Haub's leadership as CEO. The case is presented primarily with a timeline and uses the five foci approach to discuss where Haub placed his attention in strategic planning and implementation. The case is comprehensive as it deals with a large complex organization in the fast-changing environment of the retail food industry in North America. A&P is a part of the Tengelmann Group, a large European food retailer in Germany. Much of the case is presented through Haub's own narrative.

History of A&P before Christian Haub became CEO

By 1992, Jim Wood as CEO had led the company for 15 years. During that span of time he impressed his style of leadership and culture on A&P. It could be described as a command and control culture that was top-down driven, with little engagement of the people further down the chain of command. His interaction with the people at store level was non-existent. This led to a lack of accountability anywhere below the senior management level. It was also a company living in the moment without a sense of a long-term strategy. It was going from quarter to quarter, trying to achieve certain financial goals, but not really looking at where the industry and consumer behaviour were going and what implications these had on the business. The company was dealing with the crisis of the moment. Wood was finishing his career and preparing to retire.

The decision structure at that time was very much top-down driven even though the organization was to some degree decentralized with the different divisions out in the field having some degree of autonomy in the day-to-day running of the business. Any significant capital expenditure decisions or any significant people decisions were all made in the office of the CEO. Plans basically consisted of numbers, but were not substantiated by research, insights or initiatives. This led to a company in which the headquarters was very much disengaged from what was happening in the business. It was also disengaged from the employee base and middle management. There was very little movement within management; everything was frozen with little opportunity for cross-fertilization between the different functions. Within the different divisions there was not an awareness that there were other divisions. A&P was in the supermarket business and one supermarket division was a lot like the other. Because many of these divisions came through acquisition, there never had been an attempt to merge these cultures. It was always A&P as the dominant brand.

It was the acquiring companies that produced A&P's growth no matter what company was bought, i.e. Waldbaum's, Farmer Jack, Miracle Food Mart in Canada. So 40–50 per cent of the company size came through the acquisitions made from the mid-1980s through to the early 1990s. When a company was bought, it was the A&P structure, systems and processes that were installed, and the acquired company's culture was put aside and not acknowledged. This led to a lot of acquisitions going through very difficult assimilation and performance issues at the same time. A&P basically disregarded the value of the brand it had purchased. Waldbaum's, for example, because of its heritage, was very much oriented toward the ethnic/immigrant clientele, while A&P was more typically oriented toward the middle American clientele. They both had different approaches toward going to market. When A&P tried to implement its policy at Waldbaum's it backfired. The consumer became disenfranchised. This was in the early to mid-1990s. This also happened to Miracle Food Mart in Canada and Farmer Jack's in Michigan, which suffered dearly in the early to mid-1990s. The critical issue was that the CEO was not looking at the strategic issues of things that A&P had to do. The key problem was that A&P had a CEO who came in when the company was in crisis in the early 1980s, managed to save it from going out of business, and then went on an acquisition path and every 18 months acquired another company. That was the way Wood grew the company. Every time he bought a new acquisition, he went back to the suppliers and asked for more money now that the company was bigger. When that acquisition rush period came to an end, the issue then was how do you make a company out of this? How do you bring 12 divergent brands into the A&P company and build and evolve something? Jim Wood was at the end of his career, in his early to mid sixties, and did not have the outlook to develop a strategy for the next ten years.

The command and control environment that had been established at the time he took over was appropriate as the company had to be saved and this could only be done with strict controls. This same environment was not at all conducive to building a competitive organization out of what had been created.

The corporate picture of the early 1990s

In summary, the A&P of the early 1990s was one in which the corporate picture was that of a group of diverse retailing food chains, linked together in an attempt to run as one operating A&P system. Decisions were made by top management with little or no input from below. Because of the expansion, A&P was a significant market force.

Decision and implementation process from Wood 1990–1998

Christian Haub recalled his transition period to becoming CEO of A&P:

> In Spring 1998, we started the transition phase where I became co-CEO with Wood with the objective for me to become sole CEO a year later, Spring 1999. At that point, Jim would retire from an active executive role and continue as a non executive chairman of the board for three years. He also wanted to make sure that I was properly supported with the right group of executives during the transition phase and that led to the hiring of a few people who were more Jim's pick than necessarily mine. But I worked with them to figure out what they were able to offer and see where they were able to take us. So at that stage, I prepared myself for figuring out what the strategy was for going forward, i.e. what do we need to do. It was clear in my mind that we could not keep managing the company the way we had done in the past. But I had to be fully in charge before we would really be able to make any changes considering that here I had the 20 year serving CEO, a veteran with lots of experience, who while on active duty was willing to hear what anybody wanted to do even if he did not agree with it. So I engaged half a dozen or so of the senior executives in the company in a process of trying to assess where we were. Some of these were new people evaluating how we ranked in the industry. This was accomplished by benchmarking the most recent several years' performance and assessing how our performance was in relation to the rest of the industry's. They also identified what we were seeing as challenges and opportunities facing the company from a competitive and consumer's point of view. At the same time, we also engaged external consultants to help us assess the status of our people base. What are our people thinking about the company, what are their impressions, what do they see as our challenges and opportunities, and how are they viewing A&P?

Wood brought in a senior operating executive not to replace the COO, but to strengthen that area under the COO. He also brought in an executive assistant to the CEO, a very strong person on the development side. At that time, this was a very important role as A&P believed that replacing a lot of older stores was a critical, strategic initiative going forward. The decision group had a CFO that had been with the company for ten years, a COO that was with the company for ten years, and a chief merchandising officer who had been in the company for over 30 years. They were all either in their early or late fifties. Haub was in his early thirties. This was the group looking at strategy and analysis. For about 3–4 months, they went through all of the analysis and assessment of where the company was internally with employees. In August 1998, they came together to see what all of this information was showing them. As Haub expected, but had to have confirmed and verified, the company was clearly underperforming from financial measures with respect to the industry norm. This was the first benchmark. This was painting a poor picture. Haub reports:

> The internal assessment from our associates was absolutely devastating in terms of a company without vision and strategy as well as a completely disengaged workforce that felt disrespected and mistreated. As I described, it was a culture where employees were just a number on the profit and loss statement, i.e. a cost that had to be held to a minimum.

Employees felt the company was run very much top-down with no voice or opportunity for feedback. It was a company with a command and control culture and very poor treatment of people to the degree where there was a lot of resentment toward management. People looked at their job only as a way to make money with no connection to the company.

The corporate analysis to get to the new corporate picture 1998

When the senior management group sat down in April–May 1998 it set out to get the criteria for the analysis. External auditors were used for the internal analysis. For the external analysis, Haub engaged some investment bankers to help in getting competitive data that was publicly available. These were the critical benchmarks in terms of sales, growth, profitability, return on capital and market share. Haub went with external consultants in order to receive an objective view. Internally, he had a lot of long-term employees and believed they would not have an objective perspective. At that time, with the exception of the CFO, there was not a lot of interest in doing the analysis. Some of the managers questioned why they are spending their time on doing this at all. They were saying that they had other crises to deal with and crisis management was the order of the day. Some of them objected to the work of the external consultants, but Haub took this as a good sign that they were starting to make progress. He formed his conclusions about A&P and taking the company along a different path. He had to start at forming an overall concept of what direction he wanted to go and what the core mission was to be. He wanted to start developing some simple concepts that could start rallying people around in this change process. It became clear that A&P had to change fundamentally.

Framing a new corporate picture

It was clear to Haub that if A&P really wanted to change, there would need to be a massive undertaking to get buy-in from the entire management, including every store manager and mid-level manager. He also needed to buy-in from associates in the stores because they represented 90 per cent of the employee base and were the front line affecting what the real business was: selling goods and services to consumers. He wanted to get buy-in and lead a drive for a comprehensive change programme with initiatives around developing a set of core values, looking into all of A&P's people practices, store concepts, market strategies and supplier relationships. He was starting to challenge what some felt were the core drivers for the business.

The whole thrust was to change attitudes and to become the supermarket of choice. Haub started this by creating a new language. He created a word 'gaptitude', which he developed out of GAP (Great Atlantic and Pacific) and the new attitude that was needed in the company. It would articulate what was felt about where they were and where they wanted to go. This word became the symbol of the change initially. It began to establish a new mission and programme through a group of key values that were called the Great Actions and Priorities, which gave A&P a plan of nine areas that they had to improve in the organization. It was in a conference in late August 1998 where the nine As and Ps were developed. They were general and focused on customer service, improving store operations, developing new stores, putting the right merchandising approach into the business and a fundamental control of expenses. It started giving people a sense of direction and the opportunity to channel all of their activities around those areas.

What came out of this was the developing of core values. It was a huge piece that had been missing out of the foundation. People did not know how to behave. There was a culture, but it was a culture that was undocumented and driven from the behaviour of the leadership over 15–20 years. Haub recalls:

> If we wanted to change the culture, we had to start by laying out how do we want people to behave and what do we believe is important to us in this company. We developed this concept by constructing a house with the foundation, pillars and roof, symbolizing the important areas and core values. We described the values in detail in terms of the examples of behaviours. It was a major initiative to develop and introduce this into the company and to describe to our people how this was part of

the new direction we are going to take with the company. We started to develop a process where we brought in around 120 people every week (implementation now) for about 3.5 days. We got together 2,000 managers over a three month period.

Getting a buy-in for a new corporate picture

The CFO and COO presented at every conference so that they would convey the same message each time. During each conference, they would go through work exercises of what the core values were in action and people would go through self assessments to understand what their strengths and weaknesses were. This assisted in getting better engagement, buy-in and understanding of where the company was heading performance wise and why they needed to change. There were some specific initiatives around how they were going to change the business model. The development of a new business model came later. At that time, A&P was very much driven by getting allowances from suppliers, i.e. very much buying oriented. Haub recalls:

> We needed a shift to become a more sales driven organization which means that we needed to engage our store associates a lot more because that is where we wanted to win and not at the buying desk in the office where we squeezed our suppliers for allowance dollars. We started introducing the concept of net costing where we did not measure the success of our buyers by the amount of allowance dollars that they brought in, but by the amount of sales dollars they generated, i.e. the margins they were generating. This was a big culture shift in the company.

By being focused on buyers, they focused on middle management. A&P was more decentralized then and had more buying going on in lots of offices, but they had started to centralize more. Through the meetings it was realized that they would have a faster impact if they would start to consolidate and bring more of those groups together. Consolidation at the stores level was not feasible, but a lot of the backroom work could be consolidated. The ultimate goal was to create one centralized approach to the merchandising activity – one merchandising organization for the entire USA. A&P went through several iterations to consolidate buying from five to six to three to one point of purchase. Some of the delay was in generating the interdepartmental-level information systems to effect the change. These systems took four to five years to build.

Evaluation of what had been achieved in 1998–1999

When asked, 'what was realized when you finished up in 1998 and came into the summer of 1999?' Haub replied,

The organization had a broader understanding of what the challenges were for the company. The first new executive I brought in was a leader of human resources. I had to upgrade the role and get a people champion into this company besides myself. It had to be somebody who could keep driving just the people's side of this plan which dealt with implementing core values, institutionalising this new culture, and seeing how to take the next step. Then we started having fall-out, not at the top, but at the next level. We confronted this by having managers either buy in or look for other opportunities. Some did not believe in this type of culture because they lived in command and control and left voluntarily or involuntarily. One of the big challenges was to turn the words into action. If you hear the company leadership talk about new values and culture, but continue on with their day to day activities experiencing the old, they don't believe the words mean anything. A year later, the new values started coming into play because we started measuring people's performance not just based on numbers and results, but also on their values. We took a first pulse of the institution in Spring 1999 through an employee questionnaire. We got 27 per cent participation, which is low. The feedback was still very negative. The years after that, 2001–02, we engaged the Gallup organization to do the Gallup employee engagement survey. This was a short, but very focused survey. We saw tremendous success with this. We enjoyed a 90 per cent participation rate (unheard of in the industry). Over three years, we moved from the 34th to the 51st percentile in our employee ranking of A&P as a company that valued them. We saw wide-ranging improvements across the board in all geographic regions and across all categories of management. As a result, the employee engagement score is still a critical element of our performance evaluation. It's part of your performance plan, individual goals and team goals all tied together. We made great progress in that area.

Corporate words: developing critical skills in the organization. Prologue

At the end of 1998, A&P introduced its first strategic restructuring. It decided to exit certain non-core markets and close some underperforming stores. It took some decisive action to also demonstrate to the organization that change was happening. Haub was willing to take some difficult steps to change the direction of the company and to make sure that everybody realized that this was not just touchy feely stuff, but that there was also a lot of hard business stuff that was going to occur. This change process in developing new corporate skills centred around analysing their entire portfolio, from a market to market perspective. No significant changes in the managers had occurred as yet. Early in 1999, they implemented the plan that had been announced in 1998. Implementation took the first six months of

1999. It was at that point that Haub began to ask who was really on his team. He started seeing some second tier management dropping out and began to realize that he probably needed to make some changes. Why did the second tier drop out? Some of it was that they didn't fit and were not endorsing the new direction. Haub started getting feedback from the lower levels, hearing that some managers were dismissing or ridiculing the change process.

The company started to see positive sales growth for the first time in five years and there was sense of fresh air. People were starting to talk about it. They started to engage with this whole concept of 'gaptitude', i.e. their new direction and having a direction and objectives, and talking about what their common goals were. Remembering this time, Haub recalls,

> We invested a lot of time and effort to really communicate it. Communication was a big part of it. Where before there was no communication to employees in any shape or form, we now are starting to institutionalise certain forms of communication on a regular basis, informing employees of the progress of the plan and change programme.

1999–2000: Moving toward a new corporate picture and a new culture – round I

Change of this scale did not happen quickly and involved many people in the organization working together. Haub describes the process they used.

> Conferences were done every six to 12 months. In the early stages, every six months, we would call people together to review progress and introduce the next set of changes or upgrade to the next level of activities. In 1999, we then said that the culture change is under way and it would take a long time. This change was something that we needed to sustain and that was not a six or twelve months' effort. We had to get the non-believers out. We had to keep talking the talk. The first time that we let this slide, people would not take it seriously. With the business challenges, we realized that this alone would not sustain our progress. We needed to start identifying the other areas that were holding us back.

He continues addressing the resources required to make the change work.

> We did a portfolio restructuring. We started to very aggressively invest in capital, into building new stores. That was not as well thought through and not as comprehensive as the change approach made around that initiative. We thought that we had to show people that we were going to grow. They would see physical evidence of the company refreshing its store base.

The analysis phase – round I to determine the next steps

The organization up to this point was looking inwardly at core values for the first time and changing the senior team of managers. It was in the latter part of 1999 to the beginning of 2000 that the company started to move out of this inward gaze to ask what was happening out in the market place. There were also the threats of Wal-Mart, Internet shopping and home meal replacement, as well as the alternative formats and changing consumer behaviour which were causing the supermarkets to lose traffic and the number of occasions people shopped. But A&P, for the most part, still continued to analyse what the internal barriers were to its further potential with only some awareness of the external environment. This led to the next phase in early 2000 where all of the processes, systems and organization in the supply chain were so out of date, so behind the times, that no matter how good they were at doing what was their core mission of serving the customer, they were still limping behind the competitors. They needed to significantly upgrade their management information systems (MIS) and supply and distribution information capabilities to take them to the next level of merchandising, category management, store operations, distribution and supply chain activities.

At the foundation, this would consist of creating a common item database. A&P was still operating at different divisions with different data and could not compare or really work in a more unified way with their suppliers. For example, to pull information together about how much of a particular detergent they were selling at any given period was a huge effort of different systems pulling together data almost manually. So they were not really capable of executing category management as a best practice. They were recognizing that they were not using a modern form of going to market if they did not have the right information available about what their customers were buying, what were the best products to have, what the right assortment was, how to best price it, and how best to manage that process so that they would be able to grow profitably. They were still stuck in a tactical approach to business which emphasized weekly promotions' budgets, but not the analysis of the success and failure of the day-to-day, month-to-month business.

They needed to find out what the consumers were saying about their stores and their experience and how they compared to their competition and the problems consumers had when they were out of stock, or having the wrong assortment in the store, and being, in some cases, priced too high or the perception of being priced too high. They were looking at benchmarks in terms of cost in the supply chain, which was so much higher than anyone else in the industry. The amount of inventory that they were carrying to run the business was high and inventory turns were very low. These were the challenges that they set out to change in order to make the company successful. Importantly, they were starting to get people engaged and they were seeing all these issues too.

The evaluation follow-up – round I

Haub had begun to wake up people to the issues. At the same time, it became clear that, as a company, A&P had no concept of accountability, even though it had been made one of the core values. The emphasis in the first year and a half was on integrity, respect and engaging employees. Once Haub realized that it was necessary to emphasize accountability, people believed that he was counteracting what they were doing in the beginning. It looked like there was no trust. Haub relates:

> we recognized that the company was consistently missing its performance goals and there was no consequence. There were people in management positions who have not made a budget in ten years. Now you can say that part of it was that we had the wrong process in place or that we didn't know how to budget, but on the other hand we did not hold people accountable to anything.

A&P simply did not have good performance management and no measurement of goals. This was realized in 2000. A&P began to introduce a performance management system and began looking at how it was structured. Haub said:

> we were structured in a way that prevented accountability. And again, that is something that is taking us a long time to correct. I think with a new structure that's evolving, we will get to a level where we're going to have good accountability because we're flattening the organization and taking two layers of management out to ensure people are functioning at a level where they can actually have accountability. That is where they will really have control over these things and not just keep working to show results but work to manage the business.

Back to the large-scale change process – round 2, spring 2000

In the spring of 2000 the next phase began, what was called the Great Renewal Programme. This was to completely overhaul all of A&P's information systems and processes. Haub announced a four-year initiative to change the majority of the information systems and to introduce with the new systems new processes and a whole new support infrastructure in the company. This was named Evergreen.

How far had the change progressed?

Haub considered that by 2000 he was starting to have a real significant change at the senior management level because people had to be more accountable and the supply-chain business process initiative was under way. At this point, each person who reported to Haub headed up a division. They had to run a business. That was new behaviour. But this success was not without its complications. The COO, the chief merchandising officer and the head of development left. Some replacements were promoted from within, but other replacements were new people brought in from the outside. Not surprisingly, the company went through a poor performance year. The new people were learning the ropes.

Haub discusses this time period:

> In the new management information systems initiative, we engaged IBM as our main systems integrator. We also used a change management consultant and we put a team together of 150–200 people internally to work on this initiative. It's a monstrous challenge. Basically, it took three years. And we clearly underestimated what the initiative would take. Had I known then what I know today, I would have never done it. I'm glad today that I did it. The cost, the distraction, the upheaval is incredible.

Decision and implementation – round 2

Haub continues to relate:

> We had a four-year project outlined which was going to cost us about $350 million between people and capital investment. It was going to get us sustained ongoing benefits in improvements between US$150 and 200 million annually. It was going to give us a certain set of functionality that was also very critical. We finished it in three years, but that was mostly driven by change in the scope of the project. We reduced some of the functionality. The cost after three years was going to be about 10 per cent less of what we had originally projected, but we only got about 60 per cent of its benefits. Had we gone through the entire project it would have taken us about three years more and cost us about 50 per cent more. We stopped because the costs were getting so out of whack with expected returns. So this project, a year and a half into it, was completely off the rails. It turned out that the software solution provider was a small company who did not have a SAP system for retail. We ventured into uncharted waters looking for a new set of solutions that really did not exist. We first of all changed the leadership of the initiative team and within six months I changed the CIO. We put a whole new business case together. We cut back on what we thought was possible to what we could deliver in a reasonable amount of time and a reasonable cost and still preserve a majority of the potential benefits.

A&P put together a new case with a new team because all of the original functional managers, with the exception of the person responsible for distribution, had left. The new initiative was producing an information system geared toward being the best in class or the best practice in the industry around category management, around the supply chain system, and around key store operations systems like human resource management, inventory management and ordering processes. But the key was to get the merchandising infrastructure, i.e. getting a common item database and getting an assortment, pricing and promotions system that was all integrated. A&P got the foundation in, a common item database and some of the tools for managing assortment, pricing and promotion.

A&P went through another benchmark study in the spring of 2002 and had one of the best inventory turns in the industry. Haub reflects on their learning in the process:

> So the areas that were left off were in the merchandising area, i.e. merchandising solutions. Store solutions were pretty much what we wanted. Distribution solutions, the warehouse management system and the transportation management system were relatively the easiest to develop and implement. We also developed a new human resource system and a new finance system.

Evaluation round 2

The whole timing of the implementation of the new MIS was different than planned. Originally, it was envisioned to introduce the new systems on a rolling basis so as not to come all at once and overwhelm the organization. It was to have been sequenced; that did not happen. Basically, 80 per cent of the new systems hit in nine months starting in early summer 2002.

The big challenge in 2001 was a lot of new management at the senior level and the new MIS initiative coming off the rails and needing to be rescued. Fortunately, 2001 was a better year. Profits were up, people had learned and the organization had settled in. Momentum from the new leadership helped, and the external environment was more favourable than it would be in the following year.

Christian Haub, putting the results into context, stated:

> But the one area we failed to achieve and still fail in today, is that even though we've sustained the culture change in 2000 and in 2001 by introducing performance management systems that have sustained themselves pretty well through 2002 and are now going forward, we did not have enough focus on the fundamentals of our business. This business is still very much around merchandising, store execution, and the integration of that with the right leadership in place. There is a business to run while

changes are happening, even while our company transitions from its old to new culture. Just introducing performance management was a big thing. People had to learn it, understand it, adjust to it and deal with its consequences. Today, we have performance measures in place that can tell us whether somebody is performing well or not. The only thing we measured before was if there had been measurable sales and bottom line results at store level; and even then there was no consequence if a manager did or did not achieve them. Now we have those same budget goals, with a whole performance plan laid out with individual goals and objectives and being measured against those we have employee engagement scores. We introduced 360 degree feedback programme for a lot of the middle managers and just a lot more time and effort is being spent on evaluating people's performance and then tying that to compensation, promotion, stock option awards, etc. So the early period of the culture change which had very much revolved around feel good has now become the cold hard reality of 'this is a business and we are running this business for profitability and performance'. While there still is, unfortunately, a lot of change going on, with every new leadership change or senior leadership change, different personalities, ideas and directions come into play. I am still leaving out a very important aspect here. Also during 2000 when we introduced the new systems initiative, we started further developing our approach around strategy and developed a business model so that people could better understand how this all fits together.

Corporate words and corporate picture – round 3

Haub reflects:

> In 2000, we were spending quite a bit more time on strategy and framing where we wanted to go. Let me back up to the corporate strategic framework which we looked at. Typically, companies try to pursue strategies with a focus on product leadership, operational excellence or customer intimacy. We developed our strategy around customer intimacy. This is how we were going to differentiate and drive ourselves to a leadership position. And, now, this is also at the end of the period of growth in the 1990s when consumer spending was still at an all time high that we recognized that we are an industry that has not done a lot around differentiating. But on the other hand, we were being more and more dominated by Wal-Mart whose operational excellence was its competitive advantage.
>
> Out of that concept of 'this is the direction we want to go', we then developed our business model which we called 'the customer intimate business model'. This model has the customer at the core and then

has identified core activities surrounding the customer embedded in leading and directing as well as supporting and enabling initiatives and activities. This core is called identify customer requirements and develop that market which offers an understanding of the requirements of the consumer and then satisfy the demand through execution at store level. I think what has happened is that we became too consultancy/theoretically driven around these things and started translating that into what does that mean to what are we going to do. A wider and wider gap grew between people at corporate and people in the day to day business, at store level. The more strategic we became, this of course is still a tactical business, the more we lost something in the translation to going forward. In 2000, in hindsight, we did not recognize, not realize, and even in 2001 we didn't, that the whole paradigm of the economy and consumer was shifting because the ten years of growth and success of sales and growth margins going up came to an end.

The thing that was missing was that A&P had no infrastructure for measuring the external environment and its effect on the business. It changed the internal MIS, but had no way to really get to the data on the effects of economic slowdown on customers. By recognizing that the systems initiative and everything we needed to get to this point of measuring success on customer intimacy was years away, we knew that it was clearly unaffordable. By the time A&P got to working its MIS operationally, the whole environment had shifted. Where at one time customers were looking for service since they had money, they now were looking for economy and discounts.

September 11, 2001, had a dramatic effect on business. With no warning people shifted into a response mode of buying for value and not for service. This apparent change was more pronounced in lower income areas, but seemed to have endured for several years and points to real customer change. There had been a similar shift in Canada earlier.

In Canada, we've been successful in developing a complementary approach. There is a certain growth of market share we can get with a discount concept while maintaining a full service supermarket. During the holidays when people want special food, we get a bigger spike in the supermarket part of the business. This is due to our having more specialty foods, greater selections in the deli, and a broader variety with more service than we have in the discount markets. But the average growth in the discount concept versus the supermarket business has been three/four to one for the last seven years.

So if we want to have presence, i.e. market share, and profitability with the key driving force of customer orientation and customer satisfaction, we have to be able to meet our customers' economical as well as their service and greater product assortment needs. What does the analysis say is required to keep people satisfied? Is the right mix 75 per cent discount and 25 per cent conventional or mainstream full service? There is no single answer. We have to go through this market by market. I would say in places like northern New Jersey we probably are going to have a higher share of full service than discount customers, but the closer we get to an area like Newark and Patterson it's probably going to be much more the other way, more 80–20 in favour of discount.

We also need to start from the base that we have today, the markets that we are in today. If we're well positioned in Toronto and then the greater province of Ontario, and then my first objective has to be to create that same kind of presence in and around New York. First of all, we already have presence in markets which are underserved from a discount perspective. I think with the right approach of converting existing stores and developing new stores primarily for the discount format, we should be able to dominate this market place. From that strength, do Philadelphia, then Detroit and then once we would have strong dominate presence in those markets, then see if there are new market opportunities to try that approach.

As a part of this scenario, it will be essential for the managers of the stores and divisions to have a model that they could work against. What we learned from our Canadian experience was that there was a disconnection between our merchandising programme and its execution at store level. It's not that the merchandising programme in itself is necessarily all wrong, but there is not a connection between what and why. Why operations has to execute in a certain way to get us to the results that the merchandising programme is designed to achieve. So that's a management, process, and communications issue. It's going to be one of the big objectives to fix and our business is to be driven primarily by the merchandising. If that's put together correctly, then executing it at store level is, of course, will be necessary to realize it. But you can execute as good as you want, but if you do not have the correct merchandise concept approach you cannot be successful. If you have the correct merchandise concept and the wrong location approach, it won't work either. There's always a natural tension because the people in operations believe that they know more about merchandising than the merchandisers do. And the merchandisers always blame the operators that they aren't executing it correctly. If you think about the discount and mainstream mix that you have out in the market, that's a decision that you have to make earlier. If I want to capture this New York marketplace, I need to know where to have the discount and mainstream concepts and then what do these concepts have to look like so they don't cannibalize each other, but complement each other. And then as this business is dynamic, how do you keep evolving, maintaining, and keeping it contemporary with what happens around you. The discount concept will operate under a new name and concept called Food Basics.

Discussion

The A&P case provides a rich example of the strategic foci as a mechanism for large-scale change. We have followed the case from the early 1980s to where A&P is now.

Corporate evaluation: Starting with corporate evaluation the original employee surveys were being evaluated on an annual basis in terms of core values. Haub had established a link between the employee engagement score and the amount of sales and profit growth. A&P established a pretty strong correlation that the higher the employee engagement, the better the sales and profit performance of that individual store. This was based on having lower shrinkage, lower accident costs, higher profitability by each store and having higher customer satisfaction, which correlated with higher transaction sizes.

Corporate implementation: By the end of 2002, A&P was implementing the information system and was about 90 per cent finished. It was beginning to measure the functionality and testing if the information system was delivering what it was designed to do. The benefits, both soft and hard, were being detailed as the system started up. It was able to reduce working capital, reduce inventory throughout the system and speed up delivery from the warehouse to the store, and out-of-stocks were decreasing. Haub stated:

> What we did when we implemented systems was to interview the users after the implementation to find out how well the implementation worked. Were they trained appropriately? Did they understand how the system works? Did they understand how they're suppose to use the system and get feedback from that to see if we have more training needs? We are also tracking the use of the system and how many category managers are using the new category management tools, how many reports are being created and things like that.

Corporate analysis: A&P was doing analysis with the help of the new system; it was now equipped to analyse a changing environment. This analysis is different than in past years in that it is in the process of looking at what has changed in the external environment, in the customer's world. Customer surveys are employed in the analysis and this is compared to survey results from companies using the survey and sharing information in common.

Corporate words and key driving force: A&P is beginning to develop a new driving force in the discount concept called 'Food Basics'. Haub states:

I see the driving force critical in our ability to turn around our US business as it did in Canada. In Canada, the dual concept continues to be a major driving force. And again we structured correctly around price and availability, meaning location. The other driving force that I would still see in our conventional business is everything that has to do with fresh food products. Fresh I see as being the biggest differentiator for supermarkets against all other forms of retail and that is product driven. People come into the stores because they always find fresh fruits and vegetables.

Corporate picture: Who was A&P? What was A&P becoming? Haub responds:

A&P was the industry pioneer of the concept of supermarket retailing, food retailing. We are the oldest food retail company and probably the most well known. We are the company with the most heritage. Today, it has lost our historic image. Some would say that it's an image that has gathered a lot of dust and rust and doesn't know what it wants to be. I think it is due to two reasons: size and presence. Clearly, before we were national, now we are regional and only a part of the system carries the A&P name. What we want to be at our core is customer sensitive, in terms of our strategic model, customer intimacy. In today's perspective, I see that as very difficult to achieve because of the inability to measure it, and probably the amount of investment it's going to take to get there. In this concept there is the highest potential pay off and the highest margin business that you can develop, but it's also very expensive to run. It takes a lot of risk to get there. And it may not be what the customer wants. Based on where we were in the late 1990s, it was probably correct, whereas today, where the customer is going it's going to be more about delivering the minimum set of expectations at value that is at a cost saving to the customer. The drivers to be successful will be around market share because market share then drives your ability to leverage cost, leverage infrastructure, to capture attention by offering savings to the customer. That is where the Great A&P had its notoriety. It had that kind of presence. We are seeing market share not by doing it with one concept, by saying that there is the opportunity to capture more market share or maximize market share through multiple concept complementary, but multiple concepts. It looks like we were able to achieve that in our Canadian business with the combination of full service, fresh focused supermarkets, and low price limited assortment driven discount formats. And this is still going to be a business driven by how low your cost structure can be maintained.

Reflection on the change process

In chapters 3, 4 and 5 when we discussed change and large-scale change in organizations, we talked about the fact that when change is introduced by the CEO what follows is that the subordinates going through it are one step behind the CEO, and their subordinates going through it are one step behind them. The initial phase is denial. Most people when they look at new situations are in denial over the change required. By the time they become a believer and start to move to change, subordinates are one step behind. So the second phase is dodging and the third phase is doing, and the fourth phase is sustaining.

Change moved from Haub to the divisional level and then to the store level. What happened at A&P was that Haub was doing and in the initial stages his managers below the senior management group were dodging, but the stores managers, a level below them, were in denial.

Applying levels

Table 13.1 illustrates how A&P moved through the phases and levels of change described in chapter 5. Haub began his change with himself (Level I). Through the first year, he worked at and succeeded in getting the individuals in the senior management group to change. Through those individual's change, the senior management group changed (Level II) and it began to work as a Level II team during the second year. When he came to the question of getting the MIS working and faced the accountability question, he moved into the division (or interdepartmental group level). Then he was addressing Level III issues. There is a considerable difference in the amount of energy needed to change Level III as contrasted with Level I. All of the change, up to this point, was inward looking. Three years into the change programme, Haub was still internally focused. It took an external focus of what the competition was going to do to each of the actions made by Haub and A&P to move to the next level. That's when Level IV came into play. Interestingly enough, A&P is now three years into this process.

Haub saw his customer base shift after the events of September 11th. It was not a transient phenomenon as it lasted several years. This customer shift had required the introduction of a new concept of store type and brand name. The Canadian market had pioneered this approach and now it came into the US market. The scale and phases of this new change are in the early stages of implementation. A&P had reinvented itself, as most successful organizations do in time of change. The interlevel dynamics of large system change and strategy provide useful lenses for understanding and leading change in such organizations as A&P.

Table 13.1 Phases and levels of change in A&P

Phase and level of change	Actions and events
Phase 0 – Ground zero: the need for change enters the organization	In 1995, A&P was successful in acquiring other retail chains, but not successful in integrating them into the A&P concept. Profitability slipped and Wood retired as CEO.
Phase 1 – Change awareness: the key individual denying and dodging	Christian Haub moved into the CEO role and began to get an awareness of the possibility of a critical issue both inside and outside the organization.
Phase 2 – Initiation: the key individual doing and the team denying and dodging	Haub took his agenda for change to his senior management group and initiated analysis. Senior management group denied and dodged.
Phase 3 – Manoeuvring: the key individual and team doing and the interdepartmental group denying and dodging	The new senior management group started work on redoing the corporate picture and took it on the road to division, district and store managers. The lack of MIS accountability surfaced at this time.
Phase 4 – Integration: the key individual, team and interdepartmental group doing, the organization denying and dodging	The management information system was in place, but modified from the original design. Associate morale was better, but store level was still not on board. Questions were asked about non-profitable stores and changing customer needs.
Phase 5 – Achievement: the key individual sustaining, the team, interdepartmental group and organization doing	The dual concept was brought forward from the Canadian experience. It worked in Canada and now was implemented in the major US markets. The interdepartmental group worked at developing a new concept for the New York market.
Phase 6 – Follow through: the key individual and team sustaining, the interdepartmental group and organization doing	This phase is in the future where new markets will be encountered and the new dual concept deployed.
Phase 7 – Sustaining: the key individual, team, interdepartmental group and organization sustaining	This phase is in the future as A&P rolls out the new concept and removes unprofitable stores and continues in other market areas.

Finale

We began this book with the Overture, which introduced the three content themes: levels and interlevels, change and strategy.

Our opening theme was to remind you that organizations comprise these four levels of analysis and that as a manager, as an organizational member or as an ODC consultant you are constantly working with each of these levels, making them work more effectively. This involves being able to see which one might be having difficulty at any given time, knowing how to intervene to deal with the relevant issue and being skilled at a range of interventions and styles. But experience tells us that these levels are not only discrete and separate, but that what happens at one level has an impact at each of the others. The four levels are interdependent and interrelated. Each level is systemically linked to each of the others, and events at one level are both cause and effect of events at other levels.

Our second theme was large-scale and large-system change. Large-scale changes refer to changes that are deep, pervasive and complex. Large-system change involves change by individuals, teams, across the interdepartmental group, so that the entire organization may be said to have changed.

Our third theme focused on strategy. In this theme, we explored the processes by which managers, organizational members and ODC consultants create a picture of who the organization is, express that picture, analyse the external and internal environments, choose and implement actions and evaluate outcomes. We presented these processes not as linear steps, but as cyclical and systemic strategic actions, which involve iterations of individual and team actions and action between teams and with customers.

We explored several process themes that deal primarily with methodology and perspective. Attention to process is central to effective individual, team and organizational action and learning, and key to accessing the hidden world that is organizational culture. The process of change in a large system involves moving from a perceived need for change, through articulating an envisioned future, through assessing the present to determine what needs to change and getting to the envisioned future by implementing change and managing the transition. The process of change in a large system is full of interlevel dynamics in that large-scale organizational change comprises individual, team and interdepartmental group change respectively and that how change is introduced and implemented through the system is a complex movement from individual to team, team to team in the interdepartmental group and to the organization's external stakeholders over time in iterations where the movements are circular with each iteration being a cause and effect of another.

We took an action research approach whereby we invited you, the reader, to reflect on your own situation in the light of the concepts and case situations presented and see how they inform your own assessment of what is going on and what action you might plan to take.

Action research and ODC are intimately intertwined, both theoretically and through the work of those scholar-practitioners who have shaped the development of both approaches. Action research works through a series of cycles of consciously and deliberately (a) planning, (b) taking action, (c) evaluating that action, leading to further planning, action and evaluation. A second dimension of action research is that it is participative, in that the members of the system participate actively in the process. The action research approach is powerful. It engages people as participants in seeking ideas, planning, taking actions, reviewing outcomes and learning what does and doesn't work, and why. We challenged you to consider how to build participation for strategy and change by drawing on your understanding of how change moves through an organization and how interlevel dynamics contribute both a conceptual map and a practical framework to assist you.

We have framed our approach by inviting you, the reader, to engage in reflection-in-action in order that you might learn-in-action, rather than simply engage with the concepts in this book in a notional way. By taking an action research approach in this book we mean that we invited you, the reader, whether you are a senior manager, a non-executive organizational member, an external ODC consultant or a student, not only to understand the concepts developed in this book but to engage in learning-in-action by inquiring into what goes on around you, both inside and outside an organization, drawing on concepts which help you make sense of your experience and then engaging in action, evaluating outcomes, reflecting on learning and developing knowledge. As we have demonstrated, cycles of inquiry can operate at different levels of depth. A single inquiry loop looks back at actions, a double inquiry loop at goals and strategies and a triple inquiry loop at ultimate purposes and identity. We recommended that you do not do this on your own, or keep your reflections private, but that you engage others in conversations of shared reflections.

By means of vignettes and cases, we have provided examples of organizations that have worked through change processes so that you can study them and notice how interlevel dynamics shape the process of change. We have also provided the action research activities to challenge you to engage in reflection and discussion on understanding an organization with which you are familiar, so that you can take more informed action. In Appendix 3 we provide a format for using 'live' cases, where executives visit the classroom and engage with a class on the live issues of their own organizations.

It is universally accepted that change matters. In this book we have explored a neglected area of change, namely how interlevel dynamics are integral to processes of strategy and large-scale organization change with a view to enabling managers, non-executive organizational members and ODC consultants to work with and across levels in order to help organizations, of whatever sector, to change effectively and successfully.

The dynamics of insider action research

This appendix is directed to those readers who are using this book as a basis for doing action research in their own organization, where they are both intervening in their own organization and studying that intervention at the same time. The issues and process in undertaking such an approach are well described in Coghlan and Brannick (2005). That book may act as a complementary text to this one in such situations.

There are a number of significant challenges for those managers who undertake action research in their own organization that Coghlan and Brannick explore under the following headings: preunderstanding, role duality and organizational politics.

- *Preunderstanding*: Preunderstanding refers to such things as people's knowledge, insights and experience before they engage in an action research programme. The knowledge, insights and experience of the manager-action-researchers apply not only to theoretical understanding of organizational dynamics, but also to the lived experience of their own organization. The key challenge is to maintain both closeness to and distance from the data.
- *Role duality*: When manager-action-researchers augment their normal organizational membership roles with the research enterprise, they are likely to encounter role conflict and find themselves caught between loyalty, behavioural claims and identification dilemmas.
- *Managing organizational politics*: Undertaking an action research project in one's own organization is political and might even be considered subversive. This is because action research examines everything, stresses listening, emphasizes questioning, fosters courage, incites action, abets reflection and endorses democratic participation. Any or all of these characteristics may be threatening to existing organizational norms. Accordingly, manager-action-researchers need to be politically astute in deciding to engage in action research. They need to be prepared to work the political system, which involves balancing the organization's formal justification of what it wants in the project with their own tacit personal

justification for political activity. Throughout the project they have to maintain their credibility as an effective driver of change and as an astute political player. The key to this is assessing the power and interests of relevant stakeholders in relation to aspects of the project.

With that in mind, the actual processes of reflection and action may be drawn from the action research activities provided at the end of each chapter. These activities aim to stimulate reflection and provoke action by those readers who are studying their own organizations as they work at trying to change them. Engagement in these activities provides concrete structures for reflecting on the dynamics within their own organizations and to constructing interventions.

Building and using a model for corporate analysis

The most comprehensive tool for answering analysis questions is a model that portrays the diverse reality of a marketplace. The longer a model is used, with corrections made at each iteration, the more reliable it becomes. If there is some equilibrium in the marketplace this is also a help to having an effective model. This appendix lays out some of the critical issues in building and using a model in corporate analysis: purpose of the model, who should be involved, designing a use and capability and the basic software that is involved. More detailed guidelines on how to construct and use models can be found in those books that specialize in that field (e.g. Morabito *et al.*, 1999) The difficult work of putting an accurate model together for an organization has great returns in better results.

Purpose of the model

Models can fulfil several purposes:

- *An aid to participation*: With a virtual plan, a systems model is created which is accessible enough for employees to use, test and intelligently critique. This helps the organization to see the model from several different perspectives, including the all-important perspective of a less technical person.
- *Learning*: Most management simulators are created for use in learning laboratories. Typically, the model is also designed as a strategy testing device, where the case is introduced and the simulator is put into the decision mix, and as a debriefing device, where past experience is put into the framework of the model and success and failure are understood better. Often explanations of relevant causal loop diagrams and archetypes are included to help the user get a glimpse at the underlying structure of the model and the decisions it represents.
- *Practising decision-making skills*: Models give managers the chance to experiment with the results of choices, as well as learn about the structure and dynamics of the systems in which they find themselves before they

actually need to make their real decisions. By playing CEO, the managers can bankrupt the company hundreds of times and, hopefully, learn how to avoid doing it in real life.
- *Scenario planning*: In scenario planning, policies are tested against several plausible futures. A model can capture the scenarios that are of interest to the organization and permit the user to test the outcome of policy choices. One output of this is a model of virtual reality useable for rapid testing of scenarios.

Who should build a model

Systems models are not built in isolation by MIS people, but by a team of decision-makers. The team should consist of several people:

- The CEO.
- Several senior managers from the organization.
- At least one experienced model builder.
- At least one experienced computer interface designer (the interface designer should be included in all of the discussions from the beginning).

Design of the model

This is a brainstorming phase, ideally conducted with the entire planning team present. Before an organization chooses software, many options being available, it needs to begin to develop a sense of what it wants the management simulator to look like. What will people see on the screen? What reports will they be given? What decisions will they be asked to make? What plots will be introduced? What sort of events and problems should be sent their way? How fancy and elaborate should the interface be? This is a good time to run and critique some generic models as a basis for creativity and judgement.

A word of caution: fancy simulator interfaces can often hide mediocre understanding. It is important to have a very strong, validated model as the engine, i.e. either a literal mathematical model, or a well thought out and tested understanding of the causal loops and enriched archetypes of the system. If an organization has a limited budget available, the emphasis should go into a model rather than the luxury of bells and whistles in the interface with the people who use the model.

Choosing the software

Once a decision has been made on the purpose of the model, the organization is in a much better position to choose the software most useful to its purposes.

At least two separate programmes are needed. The organization should start by selecting a simulator development language. This is the program that designs the outer 'shell' of the simulator, i.e. the buttons and commands which users see. Then a modelling software package should be chosen. This is the program that creates the underlying model. Both the modelling language and the Message Format Services development language need to be compatible. These programmes constantly change, so no actual suggestions are offered here.

Appendix 3

Structuring and conducting a 'live' case

As a complement or alternative to working with cases in a book, executive programmes frequently draw on living cases presented in class by visiting executives who provide material on their companies in advance of their class visit and then, with the class, engage on issues arising from the pre-read material. In this appendix we describe an approach to the 'live' case process that has been used in EMBA classrooms for over 30 years and that is built around material from this book. We introduce the methodology of a strategy intervention – how to structure the intervention and how executive MBA students can secure a case company for the live, in-class presentation.

Steps to secure and conduct a live case

The process steps below are designed to assist executive students with securing live case studies for their strategy and change course. These process steps outline a way to start and maintain a relationship with a live case organization. The process presupposes pre-existing student learning teams; if these are not in existence they have to be formed before the process for the live case situation can take place. In this approach, the team working with the particular live case may utilize another team to act as process consultants to its work with the visiting executive and provide feedback on the performance of the live case session.

- *Meet as a team.* Discuss what type of organization is of interest to each team member, i.e. large or small, private or public, profit or not-for-profit. It is important to air your differences and make a team decision for your strategy and policy class. You do not have to fulfil everyone's wish since other teams will present other cases that will expand the experience base of the whole class.
- *Discuss the possibilities of your corporate contacts.* Determine if a team member knows someone who has a business or works in an organization that would be open to your doing a live case. Some help can be found from reviewing cases done in the past. Most students feel reluctant to ask a company to do a case. This is normal since most companies do

show some hesitancy when asked for the first time. You have something to offer them! Please keep in mind that a team member's anxiety may increase if his/her own company is asked to be the team's case study.

- *Determine if the company has ever participated in a live case study.* If so, would your team want to build upon the previous case? Is there any material on hand in the library or on the Internet pertinent to this case? The subject of the live case can be the review of an implementation or change process as well as a new strategic direction.

- *Get a commitment.* Place yourself in the position of the company and prepare to discuss how your team can be of benefit to the company. Use this material to secure your case study's involvement. Have the CEO, i.e. the owner of the problem to be studied, agree to a time and date for his/her live case presentation in class.

- *Divide the written work into parts*, assigning each team member a certain area of responsibility. Work with the strengths of each team member and assign report sections accordingly. Some written work takes place before the intervention with the organization in front of the class.

- *Set up the initial interview* with the company and see what concerns and challenges exist. What area of concern would be of interest to your team and classmates? In this interview determine (a) the issues, (b) key people, (c) internal and external information relevant to the case. In addition, obtain some of the financial statements.

- *Decide on the structure of the meeting.* What role should be assigned to each team member? How do you want the other members of the class to respond or participate? Will your team be the main consultant team or do you want to choose another team from the class to alternate with your team as consultants?

- *The live case process is conducted at this point.* In the classroom with the executive, first explore the material relating to framing the corporate picture and naming the corporate words (chapters 7 and 8). Second, explore the process of analysis, the decisions and action taken (chapters 9 and 10). Third, reflect on the outcomes (chapter 11). Fourth, explore the story of the change process in terms of the cycle of change (chapter 3) and the interlevel processes (chapters 4 and 5). This can be done by drawing on the action research activities and the questions at the end of many of the chapters. Fifth, explore what the new future organization would look like and the possible steps to get there.

- *Collect information from other teams* following the conclusion of your live case study. Other information can assist your team in writing a better report.

- *Write a thank-you* note to the CEO and other participants of the organization.

- *Write the project report* on the case. Make a copy for your instructor and your case company.

References

Adler, N., Shani, A. B. (Rami) and Styhre, A. (2004) *Collaborative Research in Organizations*. Sage, Thousand Oaks, CA.

Allen, T. (1977) *Managing the Flow of Technology*. MIT Press, Cambridge, MA.

Amason, A. A. (1996) Distinguishing the Effects of Functional and Dysfunctional Conflict on Strategic Decision Making: Resolving a Paradox for Senior Management Teams, *Academy of Management Journal*, 39(1): 123–148.

Ancona, D. G. (1990) Top Management Teams: Preparing for the Revolution, in J. S. Carroll (ed.) *Applied Social Psychology and Organizational Settings*. Erlbaum, Mahwah, NJ.

Ancona, D. and Caldwell, D. (1988) Beyond Task and Maintenance: Defining External Functions in Groups, *Group and Organization Studies*, 13(4): 468–494.

Argyris, C. (1985) *Strategy, Change and Defensive Routines*. Pitman, Marshfield, MA.

Argyris, C. (2000) *Flawed Advice and the Management Trap*. Oxford University Press, New York.

Argyris, C. and Schon, D. (1996) *Organizational Learning II*. Addison-Wesley, Reading, MA.

Bartunek, J. M. (2003) *Organizational and Educational Change*. Erlbaum, Mahwah, NJ.

Bartunek, J. M. and Moch, M. (1987) First-order, Second-order and Third-order Change and Organization Development: A Cognitive Approach, *Journal of Applied Behavioural Science*, 23(4): 483–500.

Bartunek, J. M., Crosta, T. E., Dame, R. F. and LeLacheur, D. F. (2000) Managers and Project Leaders Conducting their Own Action Research Interventions, in R. T. Golembiewski (ed.) *Handbook of Organizational Consultation*, 2nd edn. Marcel Dekker, New York, pp. 59–70.

Bateson, G. (1972) *Steps to an Ecology of Mind*. Ballantine, San Francisco, CA.

Beckhard, R. (1972) Optimizing Team Building Efforts, *Journal of Contemporary Business*, 1(3): 23–32.

Beckhard, R. and Harris, R. (1977) *Organizational Transitions*. Addison-Wesley, Reading, MA.

Beckhard, R. and Harris, R. (1987) *Organizational Transitions*, 2nd edn. Addison-Wesley, Reading, MA.

Beckhard, R. and Pritchard, W. (1992) *Changing the Essence*. Jossey-Bass, San Francisco, CA.

Beer, M. and Nohria, N. (2000) *Breaking the Code of Change*. Harvard Business School Press, Boston, MA.

Blake, R. and Mouton, J. (1964) *The Managerial Grid*. Gulf, Houston, TX.

Bolman, D. and Deal, T. (1997) *Reframing Organizations*. Jossey-Bass, San Francisco, CA.

Bunker, B. B. and Alban, B. (1997) *Large Group Interventions*. Jossey-Bass, San Francisco, CA.

Burke, W. W. (2002) *Organization Change: Theory and Practice*. Sage, Thousand Oaks, CA.

Burnes, B. (2004) Kurt Lewin and the Planned Approach to Change: A Reappraisal, *Journal of Management Studies*, 41: 977–1002.

Bushe, G. and Shani, A. B. (Rami) (1991) *Parallel Learning Structures*. Addison-Wesley, Reading, MA.

Christopher, M. G. (1998) *Logistics and Supply Chain Management*, 2nd edn. Financial Times/Prentice Hall, London.

Coghlan, D. (1996) Mapping the Progress of Change Through Organizational Levels: The Example of a Religious Order, in R. Woodman and W. Pasmore (eds) *Research in Organizational Change and Development*, vol. 9. JAI Press, Greenwich, CT, pp. 123–139.

Coghlan, D. (1997) Organizational Learning as a Dynamic Inter-level Process, in M. A. Rahim, R. T. Golembiewski and L. E. Pate (eds) *Current Topics in Management*, vol. 2. JAI Press, Greenwich, CT, pp. 27–44.

Coghlan, D. (1998a) The Interlevel Dynamics of Information Technology, *Journal of Information Technology*, 13: 139–149.

Coghlan, D. (1998b) The Process of Change Through Interlevel Dynamics in a Large Group Intervention for a Religious Organization, *Journal of Applied Behavioral Science*, 34(1): 105–119.

Coghlan, D. (2000) Interlevel Dynamics in Clinical Inquiry, *Journal of Organizational Change Management*, 13(2): 190–200.

Coghlan, D. and Brannick, T. (2005) *Doing Action Research in Your Own Organization*, 2nd edn. Sage, London.

Coghlan, D. and Coughlan, P. (2005) Collaborative Research Across Borders and Boundaries: Action Research Insights from the CO-IMPROVE Project, in R. Woodman and W. Pasmore (eds) *Research in Organization Change and Development*, vol. 15. Elsevier, Oxford.

Coghlan, D. and Mc Auliffe, E. (2003) *Changing Healthcare Organizations*. Blackhall, Dublin.

Coghlan, D. and McDonagh, J. (2001) Research and Practice in IT-enabled Change: The Case for Clinical Inquiry, in R. W. Woodman and W. A. Pasmore (eds) *Research in Organizational Change and Development*, vol. 13. JAI Press, Oxford, pp. 195–211.

Coghlan, D. and Rashford, N. S. (1990) Uncovering and Dealing with Organizational Distortions, *Journal of Managerial Psychology*, 5(3): 17–21.

Coghlan, D., Dromgoole, T., Joynt, P. and Sorensen, P. (2004) *Managers Learning in Action*. Routledge, London.

Cummings, T. and Worley, C. (2004) *Organization Development and Change*, 8th edn. Southwestern, Mason, OH.

de Geus, A. (1997) *The Living Company*. Harvard Business School Press, Boston, MA.

Dannemiller, K. and Tyson Associates (2000) *Whole-Scale Change*. Berrett-Koehler, San Francisco, CA.

DiBella, A. J. (2001) *Learning Practices*. Prentice-Hall, Upper Saddle River, NJ.

Dixon, N. (1994) *Dialogue at Work*. Lemos and Crane, London.

Duarte, D. L. and Snyder, N. T. (1999) *Managing Virtual Teams*. Jossey-Bass, San Francisco, CA.

Emery, F. and Purser, R. (1996) *The Search Conference*. Jossey-Bass, San Francisco, CA.

Finglestein, S. and Hambrick, D. C. (1996) *Strategic Leadership: Top Executives and their Effects on Organizations*. West, St Paul, MN.

Fisher, D., Rooke, D. and Torbert, W. R. (2000) *Personal and Organizational Transformations Through Action Inquiry*. Edge/Work Press, Boston, MA.

Flood, P., Dromgoole, T., Carroll, S. J. and Gorman, L. (2000) *Managing Strategy Implementation*. Blackwell, Oxford.

Floyd, S., Roos, J., Jacobs, C. and Kellerman, F. (2005) *Innovating Strategy Process*. Blackwell, Oxford.

Foster, R. and Kaplan, S. (2001) *Creative Destruction*. Currency, New York.

Fox, A. (1985) *Man Mismanagement*. Hutchinson, London.

French, W. and Bell, C. (1999) *Organization Development*, 6th edn. Prentice-Hall, Upper Saddle River, NJ.

Friedman, V. (2001) Action Science: Creating Communities of Inquiry in Communities of Practice, in P. Reason and H. Bradbury (eds) *Handbook of Action Research*. Sage, London, pp. 159–170.

Greiner, L. and Cummings, T. (2004) Wanted OD More Alive Than Dead, *Journal of Applied Behavioral Science*, 40(4): 374–391.

Hambrick, D. C. (1994) Top Management Group: A Conceptual Integration and Reconsideration of the 'Team' Label, in L. L. Cummings and B. M. Staw (eds) *Research in Organizational Behavior*, vol. 16. JAI Press, Greenwich, CT, pp. 171–213.

Hambrick, D. and Fukutomi, G. (1991) The Seasons of a CEO's Tenure, *Academy of Management Review*, 16: 719–742.

Hambrick, D., Nadler, D. A. and Tushman, M. L. (1998) *Navigating Change*. Harvard Business School Press, Boston, MA.

Harrison, M. (2005) *Diagnosing Organizations*, 3rd edn. Sage, Thousand Oaks, CA.

Hesselbein, F., Beckhard, R. and Goldsmith, M. (1995) *The Leader of the Future*. Jossey-Bass, San Francisco, CA.

Huxham, C. and Vangen, V. (2005) *Learning to Collaborate*. Routledge, London.

Jackson, M. (2003) *Systems Thinking: Creating Holism for Managers*. Wiley, Chichester.

Johansen, R., Sibbet, D., Benson, S., Martin, A., Mittman R. and Saffo, P. (1991) *Leading Business Teams: How Teams Can Use Technology and Group Process Tools to Enhance Performance*. Addison-Wesley, Reading, MA.

Kaplan, R. and Norton, D. (1996) *The Balanced Scorecard*. Harvard Business School Press, Boston, MA.

Katzenbach, J. R. (1998) *Teams at the Top*. Harvard Business School Press, Boston, MA.

Klein, K. J. and Kozlowski, S. W. (2000) *Multilevel Theory, Research and Methods in Organizations*. Wiley, New York.

Kotter, J. (1996) *Leading Change*. Harvard Business School Press, Boston, MA.

Kotter, J. and Cohen, D. S. (2002) *The Heart of Change*. Harvard Business School Press, Boston, MA.

Lane, C. (2001) Organizational Learning in Supply Networks, in M. Diekes, A. Antal, J. Child and I. Nonaka (eds) *Handbook of Organizational Knowledge and Learning*. Oxford University Press, Oxford, pp. 699–714.

Leavitt, H. (1978) *Managerial Psychology*, 4th edn. University of Chicago Press, Chicago, IL.

Lewin, K. (1948) Group Decision and Social Change. Reprinted in M. Gold (ed.) *The Complete Social Scientist: A Kurt Lewin Reader*. American Psychological Association, Washington, DC, pp. 265–284.

Likert, R. (1961) *The Human Organization*. McGraw-Hill, New York.

McCaughan, N. and Palmer, B. (1994) *Systems Thinking for Harassed Managers*. Karnac, London.

McDonagh, J. (2001) Not for the Fainthearted: Social and Organizational Challenges in IT-enabled Change. *Organization Development Journal*, 19(1): 11–20.

McGregor, D. (1960) *The Human Side of Enterprise*. McGraw-Hill, New York.

McIlduff, E. and Coghlan, D. (2000) Understanding and Dealing with Passive-Aggressive Behaviour in Teams and Organizations. *Journal of Managerial Psychology*, 15: 716–736.

Marquardt, M. (2004) *Optimizing the Power of Action Learning*. Davies-Black, Palo Alto, CA.

Marsick, V. and Watkins, K. (1999) *Facilitating Learning Organizations: Making Learning Count*. Gower, London.

Miller, J. G. (1978) *Living Systems*. McGraw-Hill, New York.

Mohrman, A., Mohrman, S., Ledford, G., Cummings, T., Lawler, E. E. and Associates (1989) *Large Scale Organizational Change*. Jossey-Bass, San Francisco, CA.

Morabito, J., Sack, I. and Bhate, A. (1999) *Organization Modeling: Innovative Architectures for the 21st Century*. Prentice-Hall, Upper Saddle River, NJ.

Nadler, D. A. (1998) *Champion of Change*. Jossey-Bass, San Francisco, CA.

Nadler, D. A., Shaw, R., Walton, E. and Associates (1995) *Discontinuous Change*. Jossey-Bass, San Francisco, CA.

Nadler, D. A., Spencer, J. and Associates (1998) *Executive Teams*. Jossey-Bass, San Francisco, CA.

Napier, R., Sidle, C. and Sanaghan, P. (1999) *High Impact Tools and Activities for Strategic Planning*. McGraw-Hill, New York.

Nohria, N. and Eccles, R. G. (1992) *Networks and Organizations: Structure, Form and Action*. Harvard Business School Press, Boston, MA.

Orlikowski, W. (1996) Improvising Organizational Transformation over Time: A Situated Change Perspective, *Information Systems Research*, 7(1): 63–92.

Owen, H. (1997) *Expanding Our Now: The Story of Open Space Technology*. Berrett-Koehler, San Francisco, CA.

Pascale, R., Milleman, M. and Gioja, L. (2000) *Surfing on the Edge of Chaos*. Crown Business, New York.

Quirke, B. (1996) *Communicating Corporate Change*. McGraw-Hill, London.

Raelin, J. A. (2000) *Work-based Learning*. Addison-Wesley, Reading, MA.

Raelin, J. A. (2003) *Creating Leaderful Organizations*. Berrett-Koehler, San Francisco, CA.

Rashford, N. S. and Coghlan, D. (1994) *The Dynamics of Organizational Levels: A Change Framework for Managers and Consultants*. Addison-Wesley, Reading, MA.

Ring, P. and Van de Ven, A. (1992) Structuring Cooperative Relationships between Organizations, *Strategic Management Journal*, 13: 483–498.

Rothwell, W. J. and Sullivan, R. (2005) *Practicing Organization Development*, 2nd edn. Pfeiffer, San Francisco, CA.

Rousseau, D. M. (1985) Issues in Organizational Research: Multi-level and Cross-level Perspectives, in L. L. Cummings and B. M. Staw (eds) *Research in Organizational Behavior*, vol. 7. JAI Press, Greenwich, CT.

Schein, E. H. (1978) *Career Dynamics: Matching Individual and Organizational Needs*. Addison-Wesley, Reading, MA.

Schein, E. H. (1987) *The Clinical Perspective in Fieldwork*. Sage, Thousand Oaks, CA.

Schein, E. H. (1992) The Role of the CEO in the Management of Change: The Case of Information Technology, in T. A. Kochan and M. Unseem (eds) *Transforming Organizations*. Oxford University Press, New York, pp. 80–95.

Schein, E. H. (1993) *Career Anchors: Discovering Your Real Values*. Pfeiffer, San Diego, CA.

Schein, E. H. (1995) *Career Survival: Strategic Job and Role Planning*. Pfeiffer, San Diego, CA.

Schein, E. H. (1996) The Three Cultures of Management: The Key to Organizational Learning, *Sloan Management Review*, 37(3): 9–20.

Schein, E. H. (1997) Organizational Learning: What is New?, in M. A. Rahim, R. Golembiewski and L. E. Pate (eds) *Advances in Management*, vol. 2. JAI Press, Greenwich, CT, pp. 11–25.

Schein, E. H. (1999) *Process Consultation Revisited: Building the Helping Relationship*. Addison-Wesley, Reading, MA.

Schein, E. H. (2003) *DEC is Dead, Long Live DEC*. Berrett-Koehler, San Francisco, CA.

Schein, E. H. (2004) *Organizational Culture and Leadership*, 3rd edn. Jossey-Bass, San Francisco, CA.

Senge, P. (1990) *The Fifth Discipline*. Doubleday, New York.

Shani, S. B. (Rami) and Docherty, P. (2004) *Learning by Design*. Blackwell, Oxford.

Shani, S. B. and Pasmore, W. A. (1985) Organization Inquiry: Towards a New Model of the Action Research Process, in Don D. Warrick (ed.) *Contemporary Organization Development: Current Thinking and Applications*. Scott Foresman, Glenview, IL, pp. 438–448.

Stacey, R. (2001) *Complex Responsive Processes in Organizations: Learning and Knowledge Creation*. Routledge, London.

Torbert, W. R. (2004) *Action Inquiry: The Secret of Timely and Transformational Leadership*. Berrett-Koehler, San Francisco, CA.

Tregoe, B. and Zimmerman, J. (1980) *Top Management Strategy*. Simon and Schuster, New York.

Tuohy, D. (1999) *The Inner World of Teaching*. Falmer, London.

Tushman, M. and Romanelli, E. (1985) Organizational Evolution: A Metamorphosis Model of Convergence and Reorientation, in B. M. Staw and L. L. Cummings,

Research in Organizational Behavior, vol. 7. JAI Press, Greenwich, CT, pp. 171–222.

Watkins, J. M. and Mohr, B. (2001) *Appreciative Inquiry: Change at the Speed of Imagination*. Jossey-Bass/Pfeiffer, San Francisco, CA.

Weick, K. and Quinn, R. (1999) Organizational Change and Development, *Annual Review of Psychology*, 50: 361–380.

Weisbord, M. (2004) *Productive Workplaces Revisited*. Jossey-Bass, San Francisco, CA.

Weisbord, M. and Janoff, S. (1995) *Future Search*. Berrett-Koehler, San Francisco, CA.

Wenger, E. (1998) *Communities of Practice: Learning, Meaning, and Identity*. Cambridge University Press, Cambridge.

Wheelan, S. (1999) *Creating Effective Teams*. Sage, Thousand Oaks, CA.

Worley, C. G., Hitchin, D. E. and Ross, W. L. (1996) *Integrated Strategic Change*. Addison-Wesley, Reading, MA.

Zand, D. E. (1997) *The Leadership Triad: Knowledge, Trust and Power*. Oxford University Press, New York.

Index